ABORTION CARE IS HEALTH CARE

ABORTION

CARE

IS HEALTH

CARE

BARBARA BAIRD

MELBOURNE
UNIVERSITY
PRESS

MELBOURNE UNIVERSITY PRESS
An imprint of Melbourne University Publishing Limited
Level 1, 715 Swanston Street, Carlton, Victoria 3053, Australia
mup-contact@unimelb.edu.au
www.mup.com.au

First published 2023
Text © Barbara Baird, 2023
Design and typography © Melbourne University Publishing Limited, 2023

Cover design by Phil Campbell Design
Typeset by J & M Typesetting
Cover photo courtesy Nikki Hartmann photography.
Printed in Australia by McPherson's Printing Group

A catalogue record for this
book is available from the
National Library of Australia

9780522878400 (paperback)
9780522878417 (ebook)

MIX
Paper | Supporting
responsible forestry
FSC® C001695

Contents

Acknowledgements

I acknowledge Kaurna people and the unceded Kaurna country where this book was written. I acknowledge Kaurna sovereignty and elders, past, present and emerging, and all First Nations people.

The thinking and writing that have made this book have been nurtured over a long period by a number of overlapping communities.

First, the book is deeply indebted to the nearly forty past and present abortion providers, healthcare professionals and managers, advocates and activists who agreed to be interviewed for my research. I have chosen to make them anonymous but that does not mean that I can't acknowledge how much I learned from their stories, perspectives and insights.

Several friends and colleagues kindly and generously read draft chapters and provided feedback. I didn't always take their advice but all contributed information, improved my analysis and/or pointed to the need for clearer expression. Thanks to Kath McLean, Judith Dwyer, Deborah Bateson, Brigid Coombe, Catherine Kevin, Prudence Flowers, Helen Calabretto, Jane Baird, Bonney Corbin and Tania Penovic. Erica Millar read and commented on several chapters and thus stands as my closest collaborator, always reliably there, always encouraging, always intellectually sharp, to whom I am particularly grateful.

Several people have responded to direct requests for information about abortion in their specific context and I am grateful for their willingness in busy working lives to assist me. This includes

Bonney Corbin, Jamal Hakim, Trish Hayes, Jo Flanagan, Jane Baird, Suzanne Belton, Pamela Doherty, Kari Vallury, Daile Kelleher, Tim Bavinton, Tahlee Blade Stevenson, Luke Grzeskowiak and Robyn Wardle.

All interpretation and analysis is mine, and I take responsibility for any errors or contestable points of view.

In addition, a cohort of academic scholars have engaged with me in discussion about abortion and related matters over many years, providing an extended community of interest and intellectual support. I am particularly grateful to my gang of Flinders colleagues, which includes Catherine Kevin and Prudence Flowers, and also Sharyn Roach Anleu, Zoe Keys, Monique Mulholland and Laura Roberts. My colleagues at Macquarie University, Michelle Arrow, Leigh Boucher and Robert Reynolds, have been great interlocutors in relation to the broader contexts of sexual and reproductive rights. Maria Giannacopoulos, Ruth Fletcher and Rebecca Stringer, with Erica Millar, have been sources of great conversations as we have planned an international research project on abortion that we hope will one day come to fruition. I have also enjoyed conversation with Sally Sheldon and Christabelle Sethna, who have both visited Australia, and welcomed me to academic life in England and Canada respectively. I acknowledge the inspiration and guidance I received from Lyndall Ryan in my early academic years for getting me started on research into abortion.

During the period of writing the book, I was devoting an increasing amount of time and energy to activist work aiming to increase access to abortion in South Australia and, to that end, working towards decriminalisation. That part of our campaign was successful when the SA parliament decriminalised abortion early in 2021. Being part of a fabulous group of people and wider community of support, including our parliamentary allies, has been a major learning experience and an immensely satisfying and rewarding part of my life. I am indebted to all with whom I worked in the SA Abortion Acton Coalition (*saaac*). Discussions with Judith Dwyer, Margie Ripper, Nola Savage, Brooke Calo, Helen Calabretto,

Leonora Herweijer, Cath Carroll, and Catherine Kevin and Prudence Flowers (fellow activists as well as colleagues), about abortion and how to make change have made a particular impact on me. I acknowledge the union women in *saaac* for their contribution to my understanding of change-making. Above all, the many conversations with my *saaac* co-convenor, Brigid Coombe, with her long history of providing sexual and reproductive health care and her detailed vision of how services must and can be patient-centred, have taught me much about the provision of abortion and the politics involved.

I have presented research related to this book at conferences and seminars over the years and am grateful to those who have listened, given feedback and made connections. I acknowledge in particular the commitment of Children by Choice in Queensland to sustain a national community of abortion providers, sexual health providers, researchers, advocates and activists.

Funding from the former Faculty of Social and Behavioural Sciences at Flinders University and from the Australian Research Council, via DP170100502 *Gender and Sexual Politics: Changing Citizenship in Australia since 1969,* have enabled research for travel, interview transcription, and research assistance for this book. Sharyn Taylor Transcribing and Secretarial provided excellent service and, at different times, Shaez Mortimer, Zoe Keys, Jade Hastings, Emily Collins and Abby Sesterka provided expert research assistance. Professional staff at Flinders University have been efficient and helpful in facilitating these aspects of the project. With many, I am deeply concerned about the future of public universities in Australia but also recognise that the permanent academic employment I have enjoyed since 1999 comes with many privileges. While critical thinking unrelated to narrow visions of economic need or national interest sometimes seems at grave risk, I have benefited from institutional as well as collegial support.

The value of the excellent editing of the manuscript provided by Kerrie Le Lievre cannot be underestimated. She worked carefully, promptly and with sensitive attention to my intended meaning. I admire her skill and am grateful for her professionalism.

I thank Joy Damousi, the History series editor at MUP, and Nathan Hollier, then Publisher and CEO, for their initial interest in and affirmation of the book. Catherine McInnis has provided clear, calm, detailed and reassuring guidance throughout the process. Melissa Faulkner was careful and supportive in copy-editing. Others at MUP with whom I have worked have made the process easy. A reviewer provided useful comment. Thanks to my friend Nikki Hartmann who took the photo for the cover.

Lots of family, friends and neighbours have shown interest in my book over the years. They have asked questions, listened, and sent links to relevant information and news. Thanks to all. Thanks too to my yoga teachers. Over the long haul, my parents Jean and Ross Baird and family, particularly my brother Graham Baird, have provided sustenance. I appreciate their valuing of education, and for making mine a well-supported life, although my comfort in this respect has come from class and race privilege as well as family background.

At home, the writing of the book in the last couple of years has been done alongside non-human companions. Jones' presence in my writing room, often in front of the heater, and sometimes walking across the keyboard, was sustaining and always lightened my spirit. Evie's and then Billie's need to be walked prompted needed breaks, physical exercise and attention to their canine worlds.

My partner, Vicki Rich, creates a beautiful garden at our home that sustains us in every way. The value of her practical support and patience during the long period of writing this book and her love and understanding is inestimable. I am in her debt.

Thinking about Abortion

I have been researching and writing about abortion since 1990. At some point about a decade ago, it came to me that while I knew a lot about the law, the politics of abortion and how we think about the issue, I knew very little about the provision of abortion services. This book is the result of my decision to explore that gap in my knowledge. It tells the story from 1990 until the present.

This turn to explore the provision of abortion coincides with the increasing prominence in the catchcries of pro-choice politics that 'abortion care is health care'. This definition and demand expands on 'a woman's right to choose', for example. 'Abortion care is health care' may seem like stating the obvious but any taken-for-granted-ness of this slogan is a recent achievement. In 1994 a sympathetic journalist wrote of a newly released and groundbreaking report on women's experiences of abortion that 'One of the more controversial assertions of the study is that women and health care providers see abortion as a health service.'[1] The focus on the provision of health care is not to displace questions of choice, rights, or justice, but to explore these as they do or do not materialise in the system of abortion provision.

The book follows the principle that the needs of the person with an unwanted pregnancy should be at the centre of our thinking about abortion. It works from the assumption that this person should have access to safe, affordable and culturally appropriate abortion care. It shifts investigation and debate away from 'the issue' of abortion. It is not concerned with who seeks abortion, nor their reasons for doing so, or how many occur each year, nor any justification of the moral value of abortion. Understanding how reproductive justice for all can be ensured, and how the needs of people seeking abortion can be met, involves grappling with more than questions of rights or morals, or debates about law and politics, or the stigma and shame that attaches to those who have abortions and those who provide them. This book therefore investigates how abortion services have been and are now provided in Australia, what this means and how they can be improved.

By focusing on abortion service provision, the book shifts our gaze to a set of problems that are not often brought into clear view. Its story of abortion services in Australia begins in 1990, the point at which the wave of liberalising legal change that began in this country in 1969 and which was different in each jurisdiction, and the accompanying liberalisation of access to abortion services, had settled. Abortion had become normalised as a lawful, albeit medicalised, service, but access was uneven and inequitable. Abortions were provided predominantly by small private providers, except in South Australia (SA) and the Northern Territory (NT), where public provision was the norm. There have been significant changes in the provision of abortion services in the thirty years since, however, and the restructuring of the private abortion-providing sector since 2000 following the arrival of international non-government organisation (NGO) Marie Stopes International (MSI Reproductive Choices since 2020) in Australia, the arrival in the mid-2000s and subsequent widespread availability in Australia of mifepristone (RU486), the drug that ends a pregnancy and leads to an abortion, and the impact of the achievement of decriminalisation in every jurisdiction, have not yet been given significant critical attention.

Neither has the lack of adequate access for many who seek an abortion, although this is widely acknowledged among pro-choice and feminist activists, researchers and commentators and the notion of a 'postcode lottery' has wide currency. While abortion has been relatively easily accessed by well-informed and economically advantaged people in all mainland Australian capital cities for the last thirty years, there are plenty of people who have needed an abortion and have not had this experience. Most people in rural, regional and remote locations have been and are poorly served, as are most who are on low incomes or find it difficult to access information, or are without residency status. The politics of geography, class and poverty, race, migration status and age shape the experience of gender that is sometimes the only power relation invoked when thinking about abortion. Those seeking an abortion later in their pregnancy also face significant obstructions that are sometimes compounded or even created by location, age and poverty. These obstructions testify to logics that are particular to the pregnant body and the way it is made socially meaningful. Calling for 'a woman's right to choose' only goes halfway in grappling with these complexities: the dignity of the pregnant person and their reproductive and bodily autonomy relies on equitable access to necessary health care. The inequities in access are becoming well documented. The other side of the story— why and how the provision of abortion services is so inadequate—has rarely been the subject of research.

The Historical Legacy

This book short-circuits over a century of professional opinion and public debate in Australia that has assumed there is (for most women) something wrong with abortion—a 'something' that boils down to pregnant women's desire to exert autonomy over their bodies and their reproductive lives. More specifically, it is *white women's* desire to refuse maternity that has been so troubling to medical, religious, legal and political authorities, and to many members of the public.[2] The tragic and brutal history of the removal of Aboriginal children from their families and communities, which is ongoing, demonstrates that Aboriginal women's relationship to maternity is thought about and experienced quite differently. As a consequence, Aboriginal women's responses to the issue of abortion have been more complex than a simple 'pro-choice' position allows for.[3] Likewise, migrant and refugee women's maternity is still today not always ideologically or materially supported in the way that white mothers' maternal status is affirmed.[4] Age, marital status, (dis)ability and sexuality also shape discourse about maternity in Australia, such that young women, those without male partners and those with disabilities have faced disapproval when becoming mothers. Sometimes abortion is considered the appropriate conclusion to their pregnancies.[5]

This history of opinion and debate includes the expectation that people should and will have an opinion about abortion. After all, it is supposedly one of the key moral issues of our society, and parliamentarians are regularly given a 'conscience vote' when they consider abortion law reform. This white Australian tradition of public debate sees abortion as a moral or religious issue, a legal issue or a political issue, but rarely as a practical matter of access to health care. I have previously argued that the regular call to debate abortion in Australia invites participation in a longstanding ritual through which the national ownership of women's bodies is restated.[6] Since the time of federation, Australian government bodies have conducted inquiries into population and the birth rate and, since the mid century, specifically into abortion. These inquiries have repeatedly assumed, and worried over, the role of white women as mothers of children and of the nation. Even if they do not explicitly oppose abortion, nearly all continue to regard it as an exception to social and cultural norms and expectations. This history might explain why parliaments are usually much more conservative than their constituents when voting on abortion. Burdened with the responsibility for the future of the nation (or their state or territory) as they imagine it, they assume ownership of not only the nation's material resources (including female bodies), but also of moral authority. The value put on white women as mothers and the shame historically associated with having an abortion reprise the privileged, if sometimes awkward, place of white women in the colonialist project of white supremacy.[7]

In this repeated national debate, abortion is frequently described as 'controversial', 'sensitive', 'emotional' and 'difficult'. I draw from the work of Erica Millar who has pointed to the way that these descriptors lock abortion into a stigmatising and shameful framework that makes it other to the norm that pregnancy leads to motherhood.[8] This representation of abortion sits somewhat contradictorily alongside the widespread normalisation of abortion among the majority of the Australian public, who have since the 1970s increasingly seen it as a 'woman's right to choose'. Sociologist Rebecca Albury wrote in 2007 that public debate about abortion in Australia between 2004 and 2006 indicated a widespread capacity to encompass 'both emotional discomfort with the fact of abortion and a rational acceptance of relatively accessible services'.[9] Many experiences related to bodies, sexuality, gender and health care can be 'sensitive' in the sense that people want privacy when they go through them, or find decision-making about them weighty or difficult, or wish to avoid the judgement of health professionals, family and friends. But none wears the mantle of 'sensitive' and 'controversial' as heavily as abortion. For the person who is pregnant and wants an abortion, and their partner, family and friends (if these are involved), abortion is about their future. It is a necessary and time-sensitive service. For those who do not have easy access to abortion, it may become an urgent, even desperate matter. So why isn't the controversy about the failure of Australian society to adequately provide it for all those who need an abortion?

Starting from the assumption that the provision of high-quality, accessible and affordable abortion services is a social good, this book sidesteps the 'both sides of the debate' approach, which is common in political debate and media representation. This approach not only suggests a false equivalency between two positions but obscures both the simplicity and the complexity of abortion politics. On the one hand, public opinion about abortion in Australia has been increasingly 'pro-choice' for decades. For the last thirty years the percentage of Australians who reported support for abortion being readily obtainable has grown from about 60 per cent to nearly 75 per cent, those who report support for abortion only in some circumstances has dropped from about 30 per cent to about 20 per cent, and that of those who oppose abortion under all circumstances has remained steady at around 5 or 6 per cent.[10] Support for decriminalisation in the last decade has been about 80 per cent. All but one piece of legislation concerning abortion that has passed through Australian parliaments in the last thirty years has been 'pro-choice' (the only exception, in the Australian Capital Territory [ACT] in 1998, was reversed four years later).[11] Some parliaments find it a difficult journey, but they eventually vote for liberal reform. 'Both sides of the debate' is a furphy. 'Pro-choice' won years ago. I do not dismiss those people who have ethical or faith-based or other concerns that lead to discomfort with or opposition to abortion, although I reserve the right to challenge their thinking about gender and the pregnant body. But there is already an international body of literature that debates the ethics of abortion, including research that makes the case for access to abortion as a human rights issue, and reproductive autonomy as a primary principle.[12] Nor do I dismiss the fervour and determination of often well-resourced groups who oppose access to abortion; we cannot afford to take our eyes away from their ideas and influence. This book argues that the views of the small minority who feel uncomfortable about or oppose abortion are not the basis on which abortion services should be thought about or provided.

On the other hand, the ongoing inadequate provision of abortion services in Australia requires an account of the complexity of the factors that have shaped these services, or their lack, so that we can see more clearly what needs to be done to improve access. Exploring this complexity involves asking new questions, seeking new information and forging new paradigms. It involves refusing the repeated return to abortion as 'an issue' while also understanding how the status of abortion as 'an issue' plays out. It involves centring the position of the pregnant person who wants an abortion, not in order to investigate them but so that their needs drive the research agenda.

The Questions to Ask

It is estimated that between one in three and one in four Australian women will have an abortion during their lifetime; some will have more than one.[13] Why has the public health system in Australia not taken responsibility for the adequate provision of abortion care? Why is abortion, unlike all other simple, common and necessary healthcare procedures, provided predominantly by the private sector in Australia, at financial cost to the patient?

Australia is an affluent country with a good-quality, comprehensive health care system. This includes excellent public hospitals and government-funded community health centres where health care is provided free to the patient, a significant private sector providing primary care as well as hospital care, the subsidised provision of pharmaceutical drugs, comprehensive regulation of quality and safety, Medicare, a universal health insurance scheme, and internationally leading medical research.[14] We have much to be grateful for, and Australians cling tightly to the entitlements and benefits which the public provision of health care delivers. Unfortunately, however, not everyone benefits to the same degree. Rural and remote communities, for example, generally do not enjoy the same access to health care as their urban counterparts. Significantly, the health system fails dismally to meet the needs of First Nations people.[15] Our public health system also faces the growing pressures of not only an ageing population but also under-resourcing, privatisation and the pressures of being in a state of 'continual reform' that delivers 'ambiguous outcomes'.[16] The COVID-19 pandemic continues to strain the public system to breaking point. None of these factors, however, explain why our public health system is negligent in relation to the provision of abortion services. In 1990 only 13 per cent of abortions in Australia were provided in the public sector. That percentage has probably declined since. Abortion has been and is provided predominantly by the private sector, which, in the main, offers good-quality and non-judgemental care for a fee. In SA and the NT abortion has been and is provided predominantly in the public sector. In very recent years both Tasmania and the ACT have introduced public provision of some abortions and/or public funding for privately provided abortion. Differences in models of provision have been only loosely related to the different legal frameworks in each jurisdiction. Recommendations that state health departments take responsibility for the adequacy of abortion services have been made regularly since the late 1970s. With one exception (see Chapter 2), they have been repeatedly ignored and then forgotten. At the time of writing, among the states and territories the Victorian government has the most detailed active policy statement relating to abortion services; other states have none or less developed commitments.[17] The prioritisation of universal access to termination services in the National Women's Health Policy 2020–2030 has received renewed attention in the wake of the election of the new Australian Labor Party (ALP) federal government in 2022.[18]

The lack of public provision of abortion services can be compared to the public provision of maternity care. The percentage of women in Australia giving birth in public hospitals grew throughout the 1990s and 2000s, from around 50 per cent to about 75 per cent at the time of writing.[19] It would be a crude argument that explained this disparity by saying that the state chooses to support motherhood to the relative exclusion of supporting women's reproductive autonomy when they wish to end a pregnancy. But in a survey of Australian state, territory and federal policies concerning reproduction conducted in 2013, Melissa Graham and her colleagues found that about half, including health policies, combined 'promoting motherhood' and 'regulating reproduction', by which they meant the 'control, monitoring and regulation' of reproductive choice.[20] They concluded that this reflected 'Australia's predominantly pronatalist ideologies' and the promotion of 'normative gender roles within family'. Notwithstanding this clear orientation, state support for mothers in Australia is hardly adequate. Some mothers face a negligent or even explicitly antagonistic state. The majority of the increasing numbers of First Nations women who are incarcerated are mothers. First Nations children are increasingly removed from their mothers, families and communities.[21] Some women have faced legal obstructions to the process of becoming mothers.[22] The public provision of maternal health care is a site of contest and advocacy by those who seek women-centred care.[23] It would be hard to argue, however, that a history of state policy in Australia in favour of maternity for respectable middle-class white women but opposed to abortion has ended, our pro-choice-ness notwithstanding.

This book asks detailed questions that emerge from this history. How is the provision of abortion services organised in Australia? Why have the great majority of public hospitals in Australia not provided abortion services? Why do so many people have to travel long distances to access abortion services? Why don't more doctors provide abortions? Is the anti-abortion movement the main obstruction to the provision of abortion services? Are there abortion-specific issues that private providers of abortion care must confront that other private healthcare providers do not? How has the provision of abortion services changed over the last thirty years? Have the changes expanded the accessibility of abortion services? Has the price of an abortion gone up in this time? Has decriminalisation made a difference? Is the availability of early medical abortion the answer? Why are people who request abortion 'late' so poorly served? What should be our priorities if we want to improve access to good-quality abortion care?

The Era of Neoliberalism
In place of public responsibility for the provision of safe and affordable abortion services and widespread delivery of abortion through public hospitals and clinics, we have *neoliberal abortion*. The book positions neoliberalism as a central framework for telling the story of how abortion has been provided in Australia in the late twentieth and early twenty-first centuries. I use the term *neoliberal abortion* to signal the centrality of the market, the relative absence of the welfare state in abortion provision and the centring of the idea of the individual with choice in my analysis of the provision of abortion.

Neoliberalism refers to a set of ideas about economic and social policy that have gained global ascendancy since the 1970s, coinciding with and mutually constitutive of the current period of globalisation and growing inequality between countries and within countries.[24] Neoliberalism also coincides with the rise of right-wing politics around the world, and in some cases political instability. Neoliberal policies give the market priority over the state as the rightful driver for management of the economy and the distribution of wealth and social goods; in this respect, they enact small government. The growing trend for governments to cut funding to, contract out or privatise health and social services is a neoliberal policy approach.[25] While they are associated with the withdrawal of the welfare state, however, neoliberal policies also deliver an intensification of state intervention into people's daily lives, especially for the poor and marginalised, evident in the increased demands for compliance from and surveillance practised on people receiving social security benefits, for example. The 1983–1996 ALP federal governments led by Bob Hawke and Paul Keating introduced neoliberal economic reform and policy frameworks in Australia. Their full force was, however, softened under ALP governments by the tempering effects of a politics of social inclusion.[26] This approach drew on a long Australian tradition of what has been described as 'social liberalism', which had been shaped significantly by white women's movements since federation and had had significant successes in the wake of the Women's Liberation Movement.[27] Since the election of the Howard Liberal National Party (LNP) government in 1996, however, major policy and economic reform in the neoliberal mode has been pursued vigorously and without social inclusion, with only a brief and mild respite during the 2007–13 ALP governments.[28] The election of the ALP government in 2022 delivered some immediate relief from the harshness of the conservative LNP government 2013–2022 but it is too soon to deliver a verdict on the depth of change.

Arguably, the delivery model for abortion services that developed in Australia from the 1970s in the wake of the liberalising court rulings and law reform was Australian-style neoliberal healthcare delivery *avant la lettre*. By 1990, abortion was provided liberally, predominantly by private sector clinics and small businesses in the east coast capital cities and Perth, with some provision by private obstetricians and gynaecologists in private hospitals. There was very little public provision, except in SA and the NT, and to a much lesser degree in Victoria. In other words, the market determined the provision of services. Clinics existed where they were profitable. They were susceptible to all the vicissitudes of the market—competition, ebbs and flows in the labour market and 'consumer' demand, changes in business costs, changes in government regulation, clinical developments that brought new modes of delivery. Private abortion clinics in small markets have been and remain particularly vulnerable. In 2018, the only remaining private provider of abortion services in Hobart, Tasmania, closed its doors. This provider's clinic in Launceston, the other major centre in the state, had closed two years earlier. The clinic's owner cited the uptake of telehealth abortion by Tasmanian women as the reason why the fortnightly clinic in Hobart was no longer financially viable. The public system did not step into the breach to address the loss of surgical abortion services until, after concerted activism, the government announced public support for access. This is a good news story told in Chapter 2.[29]

A study conducted in 2014–2015 of 2326 English-speaking women who had had abortions in the private clinics run by Marie Stopes Australia (MSI Australia since 2022) gives a snapshot of what is delivered when abortion care is left to the market.[30] One in ten women had needed to travel and stay away from home overnight to obtain abortion care, and one in three had incurred costs on top of those of the medical care. One-third of the women had experienced financial difficulty in paying for the abortion, with some sacrificing payment of household expenses to pay for their abortions; more than two-thirds relied on financial assistance from others to cover their costs, and 7.5 per cent did not have or chose not to use a Medicare card. This is what 'inadequate' and 'inequitable' looked like in the mid-2010s.

However, there is more to neoliberal abortion than relegation of the provision of health care to the private sector and financial difficulty for patients. Scholars who address the ways in which neoliberalism imagines people, including feminists who write about 'postfeminism', describe neoliberal forms of subjectivity.[31] That is, they argue that neoliberalism requires and has fostered particular ways of being and of understanding ourselves and others. The ideal neoliberal subject, around whom much policy and service provision is imagined, is a self-reliant, self-managing, self-creating rational individual who creates their own life through the exercise of choice.[32] This is contrary to an understanding of self as part of a collective, a family or a gender, for example, or as being shaped by political, social and cultural forces. This atomistic individualism is invoked by and applies to doctors and other healthcare workers who can choose whether or not to provide abortion care (although this phenomenon did not begin with neoliberalism). This sense of self can also be applied to and invoked by women who need an abortion and who think that they should be able to choose to have one with empowering effects. Many women, especially younger women who are often described as part of a postfeminist generation, believe that they enjoy both gender choice (as distinct from a defined gender role) and gender equality. They are encouraged to refuse any identification with victimhood, and many eschew the idea that they or any of their peers are victims. Women in unfortunate situations have simply made bad choices, so the script goes.[33] The position of abortion in this conservative neoliberal imaginary can, however, be contradictory because planning and control are assumed qualities of the neoliberal subject so the need for abortion has been seen as an individual failing, if not a bad choice.[34]

Political scientist Kate Gleeson describes the nineteen-year-old woman who was arrested in Cairns in 2009 for having taken medication to give herself an abortion, as 'a child of both feminist and neoliberal revolutions'.[35] When police entered her home on an unrelated matter and noticed empty pill packets with non-English labelling, this young woman volunteered that she had taken abortion medication brought from the Ukraine by the sister of her boyfriend who was also arrested. When asked by police, she willingly explained that she had made a choice, with her boyfriend and family, and had no regrets: "'It wasn't really that much of a big deal," she insisted. "Just decided that I wasn't ready for a child"'. This young woman was a self-determining neoliberal subject of choice, but also a victim of nineteenth-century Queensland law that criminalised a woman's intentional procurement of her own miscarriage. She did not know that taking pills to bring on an abortion was potentially unlawful; neither did she know that early medical abortion was at the time available for free at the Cairns Sexual Health Clinic.[36] A long eighteen months after their arrest, she and her boyfriend were acquitted by a District Court jury.

Feminist scholars and activists have long quarrelled with the limited focus on 'choice' in abortion politics as choice and indeed abstract rights are meaningless without affordable access to services.[37] In any case, choice does not exist in an ideological vacuum. As well as 'controversial' and 'sensitive', Erica Millar argues that while abortion has been normalised as a choice in Australian public discourse since the early 1970s, it has also been construed as 'an exceptional choice' and one that has increasingly been understood as an *inferior* choice in relation to the choice of motherhood. This is discursively achieved through its representation as sad, regrettable, guilt-inducing and shameful.[38] The neoliberal female subject with an unwanted pregnancy may well be judged for becoming pregnant in the first place; when an unwanted pregnancy is read as a sign of poor contraception use, or poor self-management all round, women may judge themselves as well as being judged by others. The spectre of the unruly sexual and reproductive female body is never far from the mind, in all its historically classed and raced nuance.[39] And it is not only young women who may subject themselves to self-recrimination. A magazine article about the Melbourne abortion clinic at which several women were infected with the hepatitis C virus in 2008 and 2009 following negligent practice by an anaesthetist quotes a woman who had used the clinic. At forty-nine years of age, menopausal and unexpectedly in a new heterosexual relationship, the journalist writes without comment that the woman had said 'she had not been "managing herself" very well'. Of her new partner's self-management, no word.[40]

While neoliberalism in the abstract centres individual choice and individual freedom, it has historically been accompanied by the rise of conservative right-wing political ideology and often right-wing governments. The New Right in the UK, neoconservatism in the USA and what I call renewed moral conservativism in Australia identify the gains of the feminist and sexual liberation movements as the causes of the alleged breakdown of the social fabric and urge a return to traditional family forms, and thus support the winding-back of the welfare state. These right-wing politics also manifest as racism and nationalism and, contrary to neoliberal impulses, often as anti-globalisation.[41] The election of the Howard government in Australia in 1996 signalled the introduction of a political environment receptive to the influence of conservative Christianity, and a turn away from sympathies to feminism at the federal level of government. In her book on the rise of the religious right in Australian politics, Marion Maddox writes that while 'the Market God sits enthroned in treasury' it was 'the repressive God of Howard conservatism rattling the back door of government policy'.[42] Nowhere was this more clearly evident than in the government's orientation to abortion.[43] Sociologist Margie Ripper describes a reframing of abortion in public debate in Australia during the Howard years, from a liberal and medicalised consensus to a moralising framework promoted by anti-abortionists, who were ironically aided and abetted by some feminists. Stigma and shame focused particularly on doctors, reviving the odium attached to abortion providers in the pre-liberalisation days.[44] *Giving Sorrow Words*, published in 1999 by leading anti-abortion writer Melinda Tankard Reist, was significant in this reframing, borrowing from women's health discourse to argue that abortion was bad for women.[45] In 2003, future prime minister Malcolm Turnbull revealed the persistence of racial thinking about maternity when he spoke of the threat posed to the Australian population by an increasing Muslim population, and later, when in parliament, proved ambivalent on abortion.[46]

In 2006, in the context of debate about abortion in the federal parliament, Liberal backbencher Danna Vale said Australians were 'aborting themselves out of existence', risking Australia becoming a Muslim nation.[47] In 2023 Leanne Liddle, Director of the Aboriginal Justice Unit in the NT, recounted a senior police officer's comment made to her that the way to reduce the rate of incarceration of Aboriginal people was for them 'to stop breeding for the next 10 to 15 years'.[48] The influence of anti-abortion individuals and groups may ebb and flow, but the gendered and racialised history of discourse about maternity and abortion in Australia is hard to shake. It materialises in the context of the provision of abortion services as exceptionalism.

On the one hand, private abortion providers face issues in common with other healthcare providers who operate small businesses. On the other hand, the market in which they operate is distinguished by the exceptional status of abortion. This has included the definition of abortion in criminal law, attention from regular public debates (including in parliaments), specific difficulty in finding medical staff, government regulations that include requirements not made in other contexts ... the list goes on. Roger, a retired abortion-providing general practitioner (GP) whom I interviewed for this book, told me that he has sometimes told patients that 'there's an invisible politician, lawyer and bureaucrat in the room ... one of each.' The provision of abortion services has also been distinguished by the need to deal with anti-abortion 'protesters' outside clinic premises, a burden experienced more intrusively by some clinics around the country than others. The objections to abortion of some GPs, or their ignorance on the subject, can also skew the market when information about abortion services is made hard to get, and women must visit more than one GP to access information about services. It is hard to think of another healthcare service that operates in such a complicated and obstructed context—a far cry from the idealised neoliberal free market.

A brief anecdote told to me by an abortion-providing GP lightened her frustration at the presence of anti-abortion 'protesters' at her clinic. Commenting on the attitudes to abortion that some women from Asian countries bring, Rosalie recalled patients who had made their way into the clinic through the regular barrage of 'protesters' and their placards with images of foetuses. With cultural immunity to the stigma that the protesters were promoting, they mistook the scene for aggressive marketing 'touting for another clinic'. A wry tale, abortion humour to watch out for.

An Historical Approach

Investigation into the provision of abortion in Australia since the 1960s has been of less concern in the academic and popular literature than have law, politics, attitudes, social movements, media representations, epidemiology, clinical care, experience and access. Historical literature on abortion in the period before 1970 is replete with often gruesome accounts of the provision of abortion during the illegal era, but academic literature on the period since 1970 has paid little attention to the dynamics of provision, as if we don't need to worry about that any more. Some accounts sketch the establishment of private clinics and provision in public hospitals in the 1970s and 1980s.[49] Analysis of abortion—or its absence—in public policy is mostly incidental. In recent years the promising new direction of nurse-centred models of providing abortion care has been explored, alongside research into the role of doctors in providing abortion, rarely their refusing to provide, but it is scant.[50] Psychologist Susie Allanson's monograph about the Fertility Control Clinic in Melbourne, written in the wake of the murder of the clinic's security guard by a mentally unstable anti-abortionist in 2001, is a powerful account of the workings of a private abortion clinic in crisis written by someone who worked there during the episode.[51] So is her account of 'protesters' at the clinic, and her and its role in achieving legislated safe access zones.[52] It is a valuable exception in a field where focus on the subjective, economic, social, policy and political structures through which abortion services are provided is rare.

So this history of the provision of abortion in Australia over the last thirty years sets out into relatively uncharted territory. It tells stories of how abortion has been provided in Australia during this period, and how this has changed, through a series of parallel and interweaving and overlapping chrono-thematic historical narratives. It analyses the politics, structure and logic of provision and the major changes that have taken place. It is also attentive to the more frequent minor punctuation marks that have signalled upheavals or small shifts in public and private provision over time. It picks up the story in 1990, because the changes delivered by the liberalisation of the 1970s were by that point well established, and offers an account of neoliberal abortion. It tells a story of a lack of public provision of abortion services, a theme to which I repeatedly return. It attends to both macro and micro features of abortion provision. As part of paying attention to the details of interpersonal relations and to government and commercial developments it is also concerned with political contests and the discourses that shape these contests. It is attentive to the longer history of these underlying and overt battles.

To describe the analysis they apply to social policy, feminist political scientist Carol Bacchi and her colleagues have coined the phrase 'What's the problem represented to be' (WPRB).[53] I follow their approach in many respects because critical analysis of how different key players (individual doctors, hospital managers and government bodies that regulate pharmaceutical drugs, for example) understand 'the problem of abortion' tells us much about how to intervene to address access issues. A WPRB approach assumes that the ways in which abortion services are organised don't just respond to the pre-existing needs of unwillingly pregnant people, they also (re)produce social relations and ways of being. They reproduce ideas about people who need abortions, and ways for these people to be, in the very provision of the service that they need. A WPRB approach is a 'governmentality' approach, drawing on the important work of French historian and philosopher Michel Foucault. He talks about the 'rationalities of government' and 'technologies of governing'.[54] 'Rationalities of government' refers in our case to the ideologies, logics and unquestioned assumptions that underpin the ways in which abortion is provided. 'Technologies of governing' refers to the macro practices of governing in the broad sense, including the work of market forces, and everyday micro practices which create the experience of abortion. Two key authors on governmentality write that Foucault's framework is particularly interested in 'the small and diverse events that brought something new into existence ... the vast array of petty managers of social and subjective experience ... little engineers of the human soul, and their mundane knowledges and procedures'.[55] I am particularly attracted to the idea of the 'petty managers', because the stories of abortion that I have been told by those I have interviewed are full of 'petty managers', those who manage obstruction to access and those who create new worlds of possibility for people needing abortions, in a range of micro and macro settings.

It should be clear that while the book is attentive to the 'how' of the provision of abortion, and revels in small details, it is underpinned by political commitment. This book understands the issue of access to abortion care through a framework that Black feminists in the USA have called Reproductive Justice.[56] This is a set of principles that sees human rights for all, regardless of age, ability, class, race, sexuality or gender, as inclusive of the right to continue or not with pregnancy, to be supported in providing a safe and nourishing environment in which to raise children, and to have access to adequate health care. The book focuses on abortion in the context of the full range of reproductive issues. It aims to contribute to the achievement of reproductive justice.

Sources

This book is based in a series of oral history interviews I conducted between 2013 and 2017. I travelled to different cities around the country and interviewed people who were able to tell me about the provision of abortion services in each state and territory. The book is also grounded in the analysis of documents—including media items, conference papers, activist leaflets, articles in medical journals, records of parliamentary committees and government reports. These documents provide both the scaffolding for accounts of 'what happened' and evidence of how abortion has been thought about. The book's national focus is important because models of abortion provision vary around the country. This makes it unusual in Australian research and commentary about abortion.

I interviewed nearly forty nurses, doctors, women's health workers, social workers, managers, public health professionals, activists and advocates. Most are women and most were in their forties at least, or older, at the time of interview. Their age profile reflects my historical interest and the gender profile reflects their occupations, medical doctors excepted. The male interviewees were all doctors, most of whom have had significant public profiles as medical advocates for better abortion services. Nearly all interviewees were white, as far as I know and, given their professional status, most were middle-class at the time of interview. All had been involved in providing or supporting abortion services in Australia for a significant period of time since 1990, or at particularly strategic moments. Some had begun their involvement well before 1990. Many of the interviewees expressed clearly feminist views, but those who didn't were all committed to providing a service essential for the reproductive autonomy of women and others with an unwanted pregnancy. I sought a reasonable cross-section of people who had occupied different positions in public and private providing organisations, plus activists and people who worked in community-based organisations. Some doctors worked in both the public and private sectors. Interviewees were recruited from among people I knew or had met at conferences, and via direct contact with those who had established public profiles. Permission to undertake the interviews was granted by the Flinders University Social and Behavioural Research Ethics Committee.[57]

I am deeply indebted to my interviewees for deepening my understanding of the micro and macro experience and politics of providing abortion services. The oral histories were confined to each person's professional involvement with abortion, although for many this involvement had occupied a large part of their identity and life activity over a long period. They provide information and insight without which the book could not proceed, and appear in a few different ways. They are sources of information, although once alerted to a particular event, for example, I sought documentary evidence. They are sources of insight and opinion. I also consider them to be subjective expressions of the experience of being identified with and involved in the provision of abortion services. These different uses of oral history are recognisable to those familiar with the field.[58] Some of the smallest stories told to me offered the greatest revelations. All interviewees are identified in this book by pseudonyms, even though many already had long histories of making public comment. I have done my best to disguise their personal identities, sometimes obfuscating but never lying about identifying details, and maintaining only simple references to the cities where I interviewed them and their professional identities to give some context to their voices. This was my choice, and I need to put on record that some of the interviewees were not happy with it. While some requested anonymity, most did not care whether or not they were identified. Those who wished to be identified were motivated by their belief that the stigma attached to abortion is combated by open public speech. I have overruled their preference so that I could use interview material freely without concerns about embarrassing interviewees or exposing them to criticism and to have a uniform approach to interviewees. Each were sent the transcript of their interview and gave consent for its use. A list of all interviews that I have drawn from, with minimal identifying detail, appears in the reference list at the back of the book.

Language and terminology are everything, and there are a range of terms often used when writing about abortion, all of them loaded with meaning. With respect to the experience and practice of abortion I write about abortion, not 'termination of pregnancy', which is the term more often used by doctors and in many formal documents. I use the term 'unwanted pregnancy' to describe the embodied state that leads many people to seek an abortion. I have little interest in 'unplanned pregnancy' or 'unintended pregnancy'; given the contingencies of the environments through which we

live—biological, economic, political, social, cultural, interpersonal—
singular intent, planning and control are ideals and experiences of
living that are more easily within reach for some than others (and
are not necessarily universally valued). Women and others who may
become pregnant, and their sexual partners, should have every access
to information and appropriate contraceptive technologies. Different
methods have different virtues for different people, including the
degree to which they rely on exclusively female responsibility for
birth control. Fertility is, however, not totally controllable, and most
people who have sought abortions in Australia in the last thirty years
were practising some kind of contraception when they became
pregnant. Sexual and reproductive coercion interferes with the
capacity of many people to control their fertility.[59] In addition, there
is no direct relationship between an unplanned pregnancy and abortion. Many unplanned pregnancies end, quite happily for all
concerned, in birth.[60] Some women are ambivalent about becoming
pregnant, and report being 'okay either way'.[61] And finally, a small
number of planned and initially wanted pregnancies become
unwanted often in the context of diagnoses of foetal anomaly. I also
acknowledge that it is not only those who identify as women who
can become pregnant and want an abortion. This may be an experience for people who identify as nonbinary, gender queer,
transmasculine, transgender or another gender who have bodies that
can become pregnant. Such people may experience barriers to all
kinds of health care, including sexual and reproductive health, that
normatively gendered women do not.[62] When making formal statements I therefore tend to use 'people who need an abortion', but
when discussing the experiences of these people I more often refer
to 'women' because historically and contemporarily, the great
majority of those seeking an abortion have been and are women.
'Pro-choice' is recognised by many as a limiting term to describe the
commitments needed to assure the adequate provision of abortion
services but it maintains common currency in Australia. I use it as a
broad umbrella term. Given that my discussion of those who oppose
pro-choice positions is generally confined to their public and

professional activism and is not interested in their personal views, I use 'anti-abortion' to refer to them and their activities.

The first three chapters of the book following this introduction lay out a thirty-year history of how abortion has been provided in Australia since 1990. Health sociologists Willis, Reynolds and Rudge identify the professions, the state and the market as the three major players in the healthcare system in Australia.[63] The first three chapters address the historical problem of inadequate and inequitable access to abortion through discussion of these players. The next three chapters investigate the three major developments that have changed the provision of services in Australia over the last thirty years. These are the presence since 2000 of the UK-based international sexual and reproductive healthcare NGO Marie Stopes International (MSI Reproductive Choices since 2020) as an abortion-providing organisation, the politically fraught story of early medical abortion in Australia, and the decriminalisation of abortion in all but one jurisdiction. The final chapter, 'Late', focuses on those who are marginalised and disadvantaged by the current arrangement of the provision of abortion care in Australia because they present for a service 'late' in pregnancy.

Location

My academic interest in abortion began with my PhD, which focused on the experiences and memories of South Australian women who had had abortions before they were legal. I identified then, as I do now, as a feminist scholar who is located through the privileges of middle-class whiteness, consolidated since 1999 in the security of permanent academic employment. Since my PhD I have explored contemporary discourse on abortion as evidenced in law reforms, political debate and the media, always with its pre-liberalisation history in mind. Around 2013, I shifted my focus to the provision of abortion services. I received two small research grants from the Faculty of Social and Behavioural Sciences and Flinders University that allowed me to travel to meet people and conduct interviews, and to pay for them to be transcribed. I was marginally involved in the political debates about abortion in SA in the early 1990s and more significantly in Tasmania at the end of 2001, when the threatened arrest of doctors at the Royal Hobart Hospital led to a crisis in the provision of services, and then law reform just before Christmas that year. After dipping my toes into creative activism in Adelaide in 2013 (we danced!), I joined with others to form the SA Abortion Action Coalition (*saaac*) at the end of 2015. Being among a group who led the campaign to improve access to abortion services in SA, with a focus on decriminalisation, has been a major commitment of my time and energy since then. This book's completion has been slowed as a result. The context for writing this book is not only the climax of the decriminalisation of abortion in all Australian jurisdictions (except WA), but my location in SA. As noted above, abortion services in SA in the post-liberalisation period have been provided predominantly in the public system—since 2000, almost exclusively so. There are lot of problems with abortion provision in SA, but for most people in metropolitan Adelaide provision has been of high quality, and *free*. Since 2000, over 50 per cent of all abortions in SA have been provided at the Pregnancy Advisory Centre (PAC), a freestanding abortion clinic that is part of the public system. This service is unique in Australia (see Chapter 2). Coming from SA skews my vision, as would any other state or territory location. We have direct experience of what an excellent public service might look like. South Australian abortion activists and providers therefore tend to look at provision in other states with an extra-acute eye for the inequity of their reliance on private provision. Finishing the book has coincided with the COVID-19 pandemic. The impact of this pandemic on our health system and our economy has brought to light the precarity of much about our system of abortion provision. The book has also come to fruition in the wake of the overturning of the *Roe v Wade* ruling by the Supreme Court in the US, which garnered much attention in Australia, and in the context of renewed hopes for better public policy and public provision.

A friend tells me a story of her abortion, sought in the late-1980s when she was a young woman. She had to travel a small but significant distance to the abortion clinic. She came from a Catholic family and lived in a conservative social and political environment. She worked in a typically female-dominated, low-paid occupation. She told no one of her pregnancy or her abortion, and travelled by herself on the day. I guess she paid for the abortion herself too. My first response is to express concern and sympathy that she had been so alone. She corrects me. Her aloneness made the abortion possible. She knew clearly that she wanted it. If she had told anyone, she says, they would have talked her out of it. Somehow she knew where to go and how to get there. Her wilfulness shines out of this story. Continuing the pregnancy was not the future she wanted, and the abortion clinic enabled her to embody her desire to not be pregnant when people or forces from other parts of her life might have stopped her. Her journey inspires this book, which centres on the non-negotiable necessity of the provision of abortion services. It is motivated by the desire to make journeys to abortion care easier for those who currently find them difficult, or even out of reach, and better supported for all.

Chapter 1

Neoliberal

Abortion provision in Australia has historically been defined through criminal law, making it unique in Australian health care. Like most health care in Australia, abortion care is now provided by a mixture of public and private health services. In the case of abortion, however, the balance between public and private provision is remarkably different from that of any other form of essential health care.

The 1996 National Health & Medical Research Council (NHMRC) report on abortion in Australia reports benchmark data from when this book takes off. It described an 'overwhelming predominance' of private clinics in 1990, which delivered a 'prompt service of generally good quality on day-care bases'.[1] In 1990, these specialised clinics provided over 80 per cent of all abortions across the nation. Obstetricians and gynaecologists (O&Gs), mostly in private hospitals, provided a further 7 per cent. Public hospitals that provided abortions for little or no cost accounted for just 13 per cent nationally, although the figure varied widely across jurisdictions. Interstate and intrastate travel to access abortion care was common.

This is the model of service provision I describe as 'neoliberal abortion'. Neoliberalism, with its increasing understanding of those who need care as 'consumers', expressed through government policy about funding and structure, has increasingly shaped all aspects of health care in Australia. In the case of the public health system, this has taken the form of (sometimes seemingly endless) restructuring under the principles of New Public Management.[2] However, unlike some of the health services that have been outsourced to the private sector, abortion was never comprehensively provided by the public sector to start with. This is the result of a historical legacy of moral conservatism and criminalisation of abortion care, as well as the continuation during the post-liberalisation period of the existing system of abortion provision by doctors and clinics in New South Wales (NSW) and Victoria, and to a lesser extent in Western Australia (WA), that had existed illegally in the 1950s and 1960s.

The Australian system of abortion provision can be contextualised by reference to those of similar countries. Our system is most like that in the USA, where private operators, including not-for-profit organisations, have provided the overwhelming majority of abortion care since liberalisation.[3] The major difference is that while insurance coverage for abortion care in the USA is uneven, Medicare—Australia's universal healthcare insurance scheme, previously Medibank—has included abortion as a rebatable item since its inception in 1975. In Britain, consistent with the provision of health care through the National Health Service (NHS), nearly all abortion care is provided free to the patient, although increasingly from the early 1990s it has mostly been delivered by independent sector providers under contract to the NHS.[4] In Aotearoa New Zealand, abortion is also provided free to the patient through the public health system.[5]

This chapter gives an overview of the system of predominantly private provision of abortion services that has been in place in Australia since 1990. At that time there were approximately 80,000 abortions performed annually and all were provided surgically. First trimester procedures, those up to 14 weeks of pregnancy, made up about 95 per cent of all abortions. These procedures were done by vacuum aspiration which involved gentle suction to remove the contents of the uterus. This method had a very low rate of complications, meaning that in 1990 in Australia abortion was a safe medical procedure. For patients in the mid trimester of pregnancy the safer dilation and curettage (D&C) method was replacing instillation, where saline or other fluid is introduced into the uterus to bring on labour. Abortion induced early in pregnancy by taking medication (early medical abortion), using mifepristone (RU486) and misoprostol, did not become commonplace in Australia until 2013.

Abortion Service Provision, 1990

In Victoria, in 1990, public hospitals provided about 17 per cent of all abortions, the lion's share of them at the Royal Women's Hospital (RWH) in central Melbourne.[6] The Fertility Control Clinic (FCC) in East Melbourne was the most significant player in the private scene. Established in 1972 by abortion campaigner Dr Bertram Wainer, it was a training ground for many doctors who would go on to provide abortions for years to come, with some opening their own clinics.[7] Dr Christine Healy was one of these; her clinic in North Melbourne opened in 1983. Dr Mark Jones, who set up The Women's Clinic on Richmond Hill (initially called the Wainer Clinic for Women) with Jo Wainer, Bert's widow, in 1990, was another. There were three other private clinics in Melbourne in 1990, mostly in the middle-class inner northern and eastern suburbs.

In NSW, around 10 per cent of abortions were provided in public hospitals. There were also two non-profit and six owner-operator clinics, which were concentrated in the suburbs around central Sydney. The not-for-profit Preterm, the first free-standing abortion clinic to be established in Sydney in the legal era, had become the dominant player.[8] Like the FCC in Melbourne, it trained many doctors who went on to establish their own clinics, including Geoff Brodie, who established first one clinic in Randwick in the early 1980s, then others in Camperdown in the inner west and near Penrith in the outer western suburbs in the 1990s. He also trained doctors who moved on to set up their own clinics and/or become committed abortion providers. A group of O&Gs operated a clinic adjacent to Westmead Hospital until the early 2000s, and another ran a clinic in Woollahra during the 1990s, but, as elsewhere, most clinics were run by GPs. Bessie Smyth, a feminist not-for-profit clinic, operated in Sydney's inner west.

In Queensland, public hospital provision in 1990 was described as 'rare', making up less than 1 per cent of all abortions. There were four private clinics in 1990—two in Brisbane, and one each (owned by GP David Grundmann) in Townsville and Rockhampton. The Greenslopes Fertility Clinic in Brisbane began offering abortions when GP Peter Bayliss joined the practice in 1978.[9] Both Bayliss and Grundmann came from Melbourne, where they had been associates of Wainer. However, two clinics in Tweed Heads in NSW, just across the border from Queensland, can also be included in the count. They had been established in 1976 to service women from the south-east corner of Queensland when there were no clinics in that state.[10] In 1990, some Queensland patients also travelled to Sydney to access abortion services, as they had been doing at least since the early 1970s.[11]

In WA, about 10 per cent of abortions were provided in public hospitals in 1990. There were also two private clinics in central Perth.[12] Nanyara, operated by gynaecologist Dr Victor Chan, had been established in 1973. The Zera clinic had been established in 1976 by Dr John Charters, who practised until his death in 2000.

In Tasmania public hospital provision was 35 per cent in 1990, and there was also relatively significant private hospital provision. Nevertheless, an estimated 40 per cent of Tasmanian women seeking abortion services travelled to the mainland to access care. Public provision in the ACT was described as 'minimal', and there was no reference at all in the NHMRC report to private hospital provision. Most women travelled to Melbourne or Sydney. In both Tasmania and the ACT, the opening of a not-for-profit clinic in the early 1990s made a big impact, cutting the number of women who travelled across state borders to access abortion care significantly.

In SA and the NT, public provision predominated, accounting for about 60 per cent in both cases. There were no private clinics in these jurisdictions, with private hospital provision and some travel accounting for the remaining 40 per cent (although this is surmise in the case of the NT, as there is no clear data available).[13] The opening of the Pregnancy Advisory Centre (PAC), a freestanding public abortion clinic, in SA in 1992 brought an end to the need for interstate travel, with its share of all abortion provision in SA growing throughout the 1990s.

Private abortion clinics were predominantly owned and run by male doctors until well into the 2000s: Rosalie, a GP abortion provider, commented in 2013 that 'it's the same with any sort of surgery, it's very much a male dominated sort of thing'.[14] Two leading figures throughout the 1990s and 2000s, Queensland-based David Grundmann and Sydney's Geoff Brodie, both owned more than one clinic, as noted above. By the mid-1990s, Grundmann had clinics in Brisbane, Southport, Townsville and Rockhampton in Queensland, and in Newcastle, NSW.[15] Brodie had his three clinics in Sydney. These operated into the 2000s.

Christine Healy was the only female doctor at the FCC in Melbourne in the 1980s, and the first in Australia to establish her own clinic, which she ran until retiring in 2011.[16] Sue Craig opened the Gynaecare clinic in Sydney's northern suburbs in the early 1990s; in 2013, Emma Boulton and Kath Innsley bought it and renamed it Clinic 66.[17] Sue Brumby, an abortion provider since the early 1990s who had worked with both Geoff Brodie and David Grundmann, opened her own Blue Water Medical clinics in NSW in the mid-2000s.[18] Meaghan Heckenberg established the Gynaecology Centres Australia (GCA) clinics around NSW with her partner, starting in 1998. Dr Judith Nash established her clinic in Perth in 2001. Dr Kathy Lewis established the FCC's clinic in Hobart in early 2003, and another in Albury later that year. These doctors led, but by the 2000s it was no longer unusual for women to be abortion providers.

Avowedly feminist clinics also made significant contributions in three jurisdictions until the early 2000s. Two collectively operated feminist clinics were established in Sydney in the 1970s: Everywoman's, which closed in the late 1980s, and the Bessie Smyth clinic in Homebush, which trained health professionals and students as well as providing abortion services, and struggled on until August 2002, when it was one of the first clinics to be bought by Marie

Stopes Australia on its entry to the Australian market.[19] The Women's Health Foundation (WHF), a non-profit company owned by a small group of feminist women, opened a clinic in Hobart in 1991 with doctors flying in from first Sydney, then Melbourne.[20] It closed in 2001 due to multiple factors including a local gynaecologist who started offering medical abortion using methotrexate, cutting into its market.[21] The ACT's government-funded community sector Family Planning organisation FPACT established a separate company, Reproductive Health Service (RHS), to open an abortion clinic there in 1994. However, in 1998 an anti-abortion law reform placed severe restrictions on the clinic's operation, including a requirement for a 72-hour cooling-off period after a first consultation.[22] When GCA opened a clinic in Queanbeyan, just over the border in NSW, advertising a one-visit process, the RHS clinic lost about 10 per cent of its business.[23] FPACT sold its clinic to Marie Stopes in 2004. While the geographic and political circumstances of each clinic were specific, some interviewees were of the opinion that the way feminist principles were applied in these not-for-profit clinics, including generous 'payment plans' for women who could not pay (e.g. at Bessie Smyth clinic and the RHS), was inconsistent with business survival.

As suggested above, since 1975, access to Australia's predominantly privately provided abortion services has been underpinned by abortion's inclusion as a rebatable item in Medicare. Given how little public health provision was available, this is the most significant way abortion services have been made affordable for patients. For most, the Medicare rebate has covered between one third and one half the total cost of a first trimester abortion, which would otherwise be paid by the patient.[24] Private health insurance will cover the gap between the clinic fee and the Medicare rebate in private clinics that meet certain licensing standards. Some health insurance for non-residents such as travellers and international students covers abortion, though not all.

It is standard in Australia for public hospitals to provide both emergency care in relation to all health issues, and management of complex cases that cannot be accommodated in the private sector. However, abortion has often been the exception to this rule. This has highlighted the importance of personal relationships between private providers and relevant hospital doctors. Some O&G 'champions' in the small number of public hospitals around the country that have provided abortions have historically had professional relationships with private providers. For example, Geoff Brodie's clinics had a close collegial relationship with Brian Peat at Sydney's King George V Hospital (which merged with Royal Prince Alfred [RPA] in 2002) from the 1990s until 2002, when Peat left the hospital. Patients who needed care that could not be given in a day clinic, or for whom something went wrong during the procedure, could thus be easily referred or transferred to RPA. A similar close relationship between the Perth clinics and, initially, O&G Harry Cohen at the King Edward Memorial Hospital (KEMH) operated during the 1990s, and into the early 2000s. Melbourne clinics worked with the RWH. Davina, a retired GP when we talked, who had worked in Melbourne and Hobart clinics, recalled that in the 1990s 'Hobart Hospital was there, but ... you really felt much more out on a limb in Tasmania'; this was both isolating for the doctor and the clinic, and less than ideal for patients. Rosalie, also worked in Melbourne and Hobart, reported improvement at the Royal Hobart Hospital (RHH) in the 2000s, where the senior doctor she dealt with was 'very supportive'. However, a decade later, public hospital support was still strained in some places. Ingrid, a GP provider in SA, reported a conversation with a GP in regional SA who wanted to offer early medical abortion but was hesitating 'because the two obstetricians in [regional centre] have told me that if a woman has retained products of conception after her medical abortion they will not do a D&C.'

The last element of the Australian system of abortion services provision concerns information. The criminalisation of and stigma associated with abortion have meant that information has not historically been available via the standard sources of information about health care.[25] In the 1970s, abortion information and telephone referral services were provided by Women's Liberation and pro-choice groups. Children by Choice, the Queensland-based service established in 1972, was one of these, and continues to perform this function.[26] The All Options Pregnancy Counselling, Information and Advocacy Service (All Options), which operated from 2003 to 2006 in Sydney with funds from the sale of the Bessie Smyth clinic, was the only other service that focused on abortion referral and counselling.[27] The government-funded Women's Community Health Centres established in the 1970s and 1980s have been key sources of information since then, as have the respective state-based Family Planning organisations and some youth health services.

While public and community sector resources are part of the system of abortion care provision in Australia, as a predominantly private sector service it is ruled by market forces. When new abortion providers entered the market, their impact often illustrated how precarious the viability of existing businesses was. Doctors who had worked in private clinics and/or run their own talked a lot about business—'You've gotta be making a profit, you've got to have a healthy industry and to do that there has to be reasonable profit' was how retired Sydney GP abortion provider Roger put it. Some expressed pride in the systems they developed, the quality of care they delivered and the success of their businesses. Some claimed they offered superior services to their competitors. Rosalie compared prices in Hobart during the 2000s, when there were two competing clinics, to those in Albury where there was only one during the same period and patients were charged more. She thought that competition 'probably makes the service better.'

In a finely balanced market, the profit motive impacts on the price structure for patients. In this business context, Roger described his attitude to what he called 'freebies':

I became very averse to doing freebies because a GP would ring up and say 'She's poor.' With a 2 per cent profit margin, you do that free TOP, you're behind for the week or at best zero profit. So this is where there was no largesse … so earlier on, yeah, and I still did it on selective cases … if you start making too many exceptions, an exception is an exception, the system gets rorted. Then you start raising the whole cost to everyone and then … who's winning?

Some private clinics have chosen to 'bulk-bill' abortion services to Medicare for some patients, meaning that those patients pay nothing. Viv, who advocated for women in Sydney during the 2000s, counted Roger's clinic in this group! Rowena, who worked in a non-medical role at FCC from the early 1990s, stated:

> if a woman can't pay, well, then we will try and work out a payment plan. … I know the director has just said 'that's okay, just go through with something.' … I've heard that with some clinics, they will not budge. There is no give for women on pension cards or students or whatever.

Likewise, in her account of the history of the All Options service, Margaret Kirkby wrote that 'the missing information which most women want is "which abortion service offers reduced fees"'.[28]

Abortion Provision, 2000s

Marie Stopes International (MSI) began its move into the Australian abortion-providing market in 2000 (see Chapter 4). Established in the UK in 1976, it conducted sexual and reproductive health work in developing countries and was one of the two large NGO abortion providers in England and Wales, operating through the NHS.[29] It established its operation in Australia as Marie Stopes Australia (henceforth Marie Stopes) with status as a charity, running clinics with the intention of generating financial surpluses to support its work in the Asia-Pacific area in particular.

Throughout the 2000s, Marie Stopes bought up existing clinics and/or set up new ones, first in WA and then in the east coast states and the ACT. They arrived at a time when some smaller clinics were struggling and some longstanding doctor-operators were ageing and experiencing difficulty in finding buyers for their businesses. Not all of these were bought by Marie Stopes. In 2011 Dr Christine Healy's clinic in Melbourne simply closed, so did Preterm in Sydney in 2015. The three Tasmanian clinics established in the early 2000s closed in 2014, 2016 and 2018, and the Albury clinic established in 2003 closed in 2018.[30] By the early 2020s, however, Marie Stopes occupied between 30 and 40 per cent of the market in Australia.

Marie Stopes introduced a corporate approach to Australia's private abortion-providing sector. As part of an international organisation it had access to capital beyond the reach of most existing or potential private owner-operators in Australia. In the wake of enabling federal legislation in 2006, it established MS Health, a separate company, to import the abortifacient mifepristone. Since gaining approval to do so from the Therapeutic Goods Administration (TGA) in 2012, MS Health has distributed mifepristone with misoprostol (marketed as MS-2 Step) and enabled the rollout of early medical abortion in Australia (see Chapter 5).[31]

In other words, Marie Stopes both capitalised on existing winds of change in the abortion provision sector and created its own. Roger experienced this as a cultural change as well as economic change. While he admired Marie Stopes' protocols, he described himself and his peers as 'craft men,' lamenting the end of their era. He was adamant that 'you can never replace craft with regulation':

> You have a good doctor who keeps his eyes on the ball, you know, or her eyes on the ball … They most often will pick up problems before they occur. It's just when you get mass production, corporate type that this system falls down and needs to be replaced with a far more costly and complex management structure … You can't replace a good owner-operator with a system—the former is always better both in clinical outcomes and cost effectiveness. But the owner-operator system may not suit the regulators, the regulators want you to have your bits of paper, your accreditation, you

know, this and that and this and that, and that diverts focus, time and money resources away from the core business.

He concluded, 'I look at it with sort of split emotions.'

The accreditation Roger mentions refers to the upgraded standards for the operation of day hospitals—which is how clinics that provide surgical abortions are categorised—that have been implemented in all jurisdictions over the last three decades. Regulations have not been consistent between states, and Rosalie claimed that this explains why there have been no specialist private abortion clinics in regional Victoria, where standards are higher. When establishing their clinic in the early 2000s for patients who were travelling to Melbourne from north-eastern Victoria, FCC chose to locate it in Albury, just over the border in NSW. Many interviewees described the introduction of new standards for day hospitals as putting upward pressure on prices. Some clinics closed because their operating model could not accommodate the capital investment that would be required; media coverage of the closure of Preterm in Sydney in 2015 noted that 'The costs of maintaining accreditation—including extra nurses and recovery beds—made it difficult for the centre to compete against new players in the market', the latter presumably a reference to Marie Stopes.[32]

A number of doctors commented on the coincidence between the arrival of Marie Stopes and the demise of the Abortion Providers Federation of Australia (APFA). APFA was established in the 1976 by Bertram Wainer and was in part modelled on the USA's National Abortion Providers Federation, whose conferences have been attended by several Australian doctors over the years. APFA was a national organisation resourced by membership fees and volunteer labour—most private clinics around the country were members[33]—which established and updated clinical protocols and standards, advocated for abortion providers and contributed to public debate via media commentary and other means. It also held national conferences. The 1996 NHMRC report on abortion recommended that APFA play a leading role in both clinical teaching about abortion and setting standards, indicating its standing in the medical field at that time.[34]

Davina enjoyed the APFA community and conferences:

> [It provided] a really good sense of feeling validated with what we were doing, it was scientific, it was well-done, a lot of doctors like to keep it all on a science medical side, but those things interested me anyway. ... so that was all really good, ... this was a way of networking to provide a better service really.

After the 2001 conference in Adelaide, however, energy faded. Children by Choice in Brisbane began organising national conferences at which abortion concerns were central, from at least 2008,[35] with sponsorship from Marie Stopes from 2017, but these did not necessarily have a clinical focus. In 2014, individual counsellors from the PAC in Adelaide, the RWH in Melbourne and Marie Stopes formed NAAPOC (National Alliance of Abortion Pregnancy Options Counsellors), providing support and an advocacy platform for these workers. However, neither of these has replaced APFA.

One explanation for APFA's demise may be that existing private providers, increasingly under commercial pressure from Marie Stopes, had less time and resources available to contribute to a national organisation. Leadership of APFA had circulated among the leading providers. Roger postulated that Marie Stopes, which was not involved in APFA, did not have the same interests as the smaller private providers. Davina regretted that APFA had not been more involved in opening up early medical abortion in Australia, which she thought could have been an opportunity to promote nurse- and midwife-led provision.

At the same time as Marie Stopes was coming to occupy a large part of the market, a move in the other direction was taking place. Commercial players began to operate in small markets in NSW, Queensland and Tasmania in the late 1990s. 'Everybody's then trying to open up their own centres in smaller and smaller catchment areas', as Roger put it. GCA, for example (established in 1998), had five clinics across regional NSW as well as two in Tasmania, the latter operating on alternate fortnights through the 2000s and 2010s.[36] Simon, a GP who has worked for Marie Stopes and in many private clinics in Sydney, estimated in interview in 2015 that the number of private providers doubled in about five years around the turn of the century. This coincided with a peak in the national abortion rate.[37] By 2010, with this rate in decline, the environment for new private providers offering surgical abortions was no longer so propitious. 'The market's just a little bit too uncertain,' Simon mused, and any interested person would be 'wondering what MSI [Marie Stopes] has planned.'

In the early 2000s WA became the first place where contractual partnerships between the public and private sectors for abortion provision were introduced. Interviewees Joyce and Joseph, social worker and O&G at the KEMH, both recalled that the hospital contracted first with Marie Stopes and then later also with Judith Nash's clinic to provide abortions for women who met the hospital's restrictive eligibility criteria, implementing its preference to not do any first trimester abortions at all. Since 2015, Marie Stopes has also been contracted to provide abortions which would otherwise have been provided at the new Midland Health Campus, a public hospital in Perth's north-east that is run by the Catholic St John of God company, which refuses to provide any form of birth control.[38] Some health regions in Queensland established a similar relationship with Marie Stopes in the wake of decriminalisation in 2018.[39] A much more comprehensive arrangement was established in the aftermath of decriminalisation in the NT: in 2017, the territory government entered a five-year contract with the Family Planning Welfare Association NT (FPWNT) to provide early medical abortion.[40] While public–private partnerships have been increasingly common in the Australian healthcare system in the running of entire hospitals, the outsourcing of one particular essential procedure is not so common, and these contracts to private and community providers are at the moment small in scale.[41]

When early medical abortion became available on the Pharmaceutical Benefits Scheme (PBS) in 2013, it enabled a different kind of expansion in the footprint of abortion provision, and created part of the uncertainty Simon referred to above. Some small specialist private clinics, including some operated by Marie Stopes, offer only early medical abortion, thus avoiding the need to meet the standards for surgical facilities. The provision of abortion has also extended to some public and community-run primary healthcare and sexual and reproductive health focused clinics. The Cairns Sexual Health Service, for example, led the way for this kind of public service in 2006 and continues to do so, free to the patient.[42] In 2015, Gateway Health in northern Victoria, a registered Community Health Service, also started offering early medical abortion through its sexual health clinics in Wodonga and later Wangaratta.[43] Family Planning clinics in NSW, Tasmania, the NT and WA began to offer early medical abortion in the late 2010s in and beyond the capital cities, as have some Aboriginal Community Controlled Health Organisations.[44] The volume of public and community clinic provision, however, is still small. Of potentially greater significance is the fact that GPs in private practice have also become abortion providers. Ten years after MS-2 Step was registered on the PBS, however, its uptake by GPs remains small, and some GP practices baulk at the financial, organisational and ideological challenges of integrating early medical abortion into their business model.[45] In 2023, only around 12 per cent of all GPs in Australia were registered to provide early medical abortion, and not all of these will necessarily do so. They are also disproportionately located in urban areas. Most importantly, those that do provide early medical abortion do not necessarily make this public knowledge. Significantly, the proportion of pharmacists registered to dispense MS-2 Step is also inadequate.[46]

As happened elsewhere, the availability of early medical abortion in Australia has made telehealth abortion services possible. The Tabbot Foundation, established by Dr Paul Hyland (the co-founder of GCA) in 2015, pioneered telehealth abortion services, and provided about 1 per cent of all abortions in Australia until it closed in 2019.[47] Marie Stopes has since become the most significant national provider of telehealth abortion, with others also stepping into the space created by Tabbot.[48] The health and safety issues created by the COVID-19 pandemic led to increased demand for telehealth, and the federal government's introduction of a new Medicare Benefits Schedule (MBS) item number early in the pandemic to facilitate its provision made its delivery more affordable.[49] However, most providers of abortion telehealth require that patients reside within two hours of an emergency facility, so this option is not a panacea for those in remote locations.

A detailed account of changes to clinical protocols over and above the introduction of early medical abortion is beyond the scope of this book, but I will briefly mention two. First is the move to the use of ultrasound for surgical procedures, pre-operatively for diagnostic purposes and then during the operation as a guide, which became standard during the 1990s. Second is the use of light sedatives during surgical procedures, which by the end of the 1990s had almost universally replaced the previous options of general or local anaesthetic. Viv and Davina regretted the demise of local anaesthetic, which had been used at Bessie Smyth clinic until the mid-1990s, at Preterm in Sydney, Christine Healy's Melbourne clinic and elsewhere, and was preferred by some women.[50] Viv in particular saw the unconscious or sedated patient as a move away from patient autonomy and towards medicalisation.

Several people I interviewed told me that over time, private clinics started to offer less specialist counselling. The growing recognition that most patients did not want counselling, even though the 1996 NMHRC Information Paper still recommended it, played a significant role in this shift.[51] Marie Stopes went against the trend, launching a free telephone-counselling service staffed by qualified counsellors in late 2009, but since 1990 very few private clinics have employed dedicated counsellors. In part this is for business reasons: as Roger said, 'why put a counsellor's wage on your operating costs side of things?' Instead, as Joyce noted of WA, some individual clinics have referred patients who needed counselling to public hospital social work services where the hospital services were known to be willing. In Melbourne, as Rowena recalled, some clinics referred patients who presented with particular decisional difficulties to the FCC, to see long-time clinical psychologist Susie Allanson. Government-funded abortion-specific counselling provided by community sector agencies was also an outcome of the 1998 law reform in WA.[52] While these initially included Catholic agency Centacare, since 2016 only Sexual Health Quarters (Family Planning WA) has received funding.[53] Recent thinking has turned to the need for trauma-informed approaches to abortion care, in particular to respond to patients who have experienced reproductive coercive control and other forms of domestic violence.[54]

The arrival of the internet has been a game-changer in the provision of information about abortion. Most abortion clinics developed their own websites during the 2000s.[55] Marie Stopes and some community organisations also have comprehensive websites, and offer 1800 phone lines to provide information, including Children by Choice, some women's health centres and some family planning organisations. Women's Health Victoria, an independent feminist agency, has operated the state government's 1800 My Options phone line and website under contract since 2018.[56] Similarly, Family Planning NSW operates the NSW government's Pregnancy Choices Helpline, which was established in 2019, as well as its own Talkline.[57] Women's Health Tasmania was funded in 2020 to produce a services map, similar to the Victorian and Queensland maps. However, the internet also has a downside. Some organisations that oppose abortion also have websites and offer phone and face-to-face counselling that often provides misinformation. These are known in the sector as 'false providers'.[58]

The striking decrease in the actual number of abortions performed in Australia since 1999, and the decline in the abortion rate (the number per 1000 women of reproductive age who have an abortion in any given year), demands comment for its impact on the abortion-providing sector. Simply put, there is less consumer demand. In SA—the only state that gathers and publishes comprehensive data on abortions—the number of abortions provided in 1990 was 4463: a rate of 13.4. This number reached a high point of 5660—a rate of 17.8—in 1999, but by 2021 was down to 4597, or 13.6.[59] An estimate of the national rate for the period 2014–18 showed a similar trend, although it should be noted that the accuracy of all abortion statistics is contestable.[60] This decline in the annual abortion rate may be related to the uptake of highly effective Long Acting Reversible Contraception (LARC), which includes IUDs and hormonal implants (although this is relatively small), and to a small increase in the fertility rate in the first decade of the twenty-first century.[61] Decreasing demand in the twenty-first century has combined with increasing provision of early medical abortion to put pressure on the viability of some specialist private clinics that provide surgical procedures.

Into the 2020s

In 1990 there were about twenty private clinics in Australia, plus some provision in public and private hospitals. In 2022, state-based websites that list abortion providers—some more thoroughly than others—tally well over 300. These are private clinics, community-based health services, public hospitals and GP clinics (private hospital provision of first trimester abortion has all but disappeared). The number of publicly listed providers is without doubt an under-estimate given that many GPs who provide early medical abortion do not promote this information, and the practices of public hospi-tals are not necessarily clearly stated on the public record. The number of providers belies the domination of Marie Stopes, whose clinics and telehealth service provided between 30 and 40 per cent of all abortions in the early 2020s. In every state and territory, abor-tion providers are concentrated in the large cities; surgical abortions are rarely available outside capital cities, and even there are only available in a small number of clinics—about 15 per cent of all listed clinics in Queensland and 30 per cent in Victoria, for example (these may include public hospitals where provision may not be guaranteed). State maps show that eastern Victoria, the east and west coasts and north-east Tasmania and inland Queensland are clearly poorly served.

The availability of early medical abortion, including by tele-health, has changed the horizon of possibility. In 2014–15 a survey of patients proficient in English from Marie Stopes clinics across several jurisdictions showed that 35 per cent of those eligible chose early medical abortion.[62] In 2018, early medical abortion accounted for 40 per cent of all abortions in SA and 33 per cent of those in WA.[63] In the 12 months to mid-2018, the figure for the NT was 73 per cent.[64]

The growth in early medical abortion in the late 2010s and early 2020s saw a concomitant loss of surgical services for rural and regional people. As noted earlier the three private clinics that opened in Tasmania in the 2000s, which had always relied on fly-in fly-out (FIFO) doctors, closed in 2014, 2016 and 2018.[65] The FCC clinic in Albury closed in 2018.[66] In 2021, Marie Stopes announced the closure of its clinics in regional Queensland and NSW 'because of rising costs'—an effect of the COVID-19 pandemic.[67] It had already closed its Maroondah clinic in Melbourne, which offered a unique and invaluable national service up to 24 weeks pregnancy. COVID-19 brought particular challenges to private abortion providers, involving early difficulties sourcing personal protective equipment (PPE) and workforce difficulties, including constraints on the FIFO workforce due to travel restrictions.[68] It also increased demand for telehealth abortion, as noted above.

In most jurisdictions the proportion of abortions done in the public sector in the early 2020s was less than that in 1990.[69] In half, public provision could only be relied upon when the pregnant person's health was severely compromised, or following diagnosis of foetal anomaly. Even in Victoria, where public provision of services has been both significant and historically entrenched, it is estimated to be down from the 1990 level.[70]

SA and the NT are the exceptions to the rule of declining public provision. By the early 2020s over 97 per cent of all abortions in SA were done in metropolitan public hospitals, and in the NT

85 per cent were done in public hospitals or (most) at FPWNT, where they are publicly funded. At the end of the 2010s there were also small signs of an increase in public provision and, since 2018, public funding in Queensland. Tasmania, where public provision fell dramatically when private clinics were operating in the 1990s and 2000s, also saw a dramatic increase from 2021, and the ACT government announced in 2022 that all abortions in the territory would be publicly funded from mid-2023. These increases are the result of persistent lobbying by advocates, decriminalisation and/or and sympathetic ministers.[71]

In the 2020s, in other words, the provision of abortion care in Australia is both remarkably different from what it was in 1990, and in some respects not far from where it started. The legal framework has changed, with discernible effects on provision in some jurisdictions and little or none in others. This is discussed in Chapter 6. Some clinics that were present in 1990 survive, providing early medical abortion and surgical services—Victor Chan's Nanyara in Perth, the FCC in Melbourne and Greenslopes in Brisbane, for example. Some of the NSW clinics have been around for over twenty years. All operate in a market dominated by Marie Stopes, which has one or more clinics in every mainland capital city except Adelaide and Darwin, plus a national telehealth service. The availability of early medical abortion and telehealth offsets the concentration of clinics in metropolitan centres to some degree, but currently only for those who are less than 63 days pregnant and suited for—and happy to have—a medical rather than a surgical procedure.

Inasmuch as the proliferation of small and local providers signifies a normalisation of abortion care, it is a good thing, but the decline in public hospital provision in the most populous states is concerning. So is the domination of Marie Stopes, for different reasons. Its vulnerability as an organisation, as much as its domination of the private sector, means that provision of abortion services is disproportionately affected by its financial fortunes and business direction. The need to travel has never gone away, especially for those in the second trimester. Access to abortion in WA past 20 weeks is legislatively limited, and effectively so in Tasmania and the ACT past 16 weeks, and consequently many people whose pregnancies are past these cut-off points have travelled interstate to access a service.[72]

The shape of the abortion-providing sector has changed in thirty years, and concomitantly, clinical and public advocacy leadership in relation to abortion provision has shifted. Many held hope for the NHMRC report on abortion, conceived in the early 1990s to guide policy; however, it came to a politically motivated demise in 1997 (see Chapter 2). As noted above, APFA represented private providers until the early 2000s, when it faded away. After a hiatus, Children by Choice conferences revived a national community, and from the mid-2010s the Royal Australian and New Zealand College of Obstetricians and Gynaecologists (RANZCOG) began to mobilise in relation to training and clinical standards (see Chapter 3 for discussion of RANZCOG).[73] SPHERE—the Centre of Research Excellence in Sexual and Reproductive Health for Women in Primary Care, established in 2019—has also entered this space. Located at Monash University, funded for five years by the NHMRC, employing a team of clinician researchers, and working with several national partners, SPHERE has three areas of focus, one of which is improving access to and provision of early medical abortion.[74] Marie Stopes participates in these institutional initiatives and provides research and advocacy leadership of its own, and clinical and advocacy staff speak regularly about abortion at a range of professional and academic conferences.

It is possible that the campaigns for the decriminalisation of abortion in each state raised general awareness about access to abortion services. The government-funded websites and/or 1800 numbers in Victoria, Queensland and Tasmania (less so in NSW) are good post-decriminalisation outcomes, but not the answer to all problems of access and affordability. In 2020, for example, Family Planning NSW noted the continuing 'great difficulty making contact with services' in NSW because of lack of information. In 2022

Google banned advertising of abortion by Marie Stopes (by then, MSI Australia), not for the first time.[75] In any case, rural people, those without good internet connections, and those with poor English literacy will be least able to access information.[76]

The Exceptionalism of Abortion

The definition of abortion in the criminal law of each jurisdiction is understood by many to have been the key feature that shapes the exceptional provision of abortion services. While criminalisation 'fossilises the values and assumptions of the era in which it was introduced',[77] it has not necessarily been a significant restrictive constraint on doctors in private practice. In 1990, for example, one of the women who was about to establish the WHF clinic in Tasmania—noting that gynaecologists there had performed a significant number of abortions in recent years—told a feminist conference that 'obviously the law is not the real problem!'[78] The law was a clearly a major problem during the four-year period when the anti-abortion legislation enacted in 1998 was in place in the ACT. Until decriminalisation in 2002 operations at the RHS clinic had to be compliant with a deliberately restrictive law. There were also three instances in which the mobilisation of the criminal law in the form of actual or imminent arrests lead to the temporary cessation of public abortion services—WA in 1998, Tasmania in 2001 and Queensland in 2009–10 (where only early medical abortion ceased), while the state parliaments resolved the situation (see Chapter 6). These instances were shocking, and the subsequent disruption to services caused significant hardship, but outside of these times and places the law has not overly determined the mode of practice. Most doctors I spoke to were adept at explaining their state law, and some were understandably cautious. Davina, for example, always wrote notes about the patient's reason for abortion on their medical records, 'and the only reason I was writing that down was to make sure that if I was raided that that stuff was on every file.' Roger took similar measures: 'I just feel in New South Wales until they repeal the abortion … out of the Crimes Act full stop, I think it's prudent to have the woman's words recorded'. Sally, who worked at the PAC in Adelaide through the 1990s and in the 2000s in a management role, described how this vulnerability was ever-present:

> it would be just terrible to think that a doctor would be taken to court over providing a service ... even though you talk yourself into it, that it would probably be all right in the end, common sense would prevail in the end, and it may even be better, the thought of enduring it is terrifying, really it's terrifying.

Difficulty in recruiting medical staff, which was arguably related to the criminalisation of abortion and the moral values this reflected and reproduced, was an issue raised by many. For some small clinic owner-operators this also meant difficulty organising leave for themselves, or replacing key medical staff who took leave. For example, WA GP provider Nic told me that Judith Nash's clinic in Perth relied on abortion-providing locums from Sydney and Melbourne to allow Nash to take leave. This is a particular concern outside metropolitan centres, and explains why most regional clinics have been staffed by FIFO doctors. In some cases, as several interviewees noted, doctors were willing to perform surgical abortions only up to a certain point in pregnancy, and clinics had to work around this. More than one interviewee commented that it was particularly hard to find senior doctors to take on leadership roles in the larger clinics. Roger hypothesised that this difficulty, which sometimes extended to anaesthetists, partly explained the employment of a drug-addicted, hepatitis C positive anaesthetist who, it was revealed in 2010, had infected a number of patients at the Maroondah clinic in outer Melbourne run by Dr Mark Schulberg, which provided later term abortions.[79] Roger commented, 'I would put that directly down to the fact that if you had a better choice, you wouldn't employ him'. Rosalie thought that few O&Gs would be interested in providing surgical abortions in private clinics when they could make more money in regular practice. Speaking before the take-up of early medical abortion by GPs she noted that many GPs would have invested in their commitment to general practice. Finally, while first trimester surgical abortion is a simple procedure, it requires a capacity for surgical skill that not all GPs have. This narrowed pool of potential recruits was then further limited by the stigmatised status of abortion.

While anti-abortion groups in Australia do not have the political or cultural power that they do in the USA, for example, they have been a significant irritant on clinics' business operations.[80] There were organised community campaigns against the establishment of private abortion clinics in Rockhampton in 1987 and in Hobart in 2002, and the establishment of the PAC in Adelaide was delayed from 1989 to 1992 by anti-abortion opposition.[81] However, it is the regular picketing of clinics by anti-abortionists that has had greater impact on patients and staff.[82] The FCC in Melbourne was targeted persistently over many years, as were many clinics around the country, and Rosalie told me that thinking about ways to avoid impact on patients shaped the choice of the site for the FCC clinic in Hobart.

The murder of security guard Steve Rogers at the FCC in Melbourne in 2001 by a man associated with the anti-abortion group that gathered daily outside the clinic reverberated through the community and was vivid in the memories of those I interviewed.[83] In 2015 Davina recalled exactly where she was when she took the phone call telling her of his murder, and Viv's recollection of the impact on staff at Bessie Smyth clinic, where she had worked over many years, was dramatic. Staff realised that 'if you came in with an AK47 or something, you could have wiped out two or three abortion providers at once'. Many clinics increased their security; David Grundmann reported wearing a bullet-proof vest to work.[84] Julie, who worked in a management position at FPACT told me that although regular anti-abortion protesters at the RHS clinic in Canberra had been 'polite,'

> as a result of that shooting we had to become ready for the maniac. So we brought in the Federal Police … we got

neck-based alarms so that people could hit them and there would be an immediate response. We worked with the security in the building to build that up to speed and put in CCT cameras and … in the stairwells and areas around the outside door of the building.

All this cost money. The constant, or regular, presence of anti-abortion harassment also levied a less tangible cost on staff and patients. These were financial, social and emotional imposts not borne by other healthcare businesses.

What Has This System of Provision of Abortion Services Meant for People Wanting an Abortion?

The 1996 NHMRC report identified structural features that compromised access to abortion services: poverty, rural location; difficulty accessing information, absence of Medicare entitlements or individual constraints on claiming the rebate, and lack of services for those past the first trimester of pregnancy.[85] The report noted that there was little information available about Indigenous women's experiences or 'cultural factors' affecting their access to abortion services.[86] These structural disadvantages have shifted little since the 1990s.

Margaret Kirkby wrote that workers at the All Options service in NSW in the mid-2000s 'were continually being surprised by the depth of the poverty which many women faced and by the depth of the problems which they had faced in their lives for which very little or no support had been available to them'.[87] As noted in the Introduction, a survey of English-proficient patients who had had abortions at Marie Stopes clinics in 2014–15 reported that one-third 'found it difficult/very difficult to pay for the abortion', which for some involved travel and accommodation costs.[88] The disadvantage experienced by poor people and those from Indigenous, migrant and refugee backgrounds is compounded if they live in rural or remote communities, leading regularly to patients presenting later in pregnancy, and so to more complex and more expensive procedures.[89] In

2006, Kerry Arabena wrote that 'A review of State-based policies and procedures for assisting Aboriginal and Torres Strait Islander women to access abortion services is paramount, especially for adolescents requiring second-trimester abortions'.[90] I am not aware of any such review having been conducted.

Many people I spoke with thought that the real cost of an abortion had increased since 1990. Several expressed particular dismay that early medical abortion, when the pharmaceuticals were first listed on the PBS in 2013, was not much cheaper than surgical abortion. In 2023 this is no longer generally the case, but variations in the costs of both surgical and medical abortions make the specifics hard to determine. In the early 1990s, for example, the estimated cost of a first trimester surgical abortion with local anaesthetic in a private clinic after the Medicare rebate was $185. For general anaesthesia, which most patients preferred, the cost with rebate was about $285.[91] Roughly thirty years later, the two equivalent costs are for a first trimester surgical procedure with sedation, and early medical abortion. Contemporary sources indicate that cost varies a lot.[92] In 2023 Children by Choice reports that the price for a surgical abortion up to 12 weeks for a Medicare card holder in Queensland starts at $500, while MSI Australia advertises the cost of a surgical procedure starting at $700. The costs of early medical abortion are also hard to pinpoint. At MSI Australia early medical abortion in a clinic costs from $620. Early medical abortion will usually be cheaper at a GP than at a private clinic. Children by Choice reports only the costs of the medication for early medical abortion, $6.60 for patients with a healthcare card, $41.60 for those without, stating that various pathways make costs variable, and that the cost of medications 'may inevitably continue to rise'. For telehealth, MSI Australia states the cost at $325. The Sydney-based Clinic 66 advertises early medical abortion by telehealth for $255.[93] Medical abortion provided by a public hospital or Community Health Service is generally free to the patient. Patients without a Medicare card can pay at least twice as much as those with a card; Children by Choice lists the cost of the early medical abortion pharmaceuticals at eight times as much.

Trying to establish comparability of fees across time is thus nigh impossible. Even for first trimester surgical procedures, fees have always differed from one private clinic to the next in the one city, between city and regional clinics, and between those clinics that have offered discounts or bulk-billing and those that have not. They still do. All state governments have had Patient Assistance Transport Schemes (PATS) for people who need to travel to access health care, but without a well-informed advocate these have not always been easy to access for people wanting an abortion, so travel costs can also vary from one patient to the next.[94] I have thus not tried to compare the cost of an abortion against women's wages or welfare payments in 1990 and 2020. The situation of those who need an abortion who rely on government benefit payments is, however, sobering in this respect. In March 2023 payment for JobSeeker Payment, for example, which is paid to people who are unemployed or under-employed, could easily mean that an abortion would cost 50 per cent of fortnightly income.[95] In 2020, 20 per cent of women were living in poverty, and single mothers, women suffering domestic and family violence, older women, women with disability, LGBTIQ women, recently arrived women or women from culturally and linguistically diverse backgrounds, and Aboriginal and Torres Strait Islander women were all more vulnerable than others to financial disadvantage and marginalisation.[96]

Some community organisations have created modest funds to support women. Long-time Perth activist Gwen recalled that the Abortion Law Reform Association (ALRA) channelled money to a non-government agency for this purpose in WA in the mid-2000s. Children by Choice has raised money over the years to give or lend to women and has negotiated with other organisations to provide support, as did All Options service. Marie Stopes established The Choice Fund in 2017 to support patients experiencing hardship. Some women's and youth organisations have received government grants to act as brokers: in 2019–20 Penrith Women's Health Centre received about $40,000 to manage 'referrals from across NSW'. Their funds were supplemented by fundraising and donations.[97]

At their 2017 conference Children by Choice staff presented a breakdown of how money was raised for one woman. To pay a fee of $1500, already discounted by the clinic (presumably for an abortion at around 16 weeks), six sources were noted: the woman herself ($90); Children by Choice ($300) and their No Interest Loan fund ($200); a local domestic violence service ($200); another organisation ($100); and a 'social media callout' ($640).[98]

The problem of poor information about and access to abortion services, particularly for those who are young, poor, Indigenous and/or racially and culturally marginalised, is increasingly noted in the research literature, advocacy and media discussion, although there is less reference to access issues for people with disability and LGBTIQ people who need abortion care. The culture of abortion-providing services has received less attention. A few presentations at APFA and Children by Choice conferences over the years have discussed the needs of patients with respect to differences in ability, language, religion, migration and cultural background, and the public-facing profiles of many government and community sector providers, and Marie Stopes, acknowledge cultural diversity. Private abortion services that foreground a welcome to poor people (for example, by promoting bulk-billing), or people with disabilities (for example, by noting wheelchair access or Auslan services) on their websites, or advertise languages other than English or the availability of interpreting services, are rare, and not all telehealth services will work with interpreters.[99] In other words, about half of the nation's abortion providers *appear* to pay little attention to cultural diversity and inclusion. By default, they recreate a dominant middle-class, able-bodied heteronormative whiteness as the cultural norm for abortion-providing services. While there is Australian academic literature on cultural difference in relation to sexual and reproductive health, there is little research that addresses these matters specifically in relation to abortion provision.[100] In noting the relatively low proportion of Aboriginal women accessing early medical abortion in the NT, Murdoch and colleagues draw attention to research about women's health services in general which show 'the low numbers of

Aboriginal people in the health workforce and culturally incompetent care from the non-Aboriginal workforce'.[101] Recent research on reproductive coercion (RC) in migrant and refugee families in Victoria and Tasmania reports cases of forced abortion, pointing to similar incompetency. '[P]roviders of reproductive health care may facilitate the perpetration of RC by allowing partners or family members to mediate communication in health settings and failing to ensure informed consent to health procedures.' The authors note these instances as lost opportunities to intervene in family violence.[102] The research centre SPHERE lists 'gaps in medical abortion service provision in Australia, including for women from culturally and linguistically diverse backgrounds' as one of its areas of focus, so they may generate more research in this area in the future.[103] The submission on sexual and reproductive rights from Women With Disabilities Australia (WWDA) to the Royal Commission into Violence, Abuse, Neglect and Exploitation of People With Disability refers repeatedly to the lack of reproductive autonomy experienced by women with disabilities, including coerced abortion. This has implications for abortion providers (although these are not teased out). Among many recommendations, the submission calls for governments to 'prohibit all forms of forced treatment ... [including] coerced abortion' and work with disability organisations to 'develop a national strategy to improve access for women and girls with disability to mainstream sexual and reproductive health care'.[104]

As noted in the Introduction, nearly all of the people I interviewed were, as far as I was aware, white Australians. I did not ask questions about clinic cultural norms. While interviewees referred to cultural differences among patients, such as international students and Muslim women who need a women-only service, only one drew attention to organisational issues of race and culture. This was Julie, who related the changes at the RHS clinic in the ACT following the appointment in 2000 of Torres Strait Islander woman (subsequently Professor) Kerry Arabena as Executive Director of Family Planning ACT (FPACT) and RHS. Arabena's work included building relationships with the ACT's Aboriginal community, who had previously had little engagement with FPACT. Under her leadership Julie noted there were

> peer education programs and getting [Indigenous] people engaged and employed through our organisation. And some of them ended up working across at Reproductive Healthcare Services in receptionist kind of roles as well, … having that face at the front counter really helped build a sense of trust and organisational responsiveness to a whole range of issues.

This strategy brought 'a bit more of a different-looking demographic of people who sought services across the two organisations'.[105] In other words, this period of attention to the whiteness of the organisation, even as RHS was under significant external pressure, made a difference.

That the neoliberal system of abortion care provision is driven by the need to make a profit—begrudging this need on the part of individual providers is not my point—and not by the needs of people who require abortions adds to existing inequity, marginalisation and impoverishment, and to the risk of reproductive injustice. There is no shortage of research and reports showing the way forward. Family Planning NSW's *Framework for Abortion Access in NSW*, produced in 2020, is one such report.[106] Its recommendations are predictable: coordinated information; 'accessible, appropriate and affordable abortion services' that offer choice of method enabled by workforce planning to which public hospitals contribute; improved quality of services, training and support; and research and data collection. The needs of Aboriginal and Torres Strait Islander and other marginalised women are mentioned in several places. With the exception of this new awareness of race and cultural diversity, however, the recommendations are remarkably similar to those made twenty-five years earlier by the NHMRC *Information Paper* in 1996.

Chapter 2

Public

According to the NHMRC report, as noted in Chapter 1, in 1990 only about 13 per cent of all abortions in Australia were provided in public hospitals.[1] The proportion of publicly provided abortions in 2020 was probably lower than that, although the figure is hard to pinpoint. Abortion is the only common and necessary healthcare procedure on which the public health system turns its back. As I have already noted, the proportion of babies delivered in public hospitals grew from about 50 per cent in 1990 to about 75 per cent in 2017.[2] Through the public hospital system the state supports birthing and motherhood, but while 'choice' is commonly rhetorically associated with abortion, most of those in Australia who want an abortion have no choice but to find enough money, at short notice, to pay a private provider. This chapter explains in detail how and why the public health system has failed to adequately provide abortion services since 1990.

The provision of abortion through the public health system is important for several reasons. Abortions provided in the public health sector are available for little or no cost to the patient. This is essential to ensuring that pregnant people can access abortion regardless of their financial means, as we know that for many people the cost of their abortion in a private clinic is a punishing financial burden,[3] and that private clinics are rarely present outside the large metropolitan centres and GPs offering early medical abortion can be scarce. Public healthcare facilities in these locations are an obvious way to meet the needs of those seeking an abortion.

Provision of abortion through the public health service is also a workforce training issue. The majority of nurses and doctors, including specialists, are trained in our large public hospitals, and the lack of widespread training in abortion provision in public hospitals is one reason why abortion services periodically experience medical workforce crises. It is also health professionals in the public system, who may also have appointments in university medical schools, who conduct research on abortion care and develop clinical protocols. Such work has rarely been conducted by providers outside the public sector.[4]

Finally, public provision has an ideological function: it signals that abortion is a normal part of health care that should be made available to all. The expectation that abortion will be provided though the public health system means that governments can, theoretically, be held directly accountable for the provision of abortion care; for example, through public debate and policy commitments at election time. In response to media coverage in March 2020 about the lack of abortion provision at a major regional public hospital, the NSW Minister for Health relied on the absence of this expectation to neatly sidestep government responsibility to provide this necessary health care when he said that 'Services for terminations in the early phases of pregnancy across Australia are normally delivered through the private and not-for-profit sector'.[5]

Since 2013, the subsidised availability of early medical abortion, which can be provided by a GP and now accounts for about one-third of all abortions, means that the need for a free or low-cost public surgical abortion service in Australia has lessened. But the failure of the public health system to provide adequate access to abortion remains the number one obstacle to better access for all who need abortions. This chapter offers an historical account of how abortion services have been provided through the public sector in Australia. The big question is, Why hasn't the public sector provided more?

Optimism and Its Demise

The problems with the provision of abortion services were described in the 1990 submission on abortion to the UN Committee on the Elimination of Discrimination Against Women made by the Perth branch of the Women's Electoral Lobby (WEL). It described a 'patchwork of legislation and policy—or lack of it—which makes the availability of services a "lottery" for Australian women'.[6] But in the late 1980s and early 1990s, optimism was growing among feminists involved in women's health and in the pro-choice movement about the possibility of improved access to abortion services.

The 1980s in Australia were 'a golden age in the development of women's health policies, centres and services'. In 1989, in the wake of the 1985 UN World Conference on Women in Nairobi, and after nationwide consultation, the National Women's Health Policy was announced—a world first.[7] The success of the women's health movement at this time was part of the broader strength of the 'second wave' of the Australian women's movement's 'direct engagement with the state'.[8] This strategy yielded women's advisors to ministers and government departments, and women's units which developed policy. Historian of the women's health movement in Australia Gwen Gray Jamieson acknowledges, however, that the pioneering federal women's health policy came without a 'sufficiently strong women's health policy machinery' and was never accorded priority in budgets. Initial funding was 'tiny'. In the context of the rise of neoliberalism, it delivered very little expansion of women's health programs either at the federal level, even under the ALP government, or at state level.[9] And although the Australian women's health movement had roots in the feminist abortion politics of the 1970s, in the 1980s, when it came to the development of women's health policy, abortion was often the unwanted cousin at the party. In the final report that proposed the National Women's Health Policy, written for the country's health ministers, reference to abortion is brief and comes with a moralising disclaimer.[10]

Notwithstanding this ambivalence, feminist abortion advocacy was coming to fruition. The establishment in 1992 of the PAC, a freestanding public abortion clinic affiliated with a public hospital in a western suburb of Adelaide, is arguably the most significant and innovative development of this period. This groundbreaking and still unique service was the result of a six-year push, led at community level by the Coalition for Women's Right to Choose, for the implementation of the recommendations of the 1986 report to the South Australian Health Commission (SAHC). Written by SAHC's Women's Health Advisor, Liz Furler, the report addressed the inadequacy of existing abortion services in SA.[11] The RHS clinic in the ACT opened in 1994 in government-owned premises, for which they were charged only a peppercorn rent, and the WHF clinic in Hobart, which sought no government support at all, had nonetheless benefited from association with the government-funded Women's Health Centre.[12]

Three publicly funded research and review projects, all based in SA, also commenced in the early 1990s. First, feminist healthcare administrator Judith Dwyer and feminist academic Lyndall Ryan received SA government funding for a small oral history project to uncover SA women's experiences of abortion before law reform.[13] Then Ryan, with Margie Ripper and Barbara Buttfield—two other Adelaide feminist academics—was funded by the Commonwealth Department of Health to conduct a national investigation into abortion service provision and women's experiences. Their report, *We Women Decide,* was released in 1994.[14] Their research coincided with the Women's Health Committee of the NHMRC commissioning an expert panel, chaired by Dwyer and based in Adelaide, to review current abortion service provision.[15] *We Women Decide* and the NHMRC report both recommended that regional health authorities and/or state government health departments take responsibility for the adequate provision of abortion services for all, with particular attention to the needs of women in rural areas.[16] The Furler Report in SA had already recommended this in 1986, as had the report of the federal Royal Commission into Human Relationships in 1977.[17] This provided a clear lineage of research and strong feminist advocacy on which to build.

The turn away from a political environment in which it was possible to imagine abortion services improving came quickly, however. The election in 1996 of the LNP federal government led by Prime Minister John Howard signalled a national turn to moral conservatism.[18] Soon after its election, the government made deals concerning abortion with conservative Catholic Independent Tasmanian Senator Brian Harradine. One consequence was the delay, for more than a decade, of widespread availability of early medical abortion in Australia.

In 1994 the NHMRC's Women's Health Committee was abolished as part of a restructure of NHMRC committees. The ongoing work of the abortion expert panel faced significant obstacles inside the NHMRC. The panel's report also faced an external campaign from anti-abortionists and, after the 1996 election, from the government. It was modified and released in May 1997 as an information paper rather than an NHMRC report. It was then withdrawn at the behest of the Minister for Health, released again with further diminished authority, and withdrawn again, then finally disappeared. Ryan and Ripper's analysis of 'the withdrawal method' of silencing feminist expertise on abortion places this episode in a long history of the exclusion of feminism and women's voices from medical and scientific authority.[19]

The introduction of both the National Women's Health Policy and the NHMRC Women's Committee came at a time when the Hawke–Keating ALP governments were reorienting economic policy towards neoliberalism and away from the principles of social liberalism that had prevailed in Australia in the postwar period. The reform of the federal bureaucracy in this period affected all departments, but most notably those that delivered services, including health; the federal government's investment in and capacity to redistribute wealth was downsized.[20] This was not good for feminist engagement with the state.[21] Anna, an academic women's health activist who spoke with me in 2013, described the rise of 'content-free management' which accompanied the neoliberal reform of the federal bureaucracy, in which senior bureaucrats no longer needed knowledge of the areas over which they presided. This resulted in the departure of 'key people who knew a lot about the politics and history of women's health in general, and abortion, and contraception … so a lot of that sort of historic knowledge inside the department was missing.'

By the mid-1990s the energy, networks and funding that had fuelled the development of women's health policies were 'starting to come unstuck', as Anna described it, and 'the women's advisors and the women's health services cycled into demise'. 'Mainstreaming women's health' was the new mantra. In SA this was experienced by women's health centres as 'severe budget cuts', 'policies of privatisation and contracting out for services' and the agenda to 'regionalise the health system'.[22] Anna came to the conclusion that the fate of the NHMRC report had been sealed before its eventual defeat by moral conservatives: 'Given the other political shifts … even if we hadn't had that change of government and the change of minister, and the change of the NHMRC … it wouldn't have had anywhere to go'.

At the time of writing the withdrawn NHMRC report stands as the last by a national health body or a funded research team with national focus to propose a comprehensive nationwide policy on abortion. Neither did any state or territory have policy on abortion until Victoria in 2017 (see below). In any case, professional and institutional culture can stand in for policy, or its absence. Robbie, an abortion-providing sexual and reproductive health doctor in North Queensland whom I interviewed in 2013, entertained me with a story of the mid-2000s when public provision of abortion services was being discussed in Cairns:

> They just said, 'You can't do that in Queensland.' And I said, 'Why not?' And they said, 'Well it's policy.' … So, I asked senior doctors, medical directors, and so on at the hospital, and superintendents, if they could get me the policy, and they said, 'Yes, we'll get it for you.' But they couldn't actually find it. Well, fair enough … so I then went to the policy

people in Brisbane and said, 'Can you dig up your policy on abortion for Queensland?' ... 'Oh yes, yes there is a policy, I'll get it for you.' I said, 'Great, thanks.' She got back to me a couple of days later and said, 'Oh, actually, we don't seem to have one.' And I said, 'But everyone says it's policy.' And she said, 'Well, maybe a politician a long time ago said something, but we don't actually have any written policy at all.'

This imagined policy is possibly the most effective kind: deeply embedded, outside of any formal process and peculiarly resistant to change.

You Can Get an Abortion in the Public Sector Here

Despite the absence of state or territory government policy commitment to ensuring equitable access to abortion, some public hospitals or clinics have provided abortion services over the last thirty years. In the 'lottery' described by WEL in 1990, some women get lucky.

As I noted in Chapter 1, in the small jurisdictions of SA and the NT, public hospitals have been entrenched as the main providers of abortion since the early 1970s. They accounted for about one-third of all public abortions nationwide in 1990. In Tasmania at that time, the proportion of all abortions performed in a public hospital was 34 per cent, in Victoria 17.5 per cent, in WA 10.4 per cent, in NSW 9 per cent and in Queensland 0.2 per cent.[23] The trend over the last thirty years in Tasmania (until the 2020s) and in WA was definitely downward, and there is evidence of downward trends in Victoria and NSW as well. Public provision in SA and the NT, in contrast, has consolidated since 1990, and there was very small but proportionately significant growth in public provision in Queensland from the early 2010s to about 4.5 per cent in 2016, more since decriminalisation in 2018.

Victoria

The Pregnancy Advisory Service (PAS), located in the RWH in Melbourne, was, until its dismantling in 2018, the longest-standing of only two specialised abortion services in any Australian public hospital. The PAS was established in 1975, initiating a decade of determined opposition from the anti-abortion movement.[24] It was the point of contact for people wanting abortions, and provided information and counselling for those who might then attend the outpatient Choices Clinic day surgery where the procedure was performed. The Monash Medical Centre in Melbourne's east has also consistently provided a smaller number of abortions over the past thirty years, as have a number of other public hospitals in Victoria. Some have done so less consistently, which I discuss below.[25]

Evie, a social worker who had worked in Victorian women's services for decades, thought abortion at the RWH through the 1990s was 'still the poor cousin of women's health'. The PAS was located 'in a tiny little room in the old hospital with no windows and cockroaches'. During the 2000s the PAS developed into a more professional service as a result of staff lobbying and, in Evie's view, the ideologically freeing effect of the administrative separation of the RWH from the Royal Children's Hospital in 2004. Through the 2000s and 2010s, as well as providing direct service to women, the small number of part-time workers at the PAS produced a comprehensive website, pursued advocacy in several settings and collaborated to produce research with academic, community and private partners as part of the backdrop to the campaign for decriminalisation in Victoria.[26] Evie pointed out, however, that this work was often done in individual staff members' own time. Likewise, in 2014, Bunny, a Melbourne abortion counsellor, recalled that PAS counselling staff were also involved in the establishment of the NAAPOC, again in their own time. Notwithstanding its achievements, Bunny and Evie both commented on the constraints of institutional wariness about abortion at the RWH. Difficulties in attracting medical staff to the Choices Clinic, competition with other services for theatre time, tensions around budgeting and the ongoing presence of stigmatising behaviour from other staff were constant stressors.

The RWH's commitment to a public abortion service was no guarantee for individual women. Not all phone calls were answered, and in the mid-1990s only a third who got through were able to access a service at the RWH; the rest were referred to private clinics.[27] This rate improved in the 2000s to about 45 per cent, although some women spent hours on the phone to get through. As Evie noted, the service was effectively reserved for the most socio-economically disadvantaged patients, complex cases and rural women.[28]

The PAS was dismantled by the hospital in 2018, leaving many past and present staff shocked by what one media report described as a poorly executed process. Its de facto role as a statewide point of contact was taken on in 2017 by the government's 1800 My Options phone line, the RWH having chosen not to tender to provide this service. The hospital still provides abortion services, and clinical leadership, and indeed expanded its second trimester service at this time, and again during the COVID-19 crisis. The demise of the PAS meant, however, not only the loss of a specialised service, particularly its free counselling service (which was not part of the brief for the 1800 line), and its advocacy and leadership role in the sector, but the dispersal of an expert workforce. The journalist who wrote of the closure at the time expressed the view that this 'seems to be ideologically rather than financially motivated'.[29]

South Australia

The other specialist clinic in an Australian public hospital has been the PAC, established in SA in 1992, as mentioned earlier. It pioneered a public provision model that located reception, counselling and clinical theatre services at the one site, close to but separate from the Queen Elizabeth Hospital (QEH) to which it was administratively attached. By the end of its first decade the PAC was providing nearly half of all abortions in SA and playing a leading role in the SA abortion care sector.[30]

In 1990 four other major metropolitan public hospitals were also providing abortions; this grew to five, but dropped to only three by the end of the 2010s. Ingrid, a long-time abortion-providing GP in SA, explained that Modbury Hospital, the major hospital in

Adelaide's northeast, 'used to have a service, they shut it down [in 1995] when that hospital got privatised and went to Healthscope [a large private healthcare provider]'. The hospital returned to public sector management in 2007 but did not resume an abortion service. In 2018 the Women's and Children's Hospital (WCH) closed its first trimester service and the PAC's share of all abortion provision in SA reached about 70 per cent; a radio discussion about the WCH suggested that the decision to cut abortion services had followed an internal push by a small group 'who have strong views about it'.[31] The proportion of SA abortions provided in private hospitals had dropped from about 13 per cent when the PAC opened to less than 1 per cent in 2017.

Clinicians at the PAC developed techniques using light anaesthesia which meant that by the early 2000s a same-day service was available for women, and this, Anna recalled, proved very popular. Doctors published research on their work.[32] The development of clinical expertise meant the PAC was able to offer abortions increasingly later in pregnancy. This extended to 24 weeks in the mid-2010s.[33] In 2009 the PAC also introduced early medical abortion to SA. Dr Ea Mulligan and other SA doctors spent over a year meeting the onerous requirements needed to gain permission to become individual Authorised Prescribers of early medical abortion for first trimester abortions. At this time, mifepristone could be used but was not yet commercially imported, and the TGA gave permission to prescribe only to individual doctors.[34]

The PAC was not, however, immune to the neoliberal trend that was reshaping the provision of public services in Australia. Several interviewees told a similar story. Staff workload intensified during the 1990s, partly because other public hospitals pulled back from providing abortion care. Resourcing did not increase, but patients were not turned away. Limited space had been a problem from the start. The PAC had also initially been under the oversight of an independent management committee and belonged to the section of the department which oversaw a range of specialty services, but Anna recalled that in one of many departmental restructures it was moved under the complete administrative control of the QEH. This had positive effects on clinical service delivery, but over time the service lost most of its original mandate and capacity to do research, advocacy and training, and the management committee became an advisory committee. Social workers at the PAC were at the centre of the establishment of NAAPOC in 2014, and staff contributed to the Central Adelaide Local Health Network's (CALHN) submission to the SA Law Reform Institute (SALRI) inquiry into abortion law reform in 2019, but keeping up with service provision increasingly took all available staff time.[35]

Sally, who worked at the PAC over two decades, described the relationship with the QEH and other parts of the Health Department as always being 'uncertain terrain'. One episode illustrates the tension. A woman needed to be sent to the QEH after an injury during surgery. Criticism from medical staff at the hospital was 'absolutely over the top', Sally recalled. Her sense of injustice and hurt was still palpable when I spoke with her years after the incident:

> the surgeons who criticised what the doctors at the PAC were doing wouldn't do that to doctors doing something else, they wouldn't … But they see it as their place and they wrote to the chief executive of the department, taking the moral high ground.

Sally and Ingrid both recalled another episode in the early 2000s, which affected all public hospitals. The law in SA required approval from two doctors who had examined the patient. This had become an administrative issue, with practical systems worked out to secure 'the second signature' on the government form, until one day, 'a midwife in a public hospital', who wasn't working on the abortion list, intervened.

> in one way or another she had become aware of what was going on and she went and said to the providing doctor 'I know that you don't get 2 doctors to see these women

before they go to theatre and I'm going to tell the police'.
… And the doctor went to the medical administrator who
went to risk management who rang all the other risk managers in all the other hospitals and said what do you do and
of course they went and asked people and they realised that
the letter of the law wasn't being obeyed and I think some
services were stopped for days while they worked out what
they were going to do.

The moment passed, more doctors were employed in hospital clinics,
but it illustrates the uses to which the criminal law had been put.

In 2018 a sequence of idiosyncratic events created a perfect
storm at the PAC. Against the backdrop of SA Health's 'Transforming
Health' agenda to restructure the SA health system and pressure on
the SA health budget following the brutal 2014 federal budget, the
CALHN, of which the PAC is a part, was in financial and cultural
crisis.[36] Internal events at the PAC involving staffing, maintenance of
the old building and the WCH's decision to end its first trimester
services led to 'the worst waiting times in its history' and eventually
the cessation of surgical services on site.[37]

Community activism and embarrassing media coverage put
external pressure on the department and the minister, with some
effect. By 2020 waiting times had returned to acceptable levels, but
the continuing transfer of surgical patients to the QEH (ten minutes
in a taxi) after their intake at the PAC places an unacceptable burden
on patients and the staff who follow them. The QEH is undergoing
redevelopment and a new WCH is being built, and the future location and configuration of the PAC are uncertain.

Ensuring a medical workforce willing to perform abortions is
the challenge faced by all public hospital providers in SA. Staff can
claim conscientious objection, their legal right, but institutions do
not always manage the situation well. Sally observed that

it's informal, and on any given day at any given moment
anyone can say 'I'm not doing that' and the sort of senior

people around them will go 'Oh, okay,' then suddenly you've got a situation where you should have an ultrasound being operated in the operating theatre and the sonographer saying 'I don't do that.'

Northern Territory

Staffing has been a much larger problem in the Northern Territory, the other place where public provision has been the norm since the early 1970s. In 1990, 62 per cent of abortions in the NT were performed in its two major public hospitals, most at the Royal Darwin Hospital (RDH), some at the smaller Alice Springs Hospital. The proportion provided at the Darwin Private Hospital declined to only 6.7 per cent during the 2006–11 period, and is still minimal. A number of women from the NT have always travelled interstate to access a service, usually to avoid the waiting times at the NT hospitals.[38] Until decriminalisation in 2017, all abortions performed in the NT were surgical procedures.

A large part of the history of the provision of abortion at the RDH in the period after law reform in 1973 is the story of three doctors. TT Lee joined the RDH in 1972 to lead Obstetrics and Gynaecology. He supported abortion law reform in 1973 and oversaw a steadily growing number of abortions performed at the RDH from that time on. Henry Cho joined the RDH as head of O&G in the 1990s and provided terminations until his retirement. He was continually busy and waiting times were never lower than two weeks. Geri, a long-time women's health worker in the NT, recalls that Dr Cho's holidays played havoc with waiting times: 'he might have got it down to two weeks then it'd get back up to three for about a couple of months after he came back'. The hospital did not cover the termination list in his absence. Even when he retired the hospital did not make arrangements, and he continued to perform abortions, working until he was nearly eighty, Geri thought:

so the public hospital had gynaecologists, five or six, no way were they going to do terminations ... [the hospital] wouldn't sack them and say 'Well we're getting gynaes that will do the job because that's part of our service … and it's lawful, and you're not doing your job.' They didn't seem to take the hard line with any gynaes, that's where they failed.

Dr WH Lee was eventually found and employed to provide abortions on a FIFO basis from the late 2000s. A letter to the *Medical Journal of Australia* in February 2015 notified readership of his resignation. Women's access to abortion services would again be 'severely diminished and complicated'.[39] Geri recalled that this episode replayed a long history of poor planning and uncertain provision of abortion in the NT, especially at the RDH: the lack of succession planning meant a crisis all over again. A local O&G in private practice agreed to fill in at the RDH. For a period in 2015, the situation became what Geri described as 'a complete mess'. Where Lee had been doing twenty procedures a week, the local O&G only did ten. When I interviewed her late in 2015, Geri said 'heaven knows where everyone else is going.' Women were waiting longer, and some were being sent interstate, with funding from the government's Patient Travel Assistance Scheme (PATS).

Government action in the wake of decriminalisation in the NT relieved a lot of the pressure on the NT public hospital system. There had been almost no early medical abortion in the NT, but in little more than a year after decriminalisation, over 70 per cent of all abortions were early medical abortion performed in community settings—mostly at the FPWNT in Darwin, where government funding made the service free to the patient.[40] The RDH and the Alice Springs Hospital still perform surgical abortions, and waiting times have dropped, partly because early medical abortion is now provided in Alice Springs, Katherine and Nhulunbuy (three of the largest NT towns after Darwin) as well as in Darwin.[41]

Cairns

In the middle of the first decade of the twenty-first century, Cairns, a regional city of about 150,000 people in Far North Queensland, became a centre for activism and innovation around abortion care, much as Adelaide had been in the early to mid-1990s. I discuss the leadership of O&G Professor Caroline de Costa in the next chapter. The Cairns Sexual Health Service, a public clinic, has provided access to early medical abortion for women in Cairns and surrounds since 2006. Before its doctors became Authorised Prescribers of mifepristone, clinic doctors Darren Russell and Heather McNamee began offering early medical abortion with methotrexate, a less preferred alternative to mifepristone[42] (they were not the only doctors in Australia to use this regimen at this time).[43] Until 2006, the main option for Cairns women, apart from an expensive service by a sympathetic O&G in private practice, was to catch 'the first bus to Townsville', about four hours away, as Robbie overheard a woman say. Robbie noted that women 'often came back on the bus bleeding and cramping and uncomfortable; it was just inhumane.' The clinic's willingness to offer early medical abortion was not widely advertised, but word of mouth ensured a continuous flow of patients. After ceasing the service in 2009–10 while a legal issue was resolved (see Chapter 6), Russell and McNamee went on to become Authorised Prescribers, following Dr Ea Mulligan and her SA colleagues who had paved the way for achieving this status.

The Cairns Sexual Health Clinic continues to provide early medical abortion, and while this service might seem like a good fit with a sexual health clinic, they were the only such government-funded clinic in Australia to do so until a handful of other Queensland clinics followed their lead in the wake of the 2018 law reform. During the year in which the clinic suspended its services, and for patients who are over 20 weeks and need to go to Melbourne or Brisbane the Cairns Sexual Health Clinic has funded travel for women needing to access surgical services outside Cairns using the Queensland PATS scheme.

You Probably Won't Get an Abortion in the Public Sector Here

Outside the services described above, the chances of success in the lottery of public hospital provision of abortion have been poor and/or uneven over time. An anonymous author writing for a health journal in 1989 provided a snapshot of the provision of abortion services in public hospitals in Victoria. Abortion was a low-status service, with annual quotas imposed by some hospitals and women referred to private services. Limits to the number of abortions provided were sometimes motivated by a need to '[keep] numbers at a level acceptable to [anti-abortion] staff in order to maintain their cooperation'. Services were not well publicised, and were sometimes provided on the basis of judgements about 'deserving' and 'undeserving' women.[44] Ten years later another article described a similar situation, and identified the unmet demand at the RWH.[45] In 2013, Evie described to me in interview the same uncoordinated situation in Victoria:

> Victoria has no organisation of abortion services. It's entirely up to individual hospitals and clinics to do what they do. There's no expectation of any hospital to do abortions … there's no strategy for training doctors, there's no funding. There's no statewide central service for information like there is for DV [domestic violence], sexual assault, drugs and alcohol, homelessness. We don't have a statewide service for abortion and unplanned pregnancy.

She went on to observe that in any hospital, 'someone, you know the CEO or the Medical Director, has to champion that hospital taking it on against either the real or imagined barriers.'

Across the country, in 1989 Janet Holmes à Court, the Chairman of the Board of the KEMH in Perth explained the situation in her hospital in response to a letter from WEL.[46] Holmes à Court noted that while the hospital provided abortion for a small group of women with special needs, there were three reasons why they did not to provide a standard first trimester abortion service:

1. The Hospital already has about 87% bed occupancy
    ... to admit more women for termination would mean
    other women who may be ill would miss out.
2. Most women seeking termination do not require
    hospital care and the Day Care facilities of the KEMH
    could not cope.
3. It is becoming increasingly difficult to find staff, both
    nursing and medical, who are willing to become
    involved with termination of pregnancy, particularly in
    the second trimester. Of the nine Registrars training
    to be Gynaecologists only one will perform termina-
    tions. This is in marked contrast to ten years ago when
    the ratio was reversed.

Like many Victorian public hospitals, the KEMH recommended
private clinics to women it did not accommodate. The KEMH was
evading responsibility for providing first trimester abortions when I
visited Perth in 2016. Exasperation among my interviewees was
palpable. In the words of Iona, an abortion-providing GP, 'The fact
that the women's hospital for the whole state does not perform
abortions, just boggles my mind.'

Some major capital city public hospitals, and some regional
hospitals, have performed abortions for discrete periods of time since
1990 (although not until the mid-2010s in Queensland). Ralph, an
O&G who knew the inner-city Sydney scene, recalled the RPA in
Sydney's inner west in the 1980s:

> [It had] a very strong ethos of performing terminations.
> Some of the prominent people in that hospital had been
> involved in the results of illegal abortions beforehand.

But the commitment of the old-school doctors could easily be
undone, and the reliance on individual doctors becomes clear.
Several interviewees mentioned 'the lovely Doctor Brian Peat'. He
worked at the RPA during the 1990s, with supportive management

who had seen the days of illegal abortions. Longstanding Sydney abortion activist Viv recalled:

> [He] ran a list, one day a week, I think it was a Monday, and his priorities were under 21, medical condition that means that a freestanding abortion service is not suitable, on Centrelink benefits, and any other sort of relevant issue … all of those youth-oriented services in the inner city knew so long as they got in quick enough, the women could be booked in there.

Several NSW interviewees recalled that Peat had close relationships with local private providers who were able to refer patients who needed hospital care without fear of judgement or refusal. After he left the RPA in 2002, however, the service he had maintained 'slowly fell apart'. Ralph thought that this may have been because the obstetrician who replaced Peat, who had been an abortion provider in the private sector, 'didn't want do any cases at PA because it was a nuisance.'

Sheelagh, a Sydney doctor with a long history in women's and sexual and reproductive health whom I interviewed in 2015, summed up public provision in NSW over her two decades in the field:

> it's always been a challenge. But again I would say there's been some closing up of some of the hospitals and certainly not opening up of others because again it's totally *ad hoc*, the route into the public system.

In Melbourne, the story of the Austin Hospital, a large public hospital in a north-eastern suburb which had not previously provided abortions, illustrates several elements of the idiosyncrasies and precarity of provision of abortion in public hospitals. In 2005 the Mercy Women's Hospital, a public maternity hospital run by the Sisters of Mercy, relocated from the city to a site adjacent, and connected, to the Austin. As a Catholic hospital, the Mercy has a policy that contraception and abortion services are not provided. According to Phyl, a Melbourne abortion-providing O&G, the government saves money with the Mercy as a public hospital:

> It's not funded at the same level as the Women's Hospital, so this is thereby the sting in the tail of this whole provision model. Because the government relies on the Sisters of Mercy supplying some of the money they don't have to fund as much, so it'd be just a hell of a shit fight if they said, 'No, we're not going to supply funds anymore unless you do abortions,' because the Mercy's not going to supply that. And then the government's going to have to work out how to keep running that hospital when they can pay less.

The Mercy generated need for abortion services when it tested pregnant women for foetal anomalies. A key gynaecologist at the Austin next door led a change whereby its small gynae clinic became a 'family planning clinic', offering abortion services to women diagnosed at the Mercy with foetal anomalies at 14 to 15 weeks. This was done, Phyl recalled, with implicit government support. The clinic quickly expanded to offer an ordinary first trimester service to poor local women, although only ever a fortnightly list.

> Since then the executive at the Austin have slowly been running a campaign to try and close it down, and obfuscating, and just saying, 'No, we can't remember who signed that contract, can't remember that contract, we're now going to move our funding somewhere else, because we don't want to be associated with it.' So there's a bit of a campaign of trying to kill that service by attrition—but that's another piece of politics.

According to Phyl, the service became more vulnerable when the doctor who initiated it left the hospital. At the time of writing the

Austin's abortion services were listed on the 1800 My Options phone line.

The Mercy in Melbourne is not the only case where Catholic values have clashed with public health values in relation to abortion. In 1993 the WA government announced plans to build an entirely new Bunbury Regional Hospital, to be owned and run by St John of God Health Care Systems. A community campaign including WEL opposed the move, citing 'abortion, sterilisation, fertility control and job security for women workers' as the key issues. The government withdrew the plan.[47] Twenty years later it was back in the same situation, contracting St John of God to run the new Midland Public Hospital in suburban Perth. St John of God refused to provide abortion or contraception services. In 2015 the government came to an agreement with Marie Stopes, which already had a clinic in Midland, to provide abortions to the hospital's public patients.[48] Social worker Joyce told me that the KEMH was already contracting Marie Stopes Australia to provide abortion services to women who were judged deserving. In response to a question from an anti-abortion parliamentarian in 2015, it was reported that the government had spent $783,000 in 2014–15 on construction, equipment and services to support abortion provision at Marie Stopes on referral from the KEMH, and would pay one million dollars in 2015–2016 for the service that the Midland hospital and KEMH would not provide, as well as $1.05 million to finalise the upgrade to the Marie Stopes clinic.[49]

There are currently eighty hospitals in Australia that are run by Catholic agencies; about a quarter of all beds are public, about twenty are public maternity hospitals. In 2013, Chris, a Brisbane-based abortion-providing O&G, told me that while Catholic hospitals will not perform abortions for pregnant women who are given diagnoses of foetal anomaly, it has been possible for such women in Queensland to have foeticide performed in a private clinic and then return to the Catholic hospital to undergo a stillbirth delivery by induction. An ABC report in December 2022 revealed an array of gynaecological and obstetric health care, including abortion, that Catholic-run public hospitals would not provide. This meant the need to seek services usually delivered at the same time at different hospitals as Chris described.[50]

Whether rural public hospitals are any more or less committed to abortion provision than their metropolitan counterparts is unclear. Lil, an abortion-providing GP with rural experience, pointed out that a lot less surgery of all kinds has been done in small rural hospitals over the years. In WA some interviewees suggested that rural hospitals have provided abortion more adequately than their metropolitan counterparts (although still not matching local need), and WA data backs up this observation.[51] More remote regions, where populations are small and health services are sparse, will be less likely to offer access. The submission from the Broome Regional Aboriginal Medical Service to the 2005 Senate Inquiry into RU486 stated that 'women are often required to wait several weeks for the procedure to be performed locally or when unable to be accommodated on our limited surgical lists, required to travel up to 3000 km to Perth'.[52] This was not for lack of sympathy, simply lack of resources.

Even in sizeable regional cities public hospitals abortion services can be precarious. As public health advocate Louella pointed out, abortion services at the RHH in Hobart had always depended on willing doctors, who came and went. They had stepped up when the state's only private clinic closed in early 2001, but at the end of the year the RHH doctors and nurses withdrew their services from the abortion lists when it seemed that the arrest of doctors was imminent (see Chapter 6). The law was reformed before Christmas, with retrospective effect, but the RHH doctors did not resume the abortion lists.[53] To ensure a service, management at the RHH relied on Rosalie, a GP provider, who recalled being flown in from Melbourne over the summer months:

> it was all cloak and dagger sort of stuff, you know … I had some code name in the hospital … I sort of snuck in and we had to have discussions with staff about whether they

were willing to participate in doing terminations, and we had to reassure the nurses that they wouldn't end up in jail and, you know, there was quite a lot of emotion involved with it.

Private clinics were established in Hobart and Launceston starting in 2002 and after that, as public servant Nicola noted in 2013, public hospital commitment was minimal although government funding was provided through the 2000s and early 2010s to a youth-focused community sector organisation to support those too poor to pay for a private service.

In 2007 the new CEO at the public hospital in Bendigo, about 150 kilometres from Melbourne, asked why the hospital had not been providing abortion services. About 70 per cent of women in the area had been travelling to Melbourne to access a service. Under the leadership of the Medical Director, also a new staff member, an abortion clinic was then commenced.[54] The service closed in 2012 because of the lack of a willing doctor, but re-opened in 2013 when a doctor became available. In 2017 media reports indicated that the service was far from adequate and was causing delays for women.[55] This story of on-again off-again as key staff came and went was not unique.

It is not only doctors who can facilitate or limit the provision of abortion services in public hospitals, however. Joyce, who knew the inside workings of the KEMH in Perth, recalled a ward manager (a nurse) who could be very difficult to work with. Women in their second trimester having labour induced need three consecutive days of hospital care, and the patient needs to be admitted as soon as possible. The social worker would try to make the appointment:

when she [the ward manager] was being difficult she would say, 'Well I haven't done the roster and I haven't got any staffing and I can't tell you today.' If she was being a bit more proactive, she would have already ... So there was some variations in there.

While a minority among their profession,[56] openly anti-abortion doctors can ensure that abortions are not performed at all in their hospital or even their local community. Priscilla described one of the senior O&Gs at the RDH during the 2010s as 'a conscientious objector' whose religious views had 'a very dampening effect on what can be done there,' including the decision not to allocate medical students to the termination clinic. A news report in early 2020 described how the influence of religiously conservative doctors almost completely shut down abortion provision in one NSW regional centre. The Wagga Wagga Base Hospital provides abortion only for 'medically necessary' reasons. According to the journalist, this is not just about the O&Gs at the hospital but partly because 'the hospital is worried about losing some of its pro-life specialists in other fields should it start offering elective surgical abortions'.[57]

Persistent Advocacy, Some Hope

For over two decades the withdrawal of the NHMRC report in 1998 marked the end of the possibility of a national approach to adequate and equitable abortion provision but state-based advocates did not give up looking for opportunities to intervene and seek government support. Campaigns for law reform since 1990, particularly the achievement of decriminalisation, have provided impetus for government intervention into the provision of abortion services, some more successful than others. I discuss the relationship between decriminalisation and abortion provision in detail in Chapter 6; some brief summary notes will suffice in the context of this chapter.

While the ACT government continued to subsidise the RHS clinic's rent, decriminalisation in 2002 did not involve any increase in public support. In Victoria, Evie told me that in the lead-up to the successful move to decriminalise abortion, a combination of academics, community sector and hospital stakeholders obtained state government funding to develop a model for a statewide service to oversee abortion provision: 'That seemed really encouraging at the time.' The group did the research and made recommendations, but its 2007 report 'sat on the shelf after that and got shifted around departments and no one wanted to own it. And it just disappeared.' The Victorian government made no moves to address access issues in the wake of decriminalisation in 2008. In fact, public access declined in the years following decriminalisation.[58]

Louella and Nicola noted that in the wake of hurried reform of abortion law late in Tasmania in 2001 the Tasmanian ALP government was rumoured to have given financial support for the costs of establishing a new private clinic, operated by interstate doctors. Twelve years later, after decriminalisation, health worker Petra recalled the funding by the Health Department of postcards with abortion information for community distribution and a package to be sent to every doctor in the state explaining the new law.

Decriminalisation in the NT in 2017 produced more significant government action, as noted earlier. On the occasion of decriminalisation in Queensland in 2018, the ALP government's health minister instructed all public hospitals to provide patients seeking an abortion with at least a pathway to a service, and announced an information website.[59] Access to public services since 2018 has been mixed.[60] One positive measure of decriminalisation's impact was the 55 per cent drop in the numbers of women approaching Children by Choice for financial support in the 2019 and 2020, as this indicated an increase in public support.[61] The website of Children by Choice now has a comprehensive map identifying providers across the state and including information on accessing public pathways through Queensland's fourteen health regions, although this is unclear in some cases and often advises direct contact with Marie Stopes, which is contracted to offer services. The closure of the Marie Stopes regional clinics in 2021 means that this may now be a referral to telehealth or a clinic in the southeast corner of the state. Each region has a different approach and conscientious objection among senior hospital staff can be significantly obstructive. For many hospitals, a message on the map for those who have issues when seeking care reads 'please reach out to us at Children by Choice'. Advocacy on behalf of the patient is sometimes required and the agency's counsellors spend significant time and effort securing access for clients.[62] Two websites for NSW—one for people seeking information, one for health professionals—and a Framework for Termination of Pregnancy Policy Directive (that does not require public hospital provision) followed decriminalisation in 2019 under a Liberal government.[63]

But decriminalisation has not been the only route to regulatory and policy change to improve abortion access. When I met and interviewed advocates and providers in Queensland in 2013, some were pinning hopes on the inclusion of an assessment and referral pathway for people wanting abortions in the then newly released Queensland Health Clinical Guideline for maternity-related health care, to which abortion-providing doctors had contributed.[64] Public hospitals accounted for less than 4 per cent of all abortion provision in Queensland at that time,[65] and it was hoped that the Clinical Guideline would give abortion legitimacy. O&G Chris understood that the document was only a small wedge in an otherwise almost completely closed door: 'I think it will require us to continue to push,' she said. Not surprisingly, when I checked three years later, the Guideline had not significantly opened public access. Children by Choice found that the best way to leverage the Guideline had been to support GPs in referring individual women to their local hospitals. The promise of a statewide Guideline relied on a chain of advocacy that operated case by case, which was labour-intensive and time-consuming, with no guarantee of success.[66]

In 2017 the Victorian Department of Health and Human Services launched a statement of key priorities in women's sexual and reproductive health strategy for 2017–20, with an action plan and a $6.6 million dollar budget allocation. Abortion was a key priority.[67] This statement was the first such comprehensive document to be adopted in any jurisdiction in Australia, a major achievement in this respect, although the budget allocation was small given the range of health issues it addressed. It gave the Department a mandate to let public hospitals know that abortion provision is expected, especially in rural areas. One outcome of the statement of priorities has been the establishment of the 1800 My Options phone line and website in March 2018 to deliver statewide information and connection to abortion services.[68] A second Victorian Women's Sexual and Reproductive Health Plan 2022–30 was released in 2022, reporting success in relation to the growing number of early medical abortion and the value of the 1800 My Options service and laying out continuing plans to improve information, increase access to services and develop workforce.[69]

After persistent pressure led by Women's Health Tasmania, the Tasmanian government announced in 2021 that all three major public hospitals would offer surgical abortion services. The Women's Health Tasmania website hosts a comprehensive Services Map indicating the location of abortion services.[70] Even more startling, in August 2022 the ACT Minister for Health announced a Budget Initiative that from mid-2023 would see all ACT residents including those without a Medicare card 'have access to free abortion services up to 16 week's gestation', having announced a parliamentary inquiry a month earlier. The free services came into effect just as this book was completed.[71] This commitment also came after persistent lobbying by a range of community groups, including SHFPACT and Women's Health Matters, and from young women in the ALP. A progressive ALP government, sympathetic key ministers and a moderate leader of the opposition all created political opportunity. The government will work with MSI and GPs to effect their promise but, unlike Tasmania, it is not expected that there will be any further provision in the public hospital system. Local advocates have identified options for ongoing development.[72]

In the campaign leading up to the 2019 federal election, the ALP Opposition spokesperson on women, Tanya Plibersek, announced a policy on abortion. '[A] federal Labor government would require public hospitals to offer termination services as part of their Commonwealth funding arrangement', she said.[73] While this policy did not feature in the 2022 campaign, attention to abortion has received renewed energy in the wake of the ALP's victory in the 2022 election.

The Rudd federal government had released a second National Women's Health Policy in 2010, but it was 'an action-free zone' according to Gwen Gray Jamieson.[74] References to 'termination of pregnancy' had no substance. In 2019, when the Turnbull government released the *National Women's Health Strategy 2020–2030*, reference to termination of pregnancy was brief but specified 'equitable access to pregnancy termination services' as a key measure of success.[75] In July 2022, in the early days of the new government, and in the wake of global response to the demise of the *Roe v Wade* Supreme Court decision in the USA, chair of the Australian Women's Health Network and MSI Australia's head of Policy and Research Bonney Corbin wrote an opinion piece for *The Canberra Times*. She took the opportunity to remind readers of the strategy's commitment and note that state and federal Ministers for Women were meeting to discuss 'the future of abortion access in Australia'.[76] Later in the month Sharon Claydon, the chair of the federal ALP women's caucus, was reported to be committed to 'work across party lines to ensure all women can access safe and affordable abortions' and key independent (women) members of the parliament supported the call. Assistant Health Minister Ged Kearney would work on a plan to improve abortion access, although the Prime Minister ruled out 'forcing state hospitals to provide abortions'.[77] Journalist Rachel Withers called this 'a cowardly refusal to address an inequity that Labor once campaigned against'.[78] In August, Victorian parliamentarian Fiona Patten, leader of the Reason Party, raised the bar in this context with her (unsuccessful) attempt to compel publicly funded religious hospitals to provide abortion and euthanasia.[79] By the end of 2022 three parliamentary inquiries into abortion had been announced: a Senate inquiry into sexual and reproductive health care, including abortion, established by the Greens, and government inquiries established in the ACT and WA, into abortion and reproductive choice and law reform respectively.[80] At the time of writing reports of all inquiries are pending.

Well-kept Secrets

For most of the last thirty years there has been little or no proactive health promotion anywhere in Australia to inform the public or their healthcare providers about how to access an abortion service. The postcards produced in Tasmania in 2013 are an exception. The RWH and PAC websites (and those of many private providers) have presented comprehensive information. The Children by Choice website has possibly been the best in the country, not only answering general questions but also listing abortion services in each state and territory until this became unwieldy and their site became confined to Queensland services. More recently Victoria and Tasmania also have comprehensive government funded websites that list providers. While these are only a Google search away they are not the proactive strategies used by government health promotion agencies for other issues.

The question of knowledge of publicly provided abortion services came up in several interviews. In WA, the 1998 law reform requires that women get a referral from a doctor before approaching a private clinic (or a hospital). Nonetheless, some women have rung the KEMH directly (good for them!) and got through to a social worker, who has had to direct them back to a GP. One of my WA interviewees, Joyce, recalled the social worker regularly exclaiming 'my name must be on the back of a toilet door somewhere!'

When I talked with Sheelagh in 2015, she told me that 'just in the last few days, we've found out there's two obstetrician-gynaecologists [in a NSW north coast hospital] there that will provide Medicare abortions up to 20 weeks.' She had also recently heard that it was possible to get an abortion in an outback NSW town, contrary to her existing understanding. Viv, a long-time Sydney abortion activist, described her experience over decades in similar terms.

> ...occasionally I hear a whisper on a grapevine about 'Oh, Bankstown hospital might do terminations up to 12 weeks or 3 a week or ... ' But you know, it's all kind of this secretiveness and not too many people are supposed to know.

In Melbourne in 2013, I talked to Bree and June together; they worked as women's health providers in the west, and June has been around women's health for years. Bree started, 'I didn't know until a couple of months ago that [a public hospital], provide public abortion access in the west because,' and June chimed in, 'It's secret!' Bree said that 'still health professionals or hospitals aren't willing to put their details up there, so it's still women having to navigate the back streets of who knows what, to be able to get access.' The language of 'the back streets', like Joyce's 'back of a toilet door', echoes women's experiences of abortion before liberalisation. Bree went on, 'The service's reasons for secrecy was to avoid picketers … whilst that's really important there's still this kind of morality and secrecy around public practice.'

The various state and territory government-supported online sites established in recent years has diminished this secrecy. But the NSW website does not list providers, and in 2020 the Family Planning NSW report stated that 'women are not able to easily locate abortion service information themselves' and they must navigate a range of online information which include 'a variety of sources of misinformation'.[81]

Conclusion

With the exceptions of SA and the NT, and the RWH and a handful of smaller hospitals in Melbourne, this chapter paints a picture of, predominantly, the relative absence of public health provision of abortion in Australia since 1990. The patchwork of legislation and policy that WEL identified in 1990 has shifted over the past thirty years. The opening of the PAC in Adelaide in 1992 was a high point. There has been liberal law reform in every jurisdiction but very little policy development yet at federal or state/territory level, and access problems have worsened in some jurisdictions. Starting in 2017 there have been varying levels of government commitment in Victoria, the NT, Queensland, Tasmania and the ACT to improve access through public policy and/or public funding, some of which has had immediate and significant effect, but not all. These improvements are still susceptible to all the vicissitudes of the gaps between policy or ministerial fiat, local health network and hospital culture and capacity, willingness of doctors, and implementation. Even in SA and NT, where public provision has been the norm, rural and remote people are seriously disadvantaged and public hospital provision is never smooth sailing for long.

The public health system in Australia faces many challenges, and arguably abortion is small change in this context. But for most of the period of my study it has been one of the most commonly performed surgical procedures in the country. Rural and remote women, poor women, those without access to Medicare and Aboriginal women stand out as those with significantly less access to abortion services (and poorer access to all health care) than their metropolitan, economically and residentially secure and non-Aboriginal peers.[82] The location of abortion in the criminal law in each jurisdiction until recently can only partially explain the lack of government action over the years. After all, it has not impeded public provision of abortion care where hospitals have made it available, as shown by public provision in SA and NT and the longstanding commitment to service and advocacy at the RWH in Melbourne. Nor has it impeded improvement and innovation, as shown by the SA government's establishment of the PAC in 1992 and the provision of early medical abortion at the Cairns Sexual Health Centre from 2006.

The anonymous author who wrote about public hospital provision in Victoria in 1989 concluded that women pay taxes but the government's health priorities fail them. Improvement will depend on 'the state coming to terms with its role as a provider of termination and contraception services'.[83]

The reliance on individual doctors to sustain abortion services, which hospital management has accepted—or has been powerless to shift—is a constant vulnerability. More than one interviewee told me that they had just found out about a hospital service not previously known. I don't think that this was because the timing of the interview happened to coincide with unexpected happy news. Finding out about previously unknown providers is not a breaking of silence about growing provision, but part of a constant cycle of availability and its withdrawal, secrecy and disclosure about public hospital abortion services.

The increasing delivery of early medical abortion in primary health care, in GP clinics, by telemedicine or, in the future, by nurses in community clinics, certainly decentres the place of the hospital or specialised clinic in abortion care. The innovation at the Cairns Sexual Health Clinic expanded horizons for how abortion might be provided through the public sector. But patients with comorbidities and those who seek abortions after the first trimester will need a public hospital service, as will those who do not want early medical abortion. In some rural areas the public hospital may be the only viable place for providing any such service. The broader effects of public hospital provision—normalising abortion in our large institutions, training healthcare practitioners and conducting research—cannot be adequately performed elsewhere. Access to a public service, for free or for little cost, should be a fundamental entitlement for all.

Certain public hospitals have always provided abortion services, and this is to be celebrated as well as defended. Yet the inertia in this area is hard to shift. Excellent recommendations in government-sponsored reviews and reports, data in some states that repeatedly reveals disadvantage and poor access, strategic intervention into the micro processes of policy and guidelines, ministerial announcements, piecemeal funding for information, websites and phone lines—these have been no guarantee of sustained public or affordable access. Reports and proposals for service models or health promotion about abortion have been as likely to be withdrawn, disappear, or live on only in a box of leftover postcards. At the time of writing, it is too soon to make a definitive statement about the impact of the revived federal discussion, but the smallest jurisdictions are a worthy basis for optimism.

Chapter 3

Doctors

In relation to abortion care in Australia, the problem with doctors is that not enough of them have chosen to provide it. Law and regulation single out doctors as the only ones who can lawfully do so, yet it is accepted practice that they *do not have to.*

Feminist scholarship has pointed out the particular control that doctors have historically exercised over women's bodies, never more so than in their restrictive approach to abortion.[1] There is a history of doctors who have provided abortions both legally and illegally, for a variety of motives.[2] In the postwar years, the displacement of midwives and other abortion providers by doctors was increasingly evident in Australia and similar countries. In this respect, legal liberalisation cemented and legitimated doctors' role in abortion provision.[3]

This chapter investigates how doctors in Australia have negotiated the discursive and institutional constraints on the provision of abortion care since 1990. It focuses on those who provide abortion services, and creates a story of abortion-providing doctors that is built on accounts of institutions, major public events, everyday work life, interpersonal relationships and personal reflections.

The twelve doctors I interviewed have worked in public, private and community settings. Some are GPs whose careers have been defined by abortion provision. Others incorporated provision of early medical abortion into general practice or sexual and reproductive health care, and for the O&Gs, abortion was a part of their speciality. Most began providing abortions before 2000; the oldest did so in the 1960s. The group was slanted towards those who had provided leadership over this period, either in professional and sometimes broader public settings or simply as long-time dedicated providers. I did not interview doctors who trained after 2000 because of my preference for people with a depth of historical knowledge.

British feminist legal scholar Sally Sheldon's analysis of the workings of the 1967 British abortion law reform act in England and Wales, published in 1997, delineated four different types of medical control that doctors exercise in relation to abortion.[4] These are:

> *technical* control of the actual performance of abortion operations, *decisional* control over which women should be permitted to terminate their pregnancies, and *paternalistic* and *normalising* control which may be exercised over women who request termination (regardless of whether they are granted access to it).[5]

Twenty years later, Sheldon and her colleagues' reflections on fourteen interviews with abortion-providing doctors updated her earlier analysis, leaning more on the doctors' negotiation of their position and the tension between their practice on the one hand, and the law and their professional privilege on the other.[6] As Australian law and medical cultures descend directly from the British, it is appropriate for Sheldon's analysis to underpin my own. I follow her later approach, locating the identities and practices of doctors at the negotiated intersection of interactions with the range of people, in medicine and beyond, encountered in the context of abortion; however, her earlier framework also remains relevant, as it identifies the institutional and discursive privilege, and constraints, that abortion-providing doctors must continue to negotiate.

While abortion has historically been located as a particular site of medical control in most cases, interaction with a doctor is initiated by the patient's request for an abortion. In other words, the patient understands their problem and knows how to solve it: they need access to technical expertise provided in a supportive environment. This autonomy can be a worry for doctors! Legal scholar Kerry Petersen lists 'demand for abortions' as a key factor that has led to changes in the status of abortion in Australia through the twentieth century,[7] and the force of women's demand for access to abortion services shadows this chapter, surfacing specifically in the comments of some doctors.

The Institutions, 1990s

By 1990, doctors in every jurisdiction in Australia could and did perform abortions lawfully under legislation, or interpretation of criminal law, that simultaneously authorised and constrained them.[8] The criteria under which an abortion was lawful were similar across jurisdictions, and included the requirement that the doctor believed that the continuation of a pregnancy endangered the woman's life or her physical or mental health. SA and the NT also specified foetal anomaly as allowable grounds for an abortion, required the examination of the woman by two doctors and that abortions be performed in a hospital, and legislated doctors' right to conscientious objection. The two-doctor requirement was legislatively extended to WA in 1998 and Tasmania in 2001.[9]

The institutions of medicine were central in establishing the environment in which abortions were provided. Many, including the medical schools where many providers of the 1990s had trained, had not been sympathetic. Davina, a Melbourne GP abortion provider, recalled of her study in the 1970s that 'in fifth year medicine we did gynaecology and the attitudes of the male gynaecologists, they were all male in my experience … I just found them appalling, really appalling.'

Some university medical schools in the 1990s included teaching about abortion, but it is clear that this was far from universal.[10] Public teaching hospitals that performed abortions did not necessarily offer training, and when they did it was common for students to have to 'opt in'.[11] Chris, who trained as an O&G in the 1990s, told me, 'it's never anything that you would take part in as an obstetrician when you are training in Queensland.' Doctors who trained in Catholic hospitals also received no exposure to abortion. Some hospitals, however, were committed to training. In 1990, activist Jo Wainer praised the Monash Medical Centre in Melbourne for 'rotating all its gynaecology registrars' through the abortion service.[12] Likewise, Brian Peat oversaw a ten-week program for residents at King George V Hospital in Sydney's inner west (which later became part of the RPA) during the 1990s.[13] The RWH in Melbourne and KEMH in Perth and, for GPs, the PAC in Adelaide offered less formal abortion training opportunities to doctors during the 1990s.[14]

As previously noted, the doctors providing abortions in private clinics in the 1990s were likely to have been trained in such clinics. Sydney GP Roger's pathway into providing abortions was typical. After incidental exposure to abortion during his residency, he pursued Sunday morning training organised by Family Planning NSW in the late 1970s. Hands-on experience came when he was employed at Preterm in the early 1980s. However, local opportunities for professional development were scarce, and thus a number of Australia doctors attended the US National Abortion Federation conferences during the 1980s.

This institutional reticence towards equipping doctors with knowledge about abortion practice not only conveyed conservative values about abortion, it meant that most doctors were technically, professionally and culturally ill-prepared to perform abortions. Improvements in training about abortion for GPs and O&Gs was therefore a key recommendation in both the *We Women Decide* research report, and the NHMRC report that followed it.[15]

In its assessment of the literature about abortion published in mainstream medical and health journals between 1985 and 1992, *We Women Decide* identified the overall approach as 'the catastrophisation of abortion'. The dominant framework was defined as follows:

women who seek abortions are deviant; they need counselling; they will suffer post-abortion trauma; they should be subjected to increased contraceptive scrutiny; abortions performed for 'social' reasons are bad but those performed for 'medical' reasons can be good; cultures where abortion is the main method of fertility control are represented as 'primitive' or 'uncivilised', while contraception signifies 'western' and 'civilised'.[16]

Petersen claims that 'the medical profession and individual medical practitioners [have had] a considerable influence over the shaping of abortion laws'.[17] The positions of the Australian Medical Association (AMA) and RANZCOG (then called RACOG) on abortion shifted fairly rapidly in the 1970s as legal change overtook their conservative views, but both bodies were slow to develop formal statements.[18] The first AMA position statement on 'reproductive health and reproductive technology', released in 1998, supported women's decisional autonomy, but in specific reference to 'termination of pregnancy' it also respected the 'rights of doctors to have differing views'.[19] Notwithstanding research that debunked the view that abortion necessarily had negative psychological effects,[20] the statement noted doctors' responsibility to inform patients about 'psychological consequences' of termination of pregnancy. RANZCOG did not develop a specific position on abortion *per se* until 2005.

Meet the Doctors, 1990s

Petersen noted increasing tolerance towards abortion providers in the early 1990s, but stated that 'a medical practitioner who works solely in this area is still not completely accepted by the profession'. She identified three qualities in doctors which immunised them against this 'informal regulation': absence of interest in 'professional accolades'; the pursuit of 'financial gain'; and being 'strongly motivated in an ideological sense'.[21] This lack of professional acceptance of 'abortion as a health issue' was still noted well into the 2000s, along with the consequent obstruction of 'quality improvement and the adoption of improved techniques'.[22]

Many of the pioneers of the liberalised era were still operating during the 1990s. In 1995, a news magazine article titled 'Born to Dissent' profiled Peter Bayliss.[23] An associate of Bertram Wainer, he had appeared in court in Melbourne in relation to abortion in 1965 (and was acquitted). Bayliss established a private abortion clinic in Brisbane in 1978, and when his Greenslopes clinic was raided by police in 1985, the consequent 1986 court case clarified the law in Queensland. He is described in the article as 'a cowboy', 'a maverick', and 'a self-made wealthy man', disinterested in feminism and disliked by Children by Choice, and the journalist reports that he made barely disguised racist comments about Aboriginal communities. Bayliss provided abortion services until his death in 1998.[24] Davina's comment in the early 1990s that 'some of those male abortion providers [in Melbourne] ... were just too flashy and insensitive' invokes the image of a man like Bayliss.

Among those who had practised in and/or witnessed the pre-liberalisation period, the suffering and death of women following illegal abortions left a deep impression. Prominent private provider David Grundmann wrote that as a consequence, 'I have dedicated the rest of my professional career to ensuring that the women of this country, will always have access to safe legal and dignified abortion services'.[25] Ralph, an O&G, recalled of the King George V in Sydney where he trained in the 1980s that 'if Professor [Rodney] Shearman heard you were against termination then you wouldn't get a job there ... that was the rumour.' Ironically, however, the O&G department's flexible appointment procedures were the subject of a scandal about sexism which erupted in 1992, in which one female doctor claimed that the speciality 'acted systematically to exclude women'. This exclusion may also have extended to non-white doctors.[26] June worked as a social worker in the PAS in Melbourne through the 1990s and recalled leading O&G Michael Kloss, who told stories over morning tea about abortion in the old days:[27]

[He] purposefully made himself Head of the PAS, because
... if the Head of Obstetrics and Gynae was doing it, there

would be less political argy-bargy or less attempt by the hospital or other doctors to undermine the service.

Harry Cohen played a similar role in WA as Head of the Department of Gynaecology at the KEMH during the 1990s.

I asked all of my interviewees how they became involved in providing abortion care. Joseph, an O&G at the KEMH in Perth, was motivated by seeing women suffering after illegal abortion. He had been exposed to liberal practices while working in English hospitals in the 1950s, and on his return to Australia he joined a gynaecologist in private practice who provided abortions and, once he settled in, started doing so himself.

South Australian abortion-providing GP Ingrid said, 'it was really a feminist calling to do abortions.' She grew up in Melbourne in the 1970s and was aware of Bertram Wainer:

> And then as a teenager I joined Women's Liberation ... I always knew ... that the reason for being a doctor was to promote social change ... so as soon as I was able to I start- ed making enquiries about how I could be trained to do abortions and it wasn't that easy then.

For Phyl, a Melbourne O&G, it was the process of learning to provide abortion as a trainee in the 1990s that led to her conscienti- sation and dedication:

> And that was very politicising when you were the only one and you're on the outside from the word get go, you start thinking what is going on, why is it this way? And it made me really think ... whether or not I thought it was some- thing that I could do because I was definitely a feminist, definitely supported abortion, had had my own personal experiences with abortion, there was nothing stopping me from doing abortions, except for the distaste of my colleagues.

For O&G Ralph, 'it was simply a professional duty.' The work environment added appeal, however: the part of the hospital where abortions took place was 'a sort of funky area and the midwives that worked there were a bit more interesting and you like to hang out there and talk to them.' Chris, when asked how she got involved, introduced herself as an O&G with a special interest in difficult pregnancies: 'that brought me into abortion [in the early 2000s], which then took me further to a realisation of abortion services in Queensland.'

Simon, a GP, entered the abortion-providing private sector in Sydney in the mid-1990s. He responded to an advertisement for a sedationist in the local newspaper. The ad said 'must be pro-choice.' He confessed, 'I didn't really know what that meant then.' He got the job:

> And then at that time there was quite a shortage of providers and one of the owners of one of the clinics asked if I would like to be trained in surgical termination procedures and so I was trained by that particular provider and that was finessed at Preterm who, at that stage, were the go-to place as the main training ground for abortion providers.

GP Lil also described her entrée into abortion work in SA in 2000 as serendipitous, her commitment growing over time in the context of the shortage of doctors willing to provide abortion care.

Research that has documented women's experiences of abortion since the 1970s includes stories about doctors. Many of the women from Tasmania, Queensland and SA who were interviewed for the *We Women Decide* report reported positive experiences with abortion-providing doctors in the period 1985–91. However, there were difficulties too.[28] Failure to provide accurate information and disrespectful and unprofessional behaviour were common complaints. One young woman in SA compared the hostility she experienced during her first abortion with the sympathy she received when she returned having acquired a disability and been judged as suitable for an abortion. Lectures on contraception and insistence on women taking the pill were common. More serious complaints were rare; the 1997 APFA conference was told of a doctor who had been the subject of a complaint to the NSW Health Care Complaints Commission in relation to an abortion, whose negligence, incompetence and dishonesty nearly cost the patient's life and who was eventually deregistered.[29]

Women's stories of the doctors they encountered along the way to an abortion were also a mixed bag. Those in Women's Health Centres and Family Planning clinics were discussed in positive terms, but many GPs hindered women's access through either ignorance or downright obstruction. One doctor was so fearful of retribution that the quality of their care was compromised, and plenty of GPs were opposed to abortion and made this clear. In one case, a Tasmanian woman experienced the gynaecologist's view of why she could not have an abortion as 'totally, totally humiliating'.[30]

Getting Organised

A number of abortion-providing doctors were active in creating community in the sector and providing a public presence. I discussed the formation of the APFA, an organisation of mainly private providers, in Chapter 1; after it was established by Bert Wainer in 1976, leadership was provided by abortion-providing doctors and clinic managers including FCC staff, Mark Jones and Jo Wainer, Geoff Brodie, Christine Healy, Di Jones (then manager of the PAC in Adelaide) and David Grundmann. The featured guest at the APFA conference in 1990 was the French medical scientist Étienne-Émile Baulieu, who had developed mifepristone.[31] The 1999 conference at Coolum in Queensland attracted a wide range of international presenters, most of them doctors, but was marred by political controversy when one of the invited speakers from the USA—a leading abortion provider—was temporarily detained at the airport by Australian immigration officials and only permitted to attend the conference under restrictive conditions.[32] The conference was targeted by anti-abortion protesters and organisers devised strategies to avoid disruption.

By the end of the 1990s, abortion-providing doctors were operating in an increasingly conservative national political environment,
especially after the election of the Howard government in 1996.
Sociologist Margie Ripper argues that they were experiencing a
renewed climate of stigmatisation.[33] Specific instances of controversy
contributed to this. In 1998, WA abortion clinic owner GP Victor
Chan and anaesthetist Hoh Peng Lee were arrested on criminal
charges in relation to an abortion they had performed in 1996, and
in Tasmania in 2001, unidentified doctors at the RHH were also
threatened with arrest after a medical student complained about
abortions being provided simply on the basis of a woman's request.
Neither case was prompted by patient complaints or unsatisfactory
care, and their pursuit by police and prosecutors can only be
explained by chains of conservative decision-making in the criminal
justice system. Both prompted pro-choice campaigns and eventual
law reform which allowed the doctors to avoid prosecution.[34]

Some abortion-providing doctors publicly supported reform. In
February 1998, in an open letter to *The West Australian*, Port Hedland
doctor Denis Evans declared his willingness to be sent to prison for
continuing to perform abortions. He called for other GPs to speak
out and was supported by the Rural Doctors Association of WA.[35]
When doctors at the KEMH announced that they would stop
providing abortions, demanding legal clarification from the government, O&G Harry Cohen spoke out on their behalf.[36] In Hobart,
GPs Kamala Emmanuel and Shauna McGlone, who told of her own
three abortions, and O&G Ronald Boden were all quoted as abortion providers in stories in *The Mercury*.[37] There were also letters to
the editor in *The Mercury* and *The Examiner* in Launceston in support
of law reform, from O&Gs and an oncology professor at the
University of Tasmania.

Meanwhile, in Melbourne, a case was unfolding concerning an
abortion performed at the RWH in 2000 for a woman who was 32
weeks pregnant.[38] Despite all of the procedures in the case being
lawful, ethical and professionally defensible, as was later confirmed, the
hospital CEO called a news conference and suspended the

ultrasonologist and key doctors involved, and controversy and institutional confusion ensued. The CEO referred the case to the Victorian State Coroner. Extraordinarily, a conservative member of the federal Howard government intervened and made a complaint about the case to the Medical Practitioners Board of Victoria, compounding the controversy. An article co-authored by one of the doctors involved argued that this episode harmed not only the patient, but also the doctors involved, who had been dismissed, reinstated and suspended, and generally suffered career damage and personal stress.[39] The matter was only formally resolved for the doctors in 2006.

Time for Change

In 2004 and 2005, at the height of anti-abortion activity by members of the federal government[40] and when the RWH matter was still in play, two opinion pieces written by abortion-providing doctors were published in the *Medical Journal of Australia* (*MJA*). In 2004, Melbourne O&G Lachlan de Crespigny, one of the RWH doctors, and medical ethicist Julian Savulescu wrote about the RWH case and called for clarification of the law.[41] The following year, Caroline de Costa from James Cook University in Cairns, the first female professor of O&G in Australia, wrote calling for mifepristone—the preferred drug for early medical abortion—to be made available to Australian women.[42] This proactive approach signalled an upturn in the number of articles written by Australians about abortion, in the *MJA* and in other medical journals, and in the determination of some doctors to pursue public advocacy. Both de Crespigny and de Costa continued to publish in medical journals, as have other committed providers. Authors have documented abortion practice, reported on clinical problems and innovations, and regularly called for legal and institutional change.[43]

In 2005 RANZCOG updated its earlier statement on mifepristone, supporting its availability, and released its first statement on abortion overall.[44] This included support for the inclusion of abortion 'in the education of all health professionals' and the development of 'a national sexual and reproductive health strategy—which would include supporting better equitable access to abortion services'. It also acknowledged that 'people may have strong personal beliefs about abortion'.

De Costa's 2005 article received an enormous sympathetic response and sparked a community and parliamentary campaign to change the law. In February 2006, this campaign succeeded in removing the legislation that had blocked the import of mifepristone.[45] De Costa and her Cairns O&G colleague Michael Carrette went on to become the first doctors in Australia to privately import and use mifepristone, having been granted the exceptional Authorised Prescriber status by the TGA.[46] Ingrid said of de Costa that 'She was the trailblazer, she's my hero.'

At the same time, as noted in Chapter 2, doctors at the Cairns Sexual Health Clinic started to offer medical abortion using methotrexate.[47] Robbie, who was one of the doctors at the clinic, explained how they got started, with the comment, 'it's one of our patients, as it often is' echoing Petersen's identification of demand from women as a force for change:[48]

> she had methotrexate at home ... 'I've been reading up on this. I'm pregnant and I don't want to be, and I'm going to take some methotrexate.' And so, she asked this doctor how to do it safely. ... So, I got online and looked it up and saw, oh well, there is a lot of literature, it's a good agent. ... We decided that if she was going to do it, it should be done safely, a sort of a harm minimisation model, and so, we got some misoprostol for her, she took her own supply of methotrexate and misoprostol, and it all went very well.

Doctors in private practices and at the PAC had been discreetly providing small numbers of patients with methotrexate to cause abortion before this point. The Cairns doctors, however, did so in a public setting and documented the success of the service, which subsequently used mifepristone, over the next fifteen years, as well as arguing for law reform in the *MJA* and other journals.[49]

De Costa and Carrette's application for Authorised Prescriber status was made in relation to patients for whom pregnancy was life-threatening. In SA doctors from four different hospitals, led by GP abortion provider Ea Mulligan, worked together to gain Authorised Prescriber status for the provision of ordinary abortions, becoming the first to do so, as noted in Chapter 2.[50] Ingrid, who was one of these doctors, described the process as daunting but motivated by 'consumer demand.' Applications for Authorised Prescriber status required support from a hospital ethics committee, and two of the SA committees 'went into a complete funk.' She recalled of one hospital committee that

> they spent 6 months referring it to every other committee they could think of … because they were worried about the reputation their hospital would get if it was known that medical abortions were being done there and then once they had a media plan in place then they approved it.

The application took significant time and much toing and froing with the TGA, but was successful, and the PAC began offering early medical abortion with mifepristone in 2009.[51] Other doctors around Australia, those employed at Marie Stopes, and finally doctors at various public hospitals and at the Cairns Sexual Health Clinic followed the SA lead.[52] GP Simon was working for Marie Stopes when we spoke and he acknowledged that the SA team who had shared their application had 'set the pathway.'

Meanwhile, Adrienne Freeman, an O&G in private practice in Brisbane, had been receiving national media attention for her one-woman promotion of the use of medical abortion.[53] De Costa credits Freeman with alerting her to the Authorised Prescriber possibility, but where de Costa worked through formal channels, Freeman's approach was more direct.[54] Early in 2010 she lost an appeal against the finding of the Health Practitioners Tribunal that her conduct in a 2003 case, in which she had assisted a woman to have an abortion using medication at home, was unprofessional.[55]

Later that year, concerned that women were accessing medical abortion pills from the internet, Freeman announced that she would 'launch an online DIY home abortion guide'.[56] In July 2012, after RANZCOG referred her to the Medical Board, the Queensland Civil Administrative Tribunal found that she had acted unprofessionally in relation to the website.[57] Fellow Queensland O&Gs and the pro-choice community were divided in their response to Freeman.[58] At our interview in 2013 Ingrid was 'outraged' that RANZCOG had 'invited the Medical Board of Queensland to discipline one of their members' and described the process as 'a witch-hunt.' In her view, Freeman was only following what 'responsible medical practitioners from other places in the world' were doing.

This period also saw the last time criminal charges were laid against a doctor in relation to abortion in Australia. In 2006 Suman Sood, who operated in Fairfield in Sydney, was convicted of abortion offences after prescribing medicines and sentenced to a two-year good behaviour bond.[59] While the media story of the case does not reflect well on Sood's care or professionalism, as Roger commented, she was actually convicted 'simply because she never asked let alone recorded why the woman was seeking a termination.'

Providing Early Medical Abortion

The success of MS Health's application to the TGA to import mifepristone and market it with misoprostol in 2012, and the listing of mifepristone and misoprostol on the PBS in 2013, ended the need for doctors to become Authorised Prescribers and introduced a new era. Although many doctors were still unclear on the new situation, patients were demanding the service. This process is discussed in detail in Chapters 4 and 5.

Since 2012, Australian and New Zealand conferences on sexual and reproductive health have therefore regularly included discussion and promotion of medical abortion. Dr Philip Goldstone, Medical Director at Marie Stopes since 2010, has spoken at every Children by Choice conference since 2012, updating doctors on research about and regulation of early medical abortion. Other presentations have promoted early medical abortion to rural GPs, told stories from both urban and regional medical clinics about its implementation, and reported on consumer demand.[60] At the beginning of the 2020s, however, less than 10 per cent of all eligible doctors have registered as prescribers of early medical abortion, and most of these are in metropolitan areas.[61]

The normalisation of early medical abortion has, however, enabled the development of telehealth abortion. In 2013, Cairns GP Heather McNamee became one of the first to integrate a telehealth service into her existing practice using Skype.[62] In 2015 O&G Dr Paul Hyland established the Tabbot Foundation, Australia's first national telehealth abortion provider, which quickly grew to provide about 1 per cent of all abortions in Australia.[63] When the Foundation closed in early 2019 it was not due to lack of demand, but because of the strain it placed on Hyland, for whom 'it was an expensive business to run and he did so at great personal cost'.[64] Other existing private providers around the country, including Marie Stopes, some family planning organisations and community-based healthcare services, and some GPs, have established telehealth services, demand for which has skyrocketed since the COVID-19 pandemic.[65]

The Ongoing Struggle to Improve Training

While more medical schools are training students in abortion care in the twenty-first century, and some do so well, the picture is still uneven.[66] A survey conducted in 2013 found that in some cases 'the moral stance of individual medical students allowed them to exclude themselves from abortion education' and in others 'students may not have had the opportunity to partake in abortion education'.[67] A 2020 survey showed that nearly 80 per cent of final-year medical students had received some education about abortion, although content varied and only 35 per cent had had clinical exposure, most of which was incidental. The authors concluded that 'structured and standardised teaching is still lacking. Students' confidence around abortion care is inadequate, and the majority of students showed a strong desire to have more direct abortion placement exposure'.[68]

Several interviewees provided local anecdotal evidence about the efforts being made to train medical students in the 2000s and 2010s. Sally told me of how one of the longstanding doctors at the PAC has persisted in bringing students into the PAC and family planning clinics in hospitals since the early 2000s: 'just expose, expose, expose and eventually something will come up and it has and now there's a young woman working there, she's got a permanent position.' Ingrid's story of gaining recognition among SA medical academics also signalled progress. In 2013 she told me how, because of that recognition, she had become a regular guest lecturer to students:

> I can't go to all of those lectures because there's so many of them, but I've divvied it up amongst the doctors I work with, so we're seeing every medical student now for at least 90 minutes ... I think our position within the profession is changing the more we assert that this is health care, and we're doctors, just like other doctors, and we love our work just like other doctors do.

Similarly, medical academic Max noted that Philip Goldstone from Marie Stopes has been giving lectures every year to Sydney University students, with no pushback, since the late 2000s and Laura, one of the abortion-providing GPs I spoke to in Perth in 2016, was soon making a second appearance at 'a round table on abortion provision' at the Catholic Notre Dame University. It remains the case, however, that personal dedication is required to keep abortion training on the agenda. In 2020 the formal link between the PAC and the universities and the teaching hospitals had 'essentially stopped'.[69]

The late 2010s saw significant innovation in relation to training and support for abortion provision from within mainstream institutions in Australia. The Sexual and Reproductive Health Special Interest Group of RANZCOG, established during the presidency of Dr Michael Permezel and chaired from its inception in 2013 by

O&G Professor Kirsten Black from Sydney University, has led the development of an optional Advanced Training Module in Sexual and Reproductive Health as part of its program for aspiring Fellows of the College. The module was launched in 2016, covers contraception and abortion, and is taken over 12 months.[70] At the time of writing, the module is currently available for trainees at only *two* hospitals in Australia; that is, only two institutions can provide supervision and abortion services to the level required for comprehensive training. Since 2020, however, RANZCOG's basic trainees have also been required to complete abortion training, and the online module for this group is also available to existing specialist and GPs.[71]

Several Melbourne-based institutions have developed programs to train, encourage and support doctors in providing early medical abortion. Since 2017 the Centre for Rural Sexual Health, based at Melbourne University, and the RWH, led by O&G Paddy Moore, include a focus on doctors in rural areas of Victoria.[72] SPHERE, led by Professor of General Practice Danielle Mazza, supports healthcare workers in the provision of both early medical abortion and long-acting reversible contraceptives.[73] Family Planning organisations in most states also offer accredited training for GPs with an interest in early medical abortion and related matters. In 2014, Marie Stopes was invited by Healthed, a major private health education company that provides professional development to doctors, to speak at their women's health conferences. For Simon, this signalled the mainstreaming of abortion in a commercial context.[74]

Training to perform surgical abortions, however, remains an intractable problem. In 2020, a report by Family Planning NSW and collaborators described the need for systematic training in surgical abortion as 'urgent' and called for 'a national process for accreditation' for surgical abortion, while noting that the lack of public hospital provision was a major obstacle in 'the provision of training in best practice models of care'.[75]

Public Voices

Since the early 2000s, the campaigns for the decriminalisation of abortion in Australia's states and territories have given abortion-providing doctors opportunities for public comment. Individual abortion providers from the public and private sectors have contributed to the law reform bodies that preceded decriminalisation in Victoria, Queensland and SA, and the parliamentary inquiries in Queensland, NSW and Tasmania.[76] They appeared in media coverage during the debates on decriminalisation.

RANZCOG and the AMA have been key contributors to the inquiries, supporting decriminalisation in all jurisdictions. Since 2000, their positions have been more liberal than most state and territory parliaments have been able to accept. The national AMA's formal position statements relating to abortion, for example, have become progressively more oriented to women's rights and the needs of those for whom information and access are inadequate, although in 2019 it was still emphasising 'a great diversity of views' among doctors and the right of doctors to not provide abortion care.[77] It is worth noting that this emphasis on conscientious objection is by no means universal: conscientious objection in relation to abortion is not currently available to doctors in 'Sweden, Finland, Bulgaria, Czech Republic and Iceland'.[78] RANZCOG's position statements have been less exercised by the matter of conscientious objection and more appreciative of the structural issues that impede better abortion care.[79] Abortion has also been a regular matter for discussion in RANZCOG's *Journal of Australian and New Zealand Obstetrics & Gynaecology* and its *O&G Magazine* and the *MJA* since the late 2000s, and editorials in these in favour of law reform and improved access are regular.[80] Caroline de Costa, often writing with legal scholar Heather Douglas, has kept the need for law reform in front of the medical audience for over a decade.[81]

Finally, abortion-providing doctors in the 2010s also used popular culture to talk about their work. Dr Jane, who performed abortions up to 24 weeks pregnancy at the Marie Stopes clinic in Maroondah, featured in a made-for-tv documentary about the clinic that aired on ABC television in 2015. Brisbane O&G Carol Portmann's appearance on reality television four years later was also a bold move. An elder in the Brisbane Uniting Church and a provider of later abortions, Portmann appeared in the two-part SBS program *Christians Like Us*, which initially aired in 2019. Portmann was one of ten housemates with a wide range of Christian views who spent seven days together discussing their lives and their faith; she discussed abortion. And Caroline de Costa has found time to write three books about abortion for a general audience, the third of which discusses her long career.[82]

Twenty-first Century Doctors

Stories from women who have had abortions in the twenty-first century, in both research studies and popular culture, indicate that the practice of abortion-providing doctors has improved remarkably since the early 1990s.[83] A small number of interviewees talked about abortion-providing doctors, mostly older men, whose practice was patronising, and Roger referred to a doctor assisting him who lacked courage in a life-threatening crisis. But these were outliers; nearly all interviewees spoke of abortion-providing doctors with respect. The doctors who provided abortions still faced legal and discursive constraints, especially before decriminalisation. A survey of abortion providers in Queensland and NSW about the impact of abortion law that was conducted in the early 2010s—that is, before decriminalisation—found that some dwelt on the legal requirements that allocated decision-making to the doctor while others saw abortion as a health issue and acted accordingly to meet women's needs. 'While many doctors seemed to accept that part of their role was to construct an appropriate narrative to justify a termination, many were frustrated that this was required.' Many doctors felt 'compromised'.[84]

Research into Australian doctors' attitudes to abortion in general is scant, but tells of a profession with increasingly pro-choice views, though with some variation between jurisdictions.[85] A study conducted in 2017, however, found that 'many GPs saw abortion as beyond the scope of their practice'.[86] And as late as 2017 reports continued to tell of experiences with GPs (not abortion providers) and other relevant healthcare providers that were sometimes unhelpful and 'distressing'.[87] People seeking abortions in conservative country areas are most vulnerable.[88] In the jurisdictions that legally required the signature of two doctors, obtaining the second signature was sometimes a problem. Several interviewees noted that some anaesthetists could be reticent on this matter and in general; Ingrid, her disdain to the fore, mimicked such anaesthetists at one of the smaller public hospitals in SA:

> 'we won't sign that form, we're willing to do an anaesthetic for this abortion, we don't have a conscientious objection to that. But we won't sign the form because that's about surgery and about giving permission for surgery and that's the surgeon's job and we can't check up that they've had the proper counselling and we're a bit squeamish about abortion and we think it's a bit yucky and we think that that form's a legal document and we're putting our signature on it and we don't want to.'

In 2009, 14.6 per cent of RANZCOG Fellows and trainees who responded to a survey were totally opposed to abortion, but most of the others thought that abortion should be part of O&G practice, included in training and performed in public hospitals. Only about 35 per cent of all O&Gs, however, were involved in abortion provision beyond those performed for foetal anomaly or maternal physical health issues.[89] When this survey was repeated in 2019, little had changed.[90] These doctors continued to distinguish between so-called 'social' or 'psychosocial' and 'maternal' or 'foetal' reasons for abortion. The authors therefore described the practice of O&Gs in 2019 as 'sub-optimal'.

The negative impact of doctors who are absolutely opposed to abortion is widely noted.[91] Rowena, who worked in a non-medical role at the FCC in Melbourne, knew of many cases over the years where women had encountered such doctors, in Catholic hospitals and in general practice. Priscilla's story of the internal politics of the Darwin Hospital in the 2010s, where the opposition of a senior O&G was significant and the impasse at the Wagga Wagga public hospital in NSW caused by influential doctors who were not even involved with sexual and reproductive health care are all cautionary tales.

The Emotional Landscape of Abortion Provision

Six years after the initial events, Lachlan de Crespigny talked frankly about being at the centre of the RWH episode regarding the late term abortion. At times he had been nudged into depression, and he was still angry with the hospital.[92] I am not aware of accounts of any other post-1970s abortion-providing doctor in Australia who has suffered in this way, but anger and outrage in response to institutional or professional attitudes and behaviours about abortion were common among the doctors I spoke with.

Some of the emotions that providers expressed in interview, notably anger, arise from resistance to the predominant norms and practices of the profession, and the broader health context.[93] Robbie observed that 'the well-to-do can always obtain abortions, and this, I think is what really got me angry.' After telling a story from the 1990s about a resident at the KEMH who refused to enter a room to treat a patient who had had an abortion because she didn't agree with abortion, abortion-providing GP Nic exclaimed, 'If this is *the* women's hospital in WA, the jewel in the crown of women's health, why are people employed if they can't provide a comprehensive service!' However, it was not only healthcare professionals who were angry. Roger also talked about the anger that anti-abortion picketers brought into the abortion-providing environment. He described their tactics as 'a vindictive kick in the guts' aimed at women entering the clinic.

Fear was an equally common emotion to be negotiated. Writing of the Irish situation in the late 2010s, when abortion was highly restricted, Deirdre Duffy and her colleagues identified two distinct fears among doctors. There was the fear of 'future prosecution' and damage to 'future professional status', which restricted and regulated doctors' behaviour. But there was also fear about what might happen to those who needed abortion care, which prompted 'reflection on how care can be provided within the present legal and political context'.[94] The Australian abortion-providing doctors surveyed in the early 2010s were similarly mixed in their response to the likelihood of prosecution.[95]

My interviewees, who had overcome fears of the law to respond to the need for care, still talked about it. In 2015 Davina, for example, said, 'I really didn't want to get raided,' using the word 'raided' five times in short succession—a legacy of the 1980s, when she had begun practising and when clinics in Queensland and Melbourne were indeed 'raided' by police.[96] Notwithstanding her fear, she had been ready: 'If I was raided, so be it, you take me to court then, and see what happens.'

Some doctors who worked in the public sector referred to their employers as a source of fear. Robbie, who worked at the Sexual Health Clinic in Cairns, twice told me, 'I still have a fear that I'm going to be sacked'—an apprehension, not a rational assessment, partly a joke. Ingrid described the atmosphere around services in the SA public system as having 'one foot on a banana skin at all times … There's just this huge kind of anxiety and scrutiny and stuff going on all the time.'

Ingrid led me through a long discussion about reputational fear, telling two separate stories of concern with reputation that were filtered through a range of relationships and locations. Some doctors had expressed interest in working alongside her to provide abortion care in SA hospitals; 'then they've come back to me a couple of weeks later and said "Oh, actually I can't do that, my wife doesn't want me to" or "my husband doesn't".' A doctor in private practice in a regional centre stopped doing abortions. He told her, '"I don't want to be known as the doctor who does abortions and especially now I've got a teenage daughter who's the same age as the young women who are coming for abortions and so they all know and they tell each other and I don't want that".'

The fear generated around abortion provision had a life of its own that could capture even those who did not provide abortions. In the early days of the Cairns Sexual Health abortion service, Robbie described doctors at the public hospital as experiencing 'consternation.' When I asked whether they were opposed to abortion, he replied, 'No, no, no. They were all in favour of abortion … It was more fear of retribution, I think.' When the hospital's ethics committee was approached to endorse an application for Authorised Prescriber status, it initially refused to consider it. In Robbie's view the doctors on the committee were 'Just scared … I think they just stuck their heads in the sand and said this is all too difficult.' Eventually the application was successful.

Ingrid was the only doctor who spoke about personal fear of attack from anti-abortionists. She mentioned violence against doctors in the USA and had had more than her fair share of harassment from immediate colleagues opposed to abortion. She was specific: being identified 'might be quite a risk to my health or someone might poison the dog or burn my house down or I don't know, we'll see.' Even if they were not afraid of personal attack, those who worked in clinics where protesters were a regular presence felt a toll. As part of their campaign for safe access zones, in 2014 the FCC in Melbourne engaged a psychiatrist who observed 'intermittent or ongoing medical issues or stress symptoms' in the staff he examined.[97]

GP Rosalie, who began providing abortions in 1990, was dismissive—even defiant—in the face of the law and disapproval. 'The issue isn't the legality,' she said. 'It's not, doctors don't worry about that, really, they know we're not going to end up in jail … We just go ahead and do our own thing.'

Petersen's 1993 observations about abortion-providing doctors' lack of interest in professional status, ideological commitment and/or focus on financial gain still stand as an account of antidotes to reputational fear.[98] (I confess, reader, that I did not ask doctors about financial motives.) Rosalie recognised that abortion was 'not seen as a sexy area of medicine,' but said, 'that doesn't bother me …

Somebody's got to be down there doing the real stuff.' Robbie said, 'I don't mind being an outsider and supporting rights of people.' Many stories highlight the role of doctors who are outsiders—new to the hospital, or the state, or the country, or culturally different—in creating change. As a clearly identified feminist doctor, Ingrid said, 'I had no reputation to lose. So to me, I'm not concerned about that, and I'm a hero amongst feminists and that's what I care about.'

Some of the doctors I interviewed spoke back to the mainstream. On the persistence of 'old-fashioned' beliefs about abortion, Rosalie said, 'There are a lot of naive doctors out there.' In a 2013 discussion about the lack of advocacy among O&Gs as a group in Queensland, Robbie described the profession as 'very disappointing' and said, 'I think they don't respect women's rights.' These critical views were also present in the 2018 survey of O&Gs. One respondent described the profession as 'deeply hypocritical'.[99]

Some doctors were able to hold their sense of themselves as abortion providers without experiencing tension with colleagues or professional norms. A leader in expanding public abortion provision in Queensland despite resistance, O&G Chris put faith in the power of discussion: 'I was lucky enough to have a general respect from other doctors who acknowledged that I was doing the right thing and they supported that,' she told me.

One of the most significant breaks with representations of abortion that stigmatise providers has been the increasing number of expressions of the positive nature of the work. In 2011, WA abortion provider Judith Nash concluded a letter about abortion to her local medical magazine by describing her work as 'extremely rewarding, despite the negative views of many'.[100] Likewise, Simon said of his move into becoming a full-time abortion provider, '[I] began to find it very rewarding work 'cause there's not actually many areas of medicine where women can—or patients—can come to you with a problem that you can solve on the day and they go home.'

Ralph said of the Thursday clinic at the public hospital where he worked in Adelaide that 'the atmosphere is terrific really. It's quite a lively—the whole thing around abortion—I guess you're working as a team, you've got a purpose—a few jokes,' and Robbie said of the team in Cairns, 'We're happy abortionists, that ... have made a difference to a lot of women.'[101]

I asked most doctors if their work as abortion providers had caused issues in their private lives. Davina had attended a Catholic girls school in the 1960s and '70s, and lost some friends over her work. Others became comfortable with it, though, including her family: 'My dad was a Catholic and he was negative in the beginning but maybe halfway through he totally came around.' She was not the only doctor to occasionally hide behind 'women's health' as a cover story for abortion work, however, although this tactic didn't always hold. Rosalie told me, 'I've managed to silence some dinner parties a few times when people have pushed me and said, "Well where do you work? What do you do?".' On the other hand, more than one doctor told me about being appreciated for their work. Nic said, 'My kids are very supportive ... you know my step-son, one of the girls said, "He's so proud of you and what you do".'

Conclusion

Abortion-providing doctors have changed a lot since 1990—for the better, from the patient's point of view. As well as leading improvement in the everyday practice of abortion care, they have been part of creating institutional change.

This chapter has traced three generations of abortion-providing doctors in the post-liberalisation period and three generations of leadership, although this model needs to be imposed lightly, as several doctors cross generations (and younger doctors might form a fourth). The first generation comprises those who saw the cost of the illegal era to women and pioneered early services in uncertain legal environments, in public hospitals and in private practice—all leaders in this respect. Some of these men, as they nearly all were, still practised in the 2000s. The second generation, which included more women, was made up of those who had been trained by these pioneers and matured as providers in the 1990s. Some provided leadership in APFA in its heyday, predominantly those in private practice; many enjoyed its conferences. The third generation has taken up leadership in the 2000s. Its members are more likely to be women, leading politically from positions in public hospitals, private practice and Marie Stopes. They follow the previous generations' achievement of significant institutional change in law and medical bodies, including innovations in training, and are maintaining and extending current service provision, including early medical abortion and telehealth. At best, these commitments require persistence. At worst they are tough battles.

The next cohort of medical leaders is now emerging, perhaps from the small group of RANZCOG trainees who are graduating from its Advanced Training Module and from the GPs who will become providers of early medical abortion outside metropolitan settings, expanding access to those who have been most deprived. This new group inherits well-formed medical networks and a persuasive body of research to support best practice and policy change. They can also access a critical discourse that centres the needs of those who need abortions, and speaks back to the conservative elements of the medical profession.

A triumphal narrative of the medical profession in relation to abortion is hardly justified, however. At the time of writing, it remains difficult to recruit doctors to work in abortion care. Too few GPs are becoming providers of early medical abortion. Training in surgical provision is an intractable issue. And abortion-providing doctors are still often required to perform emotional labour that would be unusual for most other healthcare professionals. As many interviewees stressed, many services (public and private) are maintained, and change comes, only because of the persistence of 'champions'. In the absence of government health departments taking responsibility for sustaining and improving abortion care, it is individuals, including those in the private and NGO sectors, who do so, often inadvertently becoming the 'entrepreneurial employees' upon whom institutions that are being reshaped by neoliberal forms of government rely.[102]

At the end of this chapter it seems to me that the greatest obstacle to change and improvement in the adequacy of abortion services in Australia could be the entrenched conservatism of the medical profession as a whole. While there are individual doctors who hold anti-abortion views and who obstruct the provision of abortion care, they are the minority. The majority is pro-choice. It is not their professed attitudes to abortion that are the problem; it is their action, or lack of it. And this inaction is guaranteed by the provision for conscientious objection in the legislation which has decriminalised abortion. In 2022 a doctor's right to conscientious objection to providing abortion is legislated, uniquely—and some would say unnecessarily—in all jurisdictions. While these provisions do protect patients by requiring those with an objection to refer them on (in most jurisdictions), a 2017 study of abortion in Victoria post-decriminalisation suggested that they had 'increased the legitimacy of "opting out" of abortion provision ... and whole institutions could justify not providing abortion services'.[103] This unintended effect draws on a history of medical privilege that elevates the judgement and desires of individual doctors above those of their patients. At a minimum, this historical legacy sits alongside the intransigence of the state and the harsh realities of the market in relation to those who need abortion care.

Decriminalisation has formally removed the decisional control over abortion that Sheldon identified as one of the types of medical control exercised by doctors. Their exercise of paternalistic and normalising control has probably waned over the years. Their technical control, however, remains for the time being. Notwithstanding this change, the paradox I spelled out in the introduction to this chapter thus continues to frame the problem with doctors: they still have the exclusive right to provide abortions; and their specific right to not provide abortions has been further entrenched.

There were a few—not as many as I expected—hints among my interviewees at frustration with the ongoing presence of the historical privilege accorded to doctors. Evie, social worker at the RWH, commented wryly, 'I still feel like we're sometimes the handmaidens to the medical profession.' In a discussion about nurses becoming providers of early medical abortion, Sally noted that doctors are 'pretty expensive,' costing 'really a vast amount more [than nurses].' There was an edge to her comment. I haven't discussed nurses in this chapter—I will do so in Chapter 5, which focuses on early medical abortion. Nurses are poised to take over from doctors as providers of early medical abortion, and not only because they are cheaper to employ. Some of the clinics that pioneered the provision of early medical abortion in Australia have been doing so through nurse-led models and some overseas studies show that 'women prefer nurse- or midwife-led services'.[104] And while legislation and/or regulation still require a doctor's oversight, this may change, and nurses may be able to become fully fledged providers, as is the case in some other countries. Internationally, doctors are also challenged by the call for 'self-managed abortion', which can mean telehealth abortion supported by healthcare workers who are not necessarily doctors.[105]

A friend who is a longstanding abortion activist and public health advocate said to me that she felt abortion-providing doctors were different from other doctors. For my part, although I enjoyed meeting and talking with all the doctors I interviewed, I hadn't expected to be as impressed by them as I found I was when I returned to the interviews to write this chapter. I did not expect to be documenting so much persistent professional and political activism on their part, in some cases over decades. Abortion-providing doctors have supported and been active collaborators in many struggles over abortion. In specifically medical arenas, they have led. It is ironic that their leadership is underpinned by their historical privilege, which they cannot always surrender to the autonomy of women and others who need abortions, and that this means there is little chance of change without them and their medical associations and colleges. But doctors who are abortion providers are the ones most directly and personally addressed by people who need abortion care. They are thus important conduits for these peoples' demands for better access to care, and indeed to reproductive justice.

Chapter 4

Marie Stopes

When the charity Marie Stopes International (MSI) arrived in Australia in 2000, it initiated a significant change in the landscape of abortion provision. The progressive impetus in understanding abortion as a matter of health care in Australia, which had peaked in the early 1990s, had stalled. Longstanding private providers in three states were close to retirement, and there were no likely buyers for their businesses. The period of expansion in private clinics was coming to an end. Marie Stopes Australia both responded to this context and remade it.

Founded in London in 1976, MSI is one of the largest global providers of sexual and reproductive health. It is highly regarded for its work in developing countries, and in particular for its provision of abortion care.[1] MSI's abortion clinics in England and Wales, and in Australia, Austria and Romania, are self-sustaining programs, run to make a surplus—as profit is described in the not-for-profit sector—that is reinvested into their work in developing countries.[2] In Britain they have been one of two large charities contracted by the NHS since the 1980s to provide publicly funded abortions. Following a re-evaluation of the legacy of Marie Stopes—the mid-twentieth-century British birth control campaigner who was also a committed eugenicist—prompted by the Black Lives Matter movement, in 2021 the charity changed its name from Marie Stopes

International to MSI Reproductive Choices.[3] In 2022 the Australian branch followed the parent body in removing the name 'Marie Stopes' from their name and became MSI Australia. For reasons of historical accuracy, I will continue to use 'Marie Stopes' to refer to the Australian body until 2022.

Marie Stopes Australia was established in 2000, and just over a decade later had purchased existing abortion clinics in all mainland jurisdictions except for SA and the NT and opened some new ones, branded as Dr Marie clinics, led the provision of early medical abortion, and established a company that would import and distribute the pharmaceutical drugs necessary for this form of abortion. Thus far, I have bracketed Marie Stopes Australia's operations in Australia with those of other private providers, but in truth they are a charity—an NGO operating with tax-free status, with a mission and culture quite distinct from the private sector, although there are some similarities. This chapter tells the story of the growth of Marie Stopes in Australia, and its sometimes contested position in the local abortion-providing sector.

In Australia there are three separate corporate entities all owned by the London-based organisation, each with separate (though sometimes overlapping) executive leadership and advisory boards: MSI Australia (previously Marie Stopes Australia), MS Health and MSI Asia Pacific (previously Marie Stopes International Australia). Marie Stopes is the only large-scale national private provider of abortion services, occupying upwards of 30 per cent of the abortion market at the time of writing, and providing advocacy in relation to sexual and reproductive health care. It also provides contraceptive and related sexual health services and is the largest Australian provider of vasectomies, both in clinics which also provide abortions and in separate facilities. MS Health opened in 2012 as a not-for-profit pharmaceutical company to import and distribute mifepristone and misoprostol, the pharmaceutical base for medical abortion. Both Marie Stopes Australia and MS Health aimed to contribute financially to Marie Stopes International Australia, which was established in 2004 and became MSI Asia Pacific in 2021. This body works with other MSI companies to deliver sexual and reproductive health care in developing countries in the Asia-Pacific region. Except where explicitly noted, however, this chapter focuses on the network of abortion-providing clinics and related services in Australia.

As far as I have found, there has been no history or critical appraisal done of the last fifty years of MSI worldwide, its operations in the UK, or its work in Australia. While published research has documented and evaluated its work in developing countries, and research about abortion in Australia based on patient surveys and similar has been published by Marie Stopes since the early 2010s, the lack of existing research *about* rather than *by* Marie Stopes in Australia reflects the lack of critical attention to the structure of abortion provision in this country. (This also seems to be the case in the UK).[4] I am aware that this lack of critical attention to MSI and Marie Stopes *as organisations* may arise from the often precarious position of all abortion provision, which renders critical analysis of abortion-providing organisations a low priority and may even be politically ill-advised. I am persuaded, however, that the value of insight into the provision of abortion care in Australia outweighs the risks of exposure to unfriendly readers.

Two bodies of literature which describe the neoliberal forms of government that have shaped the provision of health, social and welfare services globally over the last thirty or more years suggest questions to use in thinking about Marie Stopes in Australia, which began as a commercial operation, but has connections and shares values with local and global movements for reproductive rights in ways that make it distinct from private providers. The critical literature on 'NGOization' describes the process of the 'institutionalization, professionalization, depoliticization and demobilization of movements for social and environmental change'.[5] The term has been applied to the operation of NGOs in developing countries and to feminist activism, where Nancy Fraser calls it 'NGO-ification', and INCITE! has coined the term 'the non-profit industrial complex'.[6]

Marie Stopes arrived in Australia at a time when governments were increasingly outsourcing welfare and employment services to the community and private sectors. The literature on this trend asks questions about the impact of being brought into the neoliberal model of outsourcing—and into dependence on government funding—on the values and practices of NGOs. Two such impacts are constraint on the potential advocacy roles of progressive NGOs, and downward pressure on wages and conditions in the sector.[7] The NGOisation literature also asks questions about 'whether or not NGOs open up political space or represent specific forms of regulation and containment in the interest of a contemporary capitalist (re) colonization'.[8] Both literatures raise questions about accountability in the face of pressure from funding bodies. But Marie Stopes operates as a private business and has historically been mostly unconstrained by the pressures that come with government funding. Neither the NGOisation nor the community sector literature therefore exactly captures its nature. The nascent body of commentary on the corporatisation of medical general practice in Australia—a trend since the late 1990s—might be a useful third source of input given that it deals with tensions between health professionals in corporate employment and the forces driving the corporation.[9] Taken together, these bodies of literature raise questions about the broader historical forces that Marie Stopes embodies in Australia, the political space it creates, its relationship with government and other players in the sexual and reproductive health sector, and its impact on service provision.

Like previous chapters, this one draws on a range of government and organisational documents, media stories, and oral history interviews. Among the forty or so people I interviewed for this book, nine had worked for Marie Stopes in Australia or for MSI, either in the past or at the time of interview, across a range of professions, including senior roles. Many others also had experiences and opinions to share.

Origin Stories

The MSI website tells the organisation's story of its origins: 'Our story starts with three reproductive health pioneers, Tim Black CBE, Jean Black and Phil Harvey. In 1976, they set out on a mission to bring choice to women around the world'.[10] Its accounts often begin the Australian story by saying that the organisation was 'invited' to buy a clinic in WA.[11] However, several of the people I interviewed told a tale which, although not necessarily contradictory, has a different slant. Roger, a GP abortion provider at the centre of the Sydney scene at the time, started with a story of MSI having some money to play with—about £20 million, he thought:

> they sent one of their nurses that does quality assurance in their global network, came to Australia, came to a conference, started to talk to people, probably had the overview that the next generation were not probably wanting to buy in to the current operations so no succession options for those who wanted to sell and/or retire.

Helen Axby, listed as MSI UK's Deputy Chief Executive, presented a paper about abortion provision in the UK at the November 1999 Abortion Providers Federation Australia conference in Queensland, but she was not the person to whom Roger was referring.[12] Viv, an activist then closely associated with the Bessie Smyth clinic in Sydney, explains:

> Well, what actually happened with Marie Stopes, in 1999 they sent a male nurse out from the UK to basically go to every abortion service across the whole nation ... Basically he went to every state, and it was really just this complete sussing out of the financial position, really, of the different clinics with a view, obviously he was going back to MSI, to report which ones were OK financially and might be worthwhile buying out.

Davina, a GP who worked in the private sector, told the story from a Melbourne perspective, filtered through her commercial interest and subsequent jaded view: 'they came to Christine Healy's clinic, they came to Fertility Control's clinic, they went to Mark Jones' clinic, and we all in a naive way gave them tons of information about our practices.'

Buying Up Clinics

Marie Stopes established itself in Australia in 2000, purchasing its first clinic in Perth, WA the next year.[13] John Charters, the GP who had run the Zera clinic in Midland since its inception in 1976, was unwell and had started to negotiate with Marie Stopes.[14] Nic, who worked in the O&G department at the KEMH with senior O&G Harry Cohen, recalls her start at this clinic:

> Harry Cohen was going around asking people if they would be prepared to help out … So he organised for me to go up there on a Wednesday with him just to have a look and see how it ran, how I'd feel about it. I went in there, we went in there, and John had gone into hospital the night before. So Harry and I did the list.

John died a week or so later; Nic stayed on. Roger recalled that he had been 'operating whilst breathing oxygen' and thought that he had 'no local doctor to sell to.' This is the first of a handful of stories in which Marie Stopes 'saved' a clinic and the service that it provided.

Joyce related how Marie Stopes secured a small contract with first the KEMH and then later for the new Midland Public Hospital, which was run by the Catholic St John of God organisation (mentioned in the previous chapter).[15] A similar arrangement was established in Queensland when abortion was decriminalised there in 2018. In some respects, these contracts mirror MSI's arrangement with the NHS in Britain, where in 2020 independent organisations provided 77 per cent of all abortions in England and Wales under contract to the NHS, around 35 per cent by MSI and most of the rest by the British Pregnancy Advisory Service (BPAS).[16] In WA the KEMH's contracting out to Marie Stopes was represented to me by the local healthcare providers with whom I spoke as a sign of the public hospitals' distaste for or indifference to providing abortion care as much as it was a sign of commitment to the service.

More or less at the same time as it purchased Zera in WA, Marie Stopes was investigating a clinic in the small state of Tasmania. Nicola worked in the government at the time and recalled, 'I think they were going to be treating Tasmania as a developing country because the business case didn't really look like they would make much money out of it, but they were still very keen to do it.' Negotiations did not proceed.

Marie Stopes moved into Sydney shortly after its initial purchase in WA, purchasing two clinics in short succession in 2002—the clinic near Westmead Hospital, northwest of central Sydney, which had been operated by O&Gs Simcock, Kuah and Ng, who had been in practice since the 1970s, and the independent feminist Bessie Smyth clinic at Homebush, closer to the city centre, which had opened in 1977. In her unpublished history of Bessie Smyth, Margaret Kirkby writes that

> By Feb 2002 it became evident to the Directors that the financial position of the company was slipping badly. Eventually an offer came through from the British multinational [*sic*], Marie Stopes International (MSI), to buy us out … the business and premises were sold and [we] moved out on Monday 26th August 2002.[17]

The other purchase in Sydney at this time was doctor Suman Sood's clinic at Fairfield. Sood would be convicted of abortion offences in 2006 in relation to an abortion conducted in 2002.[18] Finally, in 2007, after a period of negotiation, Marie Stopes bought Geoff Brodie's clinics in inner-city Camperdown and Penrith in the outer west. Roger recalled that Brodie was ready to retire and 'None of the doctors wanted to pay up money.'

Marie Stopes had also bought the Reproductive Health Services clinic in Canberra, previously owned by Family Planning ACT, in

2004. Like the Bessie Smyth clinic, RHS was struggling to survive. Julie, who worked there in a management role at the time, recalled:

> We did a great negotiation with Marie Stopes who were able to come in then and takeover the equipment, the premises. The government was still able to offer a peppercorn rent ... They did a financial view; the fact that they're a global organisation and were able to purchase insurance at a much different rate [was important].

Julie said of Marie Stopes that 'they saved the space where women could access services in the ACT.' In Queensland Marie Stopes first established a clinic in Caboolture, north of Brisbane, and later bought the Salisbury clinic in suburban Brisbane in the mid-2000s. In WA a clinic was opened in Kwinana, south of Perth. In Melbourne, presumably due to the lack of a suitable clinic willing to sell, it established its own new clinic in East St Kilda in 2007.

As well as buying up clinics, Marie Stopes began to start offering early medical abortion. In mid-2006 senior doctor Philip Goldstone commenced a trial in Sydney of early medical abortion using methotrexate, which was available in Australia as a cancer drug.[19] The following year it announced that it would be offering methotrexate abortions in its clinics in all states.[20] As noted in Chapter 3 Marie Stopes' doctors then followed the South Australians in becoming Authorised Prescribers and started importing mifepristone from Aotearoa New Zealand, offering it across all jurisdictions where they were present.

By the end of 2009 Marie Stopes had eleven clinics across the country. Its revenue for the year ending December 2009 was about $19 million.[21]

New Horizons, Unexpected Challenges

In August 2009, Maria Deveson Crabbe, who came from the corporate sector, was appointed by the UK Board as the new CEO of Marie Stopes in Australia.[22] She oversaw its application to the TGA to import mifepristone, working with French activist doctor and pharmaceutical manufacturer André Ullman,[23] and the establishment of MS Health as a pharmaceutical company to do so. This was a multi-million-dollar undertaking. According to Yolanda, who worked at Marie Stopes in a management role at this time, Deveson Crabbe's leadership brought in new staff, a new culture and higher rates of pay than had previously been the norm. She was appointed as CEO of both international and domestic wings of the organisation, following former UN and government NGO manager Suzanne Dvorak (2002–09) as CEO of the Australian clinic business, and development practitioner and academic Julie Mundy as CEO at MSI Australia (2000–10).[24]

In 2006 a successful campaign in federal parliament had removed the near-decade-long necessity for the Minister for Health to approve the import of mifepristone, but with conservative Catholic Tony Abbott as Health Minister 'not one drug company was prepared to register it,' as Yolanda exclaimed. GP Simon, also at Marie Stopes at the time, said of the initiative to import mifepristone that 'I'm sure there was a commercial aspect [but] ... a massive part of it was about improving access for Australian women.'

Partway in, the process became much more complicated.[25] Where Marie Stopes had sought approval to import and distribute mifepristone, which would be marketed with misoprostol (which was already on the market to treat stomach ulcers), the TGA now required that it also seek approval to use misoprostol as a gynaecological drug, as it was not prepared to endorse a regimen that depended on off-label use of another medication. Simon commented with a laugh that, at that time, 'nowhere else in the world is that a requirement.' But there was no turning back. In 2010, the death of a woman who had accessed early medical abortion from Marie Stopes but could not be contacted for follow-up after the procedure and had developed sepsis contributed to the TGA's cautious approach.[26] Yolanda estimated that because of the TGA's requirements, 'the whole process took like three and a half years instead of eighteen months.' As many interviewees acknowledged, it also increased the cost of the application: the most reliable figure I have been told is $6 million.[27]

The TGA gave approval to import and distribute the drugs for early medical abortion in August 2012. MS Health had already been established to launch their sale.[28] The TGA's conditions of approval were many (see Chapter 5). The cost of the process and the ongoing TGA requirements to manage risk are partly what led to the sixfold increase in price over what Authorised Prescribers had been paying to import the drug from Aotearoa New Zealand. Patients and others in the sector were dismayed.[29] However, the cost of the drug to patients was reduced in 2013 following the success of Marie Stopes' application to have it listed on the PBS. In early 2015 Marie Stopes began piloting its telemedicine abortion service.

The process of purchasing GP Mark Schulberg's clinic at Maroondah in the outer eastern suburbs of Melbourne was another complex matter that occurred early in Deveson Crabbe's period as CEO. In 2009, Schulberg's clinic was the only one in Victoria—indeed in Australia—which conducted 'late' abortions for so-called 'psychosocial' reasons, including abortions over 24 weeks. Prior to initial negotiations with Marie Stopes, the Medical Practitioners Board of Victoria had found Schulberg guilty of serious unprofessional conduct in relation to an abortion he had conducted in 2005.[30] A history of other problematic practices was yet to surface. In early 2010, however, it became public knowledge that the anaesthetist employed by Schulberg had infected several women at the clinic with hepatitis C over a number of years. Marie Stopes continued with the purchase of the business and worked with the Department of Human Services, which was contacting patients who had used the clinic. Yolanda recalled that 'thankfully' the department 'saw [Marie Stopes] as a white knight and not as part of the problem ... and agreed that the services needed to go on while we dealt with this hideous case.' Shortly after taking control, Yolanda also noted, Marie Stopes made a decision to limit the service to 24 weeks in the interests of clinical safety.

Schulberg continued to work at Maroondah until 2013, when he was struck off the medical register for one year for improperly prescribing drugs to patients between 2000 and 2009.[31] His last years had been marred by two clinical emergencies, including the death of a patient after he had performed her late term abortion.[32] Both incidents received media coverage. The Victorian Civil and Administrative Tribunal found his conduct unprofessional in relation to the non-fatal case; the coroner's inquest into the death made no adverse finding against him although the anaesthetist's practice was described as a 'gross departure' from clinical standards.[33] Schulberg was replaced by doctors who flew to Melbourne once a week from interstate.

Maria Deveson Crabbe's go-ahead for the launch of a free phone-counselling service in late 2009 was much less stressful. As in most private clinics, Marie Stopes nurses had provided counselling when needed over and above what was legally required of doctors. The phone service was available to anyone who rang Marie Stopes and requested it (not all of whom would go on to have an abortion), for clinic workers needing to refer patients, and for post-abortion support. The federal Health Minister Tony Abbott had introduced a Medicare item number for pregnancy counselling in 2006, but this was only available for counselling provided separately from abortion-providing organisations, as it was intended to reduce abortion numbers.[34] Simon commented that the counselling service was provided 'at quite a cost to us.'

Deveson Crabbe oversaw the last major purchase of clinics when Marie Stopes bought David Grundmann's suite of clinics on his retirement in 2011. This included the clinics in Townsville and Rockhampton, the Bowen Hills clinic in inner-city Brisbane, the clinic on the Gold Coast, and the one in Newcastle in NSW. The east coast clinic footprint was adjusted at this time, three of the five clinics that had been bought during Marie Stopes' entry into the Sydney market closed as did the Salisbury and Caboolture clinics in Queensland. Clinics that offered medical abortion only opened in

Sydney's CBD, Woolloongabba in suburban Brisbane and two in Melbourne.

Review and Re-orientation

Marie Stopes' period of expansion eventually morphed into a period of internal review. A new CEO in London was a key marker of change. Dana Hovig, who had replaced Tim Black in 2006, bringing developing-world NGO experience in sexual and reproductive health, was replaced in 2013 by Simon Cooke, who brought experience in sales, marketing, fundraising and general management roles in the international corporate sector.[35] These changes filtered through to the Australian operation.

The departure of Mark Schulberg from the Maroondah clinic in 2013 was followed by a volatile period in that clinic. GP Alex, who worked at Maroondah, recalled that new doctors revised clinical protocols and worked to establish a better relationship with the local hospital. This was in the context of absorbing the fallout from the two emergency cases at the clinic, and managing budget concerns and staff turnover—including at management level—until a manager was found who stayed on and was 'fantastic'.

By 2017 Michelle Thompson had replaced Maria Deveson Crabbe as CEO at Marie Stopes. Thompson came with a background in health sector management, in both Australian and international settings.[36] After a period in which the counselling service was under review, there was significant movement in the counselling team in mid-2016. Bunny, a counsellor who has worked at Marie Stopes and in public and private settings, recalled that the counselling coordinator 'had been fighting for it for a number of years.' A new head of counselling appointed in 2017 re-established stability.

The second half of the 2010s saw shifts in Marie Stopes' orientation in relation to its social mission in Australia. Where donations had previously only been sought for international operations, in 2017 Jamal Hakim, then Chief Operating Officer, championed the establishment of The Choice Fund to provide support to individuals in Australia needing abortion care who were experiencing financial difficulty.[37] This fund combines some of Marie Stopes' own money with tax deductible donations solicited from the public. According to several interviewees from NSW and Victoria, including some who worked for Marie Stopes, prior to The Choice Fund responses to individuals or advocates seeking discounted fees from Marie Stopes clinics were generally, though not always, inflexible. The Choice Fund, however, established a systematic approach and was gaining momentum until 2020, when it suffered from the downturn in donations experienced by a lot of charities during the COVID pandemic. In 2019 it provided bursaries in excess of $561,000 to close to 1100 patients, the majority in NSW. It also underwrote $71,000 worth of no interest payment plans.[38] A year later, the organisation commented that 'this level of hardship support is not financially sustainable'.[39] At the beginning of 2022 the fund was empty, and Marie Stopes made a social media callout for assistance for a particular patient—a method common to other organisations that support people who need abortion care.[40] It re-gained momentum with generous donations made in the wake of the widespread response to the overturning of *Roe V Wade* by the US Supreme Court.[41]

Marie Stopes also expanded its involvement in advocacy at this time. It contributed to campaigns for abortion law reform, made pre-budget submissions to government, and wrote media releases and opinion pieces. The November 2018 'white paper' *Hidden Forces: Reproductive Coercion in Contexts of Family and Domestic Violence*, re-released in 2020, was a notable contribution and detailed the organisation's commitments to address reproductive coercion and trauma in their delivery of care.[42] Their 'legislative scans' published in 2020 regarding safe access zones and nurse-led models of abortion care were also designed to guide change.[43] Most were prepared collaboratively with individuals and organisations working in the relevant sectors, including SPHERE, The University of Queensland Pro Bono Centre, Australian Women Against Violence and the Australasian Society for HIV, Viral Hepatitis and Sexual Health Medicine.

This attention to Marie Stopes' social mission in Australia also took internal form. The *Impact Report* for 2019 reported that the organisation conducted a Reflect Reconciliation Action Plan, in the acknowledgement—admirable in its frankness—that 'as an organisation set up in 2001, we did nothing to truly understand and respect Aboriginal and Torres Strait Islander people, lands and cultures when we established the organisation'. The organisation also conducted a survey of discrimination in the organisation which showed that 'racism was a key area of concern'.[44] In August 2022 they issued an apology for the history of reproductive injustices inflicted on First Nations people through systematic racism, acknowledging trauma and committing to preventing 'further re-traumatisation'.[45]

The other development of note in the very late 2010s was the previously mentioned contracts that Marie Stopes signed with Queensland hospitals/regions in late 2018.[46] In early 2018, in an opinion piece in the *Sydney Morning Herald*, CEO Michelle Thompson had argued for a model of public provision for complex cases and public support to enable those in financial difficulties to access services through Marie Stopes, with most patients finding a service from private clinics.[47] By the end of the year the model was coming to fruition in Queensland.

In 2019 the senior leadership at Marie Stopes changed again. Jamal Hakim, Chief Operating Officer since 2013, replaced Michelle Thompson, taking on the new title of Managing Director (MD) of both Marie Stopes Australia and MS Health. Like his predecessors, he was appointed by and reported to the London-based board. His appointment coincided with the arrival in 2019 of Clare O'Neill from the UK, where she had been Global Head of HR Operations at MSI. The Marie Stopes website says Clare came to Australia 'to assist with our Change Management program', staying on as Executive Director of People and Culture.[48] A media release in late 2020 signalled more changes in leadership roles; some appointments were to be short-lived.[49] At the time of writing, the Executive Team comprised Hakim and Medical Director Philip Goldstone, who has held his position since 2010, and three more recent appointments, including O'Neill.

The latter part of the 2010s saw international events shift the global context for Marie Stopes in Australia. The parent body went through significant challenges at this time, which I have found mention of in only the very conservative Australian media.[50] In August 2016 some services at MSI clinics in Britain were temporarily suspended on the instruction of the Care Quality Commission, the independent regulator of health and social care in England.[51] The following year MSI denied media allegations that staff were paid bonuses for encouraging women to have abortions, a regular accusation from anti-abortion groups.[52] In late 2019, The Charity Commission criticised MSI for a lack of transparent process regarding the CEO's pay package.[53] The re-establishment of the 'global gag rule' with the commencement of Donald Trump's presidency of the US in 2017, expanding its prohibitive reach, also had significant consequences for the international operations of all sexual and reproductive health agencies including MSI. This rule prevents USAID assistance to agencies that provide or refer to abortion services, and has come and gone with Republican and Democrat presidents since Reagan in 1984. Marie Stopes in London estimated that its refusal to comply with the gag rule in 2017 cost it $US80 million over the next three years.[54] Then, in 2020, the arrival of COVID-19 posed serious challenges to sexual and reproductive health services around the world, including Marie Stopes in Australia.[55]

COVID-19—Before and After

As Australian governments responded to the pandemic by putting communities into lockdown and restricting people's movement, with far-reaching personal, social and economic effects, Marie Stopes produced and updated situational reports on sexual and reproductive health throughout 2020. It reported the impact of the pandemic on people's abortion needs, including situations of delayed presentation for abortion and associated complexities, patients experiencing sexual and reproductive coercion, clinics needing to care amidst rapidly changing localised movement restrictions and physical distancing requirements, and significant increased demand for medical abortion via telehealth. Like other private providers, Marie Stopes experienced pressures on its capacity to provide services, some of which were specific to abortion, such as discrimination from private medical goods suppliers who did not see them as essential services. Marie Stopes had to

1. Charter private flights for clinical staff in order to keep regional clinics open
2. Navigate reduced availability and high costs of PPE
3. Reduce in-clinic list capacity and cancel surgical abortion care lists
4. Reduce our national gestational limit for surgical abortion to 22 weeks
5. Reduce financial support for clients experiencing financial hardship.

It argued that obstructions to care and other factors amounted to 'structural reproductive coercion'.[56]

At the end of 2019, Marie Stopes was providing abortion care in sixteen clinics around the country and a telehealth service, plus its vasectomy services. The turnover of the clinics and MS Health together that year was close to $42 million dollars.[57] A donation of $1 million was made by the domestic body to Marie Stopes International Australia. The amount donated had varied over the preceding decade, peaking at nearly $3 million in 2014 and dropping to $900 000 in 2017.

In 2020, revenue increased to over $44 million, which included more than $4 million in 'viability guarantee funding' in response to the COVID-19 pandemic from the WA, ACT, Victorian, NSW and Queensland governments. Employees received income from the federal government's JobKeeper wage subsidy scheme. The organisation reported increased expenses in staffing, general costs and finance. The donation to Marie Stopes International Australia dropped to under $80,000. In 2021 revenue was down to $41 million, after reduced support from governments, and the donation to the international body was up a little.

In 2021 COVID-19 exacerbated existing vulnerabilities in clinic viability and led to the closure of five clinics where surgical abortions had been provided, contracting the Marie Stopes clinic footprint to ten nationwide. In 2022 I was told that most surgical services were barely viable from a financial point of view and are heavily subsidised by the rest of the operation.[58] Presumably selling clinics to private buyers was not an option. All remaining clinics except for the one on the Gold Coast are in capital city locations, and only one in each state provides surgical abortion. The Maroondah clinic closed first, and the clinics in Rockhampton, Townsville and Southport in Queensland and Newcastle in NSW followed, all ceasing operation at the end of August.

In January 2023 MSI Australia announced that Managing Director Jamal Hakim was set to leave the organisation. The media release was upbeat about the organisation's role in progress towards universal access to abortion care. Hakim is quoted taking credit for steering MSI Australia from 'a traditional, aggressively competitive organisation to a dynamic, diverse and collaborative one'.[59]

Marie Stopes in Australia in Context

Marie Stopes has made unique and valuable contributions to the provision of abortion in Australia, and to advocacy. It presents itself as a leader in the national sexual and reproductive health sector—with just a small dose of hubris. In its 2020 *Impact Statement* it wrote, 'We have a commitment and responsibility to lead the national conversation on sexual and reproductive health and rights'![60]

However, the 2020s, to the time of writing, have seen periods of internal uncertainty and change at Marie Stopes, signified by periods of significant staff turnover—not necessarily unusual in times of change—exacerbated by COVID-19. The pandemic stressed the organisation's medical workforce issues to breaking point, as it no doubt did to other providers, and this impacted both individual staff members and clinic services. But both the website in 2022 and the *Australian Strategic Plan 2021–2023* also draw attention to the lack of government commitment to sexual and reproductive health. The MD's introduction to the *Strategic Plan* states that change is necessary to deliver Marie Stopes' goal of 'bodily autonomy and reproductive justice':

> Which is why we can no longer subsidise chronic underinvestment in abortion and contraception access. We have supported hundreds of thousands of people access essential healthcare that should be provided by the public system. This has been to the detriment of our viability and mission, and it perpetuates a policy context that harms our clients and communities.[61]

This is a new strand in Marie Stopes' public commentary. In July 2022 Bonney Corbin, MSI Australia's head of policy, told a journalist that 'ideally the organisation [MSI] would "run itself out of a job" by advocating for universal public access to abortion'. She went on 'there'd likely still be a need for private clinics and specialist providers given there are still so many gaps in care for people who are gender-diverse, from linguistically diverse backgrounds, in prisons, with disabilities, and/or are from Indigenous or Torres Strait Islander communities'.[62] At the time of writing, however, it is unclear to me what the bold criticism of the failures of the public healthcare system means for MSI Australia.

Why then, against this history of significant contribution to the provision of abortion services in Australia and visible advocacy, has Marie Stopes sometimes been challenged by individuals in the sexual and reproductive health and abortion-providing sector, and at other times attracted expressions of wry ambivalence? These have been evident both in debate and minor dispute in academic journals over the adequacy of Marie Stopes' model of follow-up care for medical abortion patients and the degree to which medical abortion is provided across Australia, and at sexual and reproductive health conferences.[63] I have observed the latter in relation to the cost of medical abortion pills, the presence of Marie Stopes in the NT, and the way the Australian operation runs to contribute to MSI Asia Pacific. This disquiet was also evident in the interviews I conducted between 2013 and 2017.

Ethics

Some people expressed clear ethical opposition to the basis on which Marie Stopes operates in Australia. Public hospital abortion-providing O&G Phyl did so most clearly, saying:

> I think Marie Stopes' model is not ethically defensible. I understand their argument about you generate the funds in the developed world and you spend it elsewhere but it doesn't sit with me, I don't think it's actually a valid argument if you carry it through because it's the vulnerable in the developed world who pay the cost.

Others, including those who worked for Marie Stopes, had 'in-between' views. Bunny, for example, offered a pragmatic summary:

> At least they are open and transparent that they're a social business—they use this money for working in developing countries. Now that is extremely problematic for women, marginalised women in Australia ... [But] they are not doing anything they're not saying they're doing and they're not using that money for bloody private jets and they are doing some great work.

I did not inquire whether the 'bloody private jets' were a metaphor or belonged to a real-life private abortion provider.

Yolanda also made an offhand comment about the profits made by private providers—'So they're taking it home and buying a Mercedes ... And we're taking it and putting it into starving women's lives'—along with giving a full explanation, justification and defence of the organisation's model:

> When you go to the Philippines and you see the midwives from Marie Stopes, well they spend ... five nights a week away from home and then one day in the office—reloading the supplies. They take 20-kilo bags of family planning and they're out in the heat and they're climbing up mountains and they walk for miles and miles and miles and then they deliver these lifesaving services to women who are living on less than $2.50 a day. And you know that that wouldn't happen without the work we did in Australia.

She attributed the Marie Stopes business model to founder Tim Black, who believed that 'because we were abortion providers in developing countries ... he was like, we have to have our own money.' MSI's global strategy for 2021–30 includes 'having sufficient financial resilience to withstand shocks and funding shortfalls and, wherever possible, to be able to generate income from services provided from those who can afford to pay'.[64] Yolanda acknowledged that Australian staff might and did feel discomfort with the model, but for her the Marie Stopes social contract was a fair deal, if always a difficult balance:

> ... we've invested a huge amount of money in Australian women with RU486 as well so, like with a commitment, but in the long term, yes, some of that's going to go overseas. I also think that it is really hard to think local and act global and all that sort of stuff ... we were pretty tough in a local sense because we were always thinking globally.

Discussion of MSI's significance as a global provider of sexual and reproductive health was rare among those of my interviewees who had not worked for the organisation. Ingrid told me, 'So they're providing abortions in forty-two countries, they're the only people I think providing abortions in Addis Ababa for instance,' and Roger talked about the challenges posed by the global gag rule, but these were the exceptions.

The Choice Fund could be seen as one way of mitigating the critique that Marie Stopes' model of generating surplus to support overseas projects comes at the expense of marginalised and poor women in Australia. The fund was in part initiated as a result of concern within the organisation about this issue.[65] The 'bursaries' offered, however, create a divide, as all concession schemes do, between those who can self-finance and those who must demonstrate their need and become supplicants to the concession-granting body. My interviews were conducted before the fund was established, however, so I cannot report on interviewees' views on the fund's impact.

Market Dominance

A different thread of criticism came from those interviewees for whom Marie Stopes was a direct competitor. Rosalie, a GP operating in the private market, said, 'They're very competitive.' Roger, recalling Marie Stopes' arrival in the Sydney market, reflected on 'what you learn when people want to move into, when somebody bigger than you wants to move in … they nudge you aside.' Yolanda acknowledged that the organisation 'wanted to have as much of the available unmet need market as possible and we really did go hard against other providers that were in our geographic region.'

Some perceived a contradiction between Marie Stopes' rhetoric and its commercial orientation. Rosalie was disgruntled:

> I mean if they want to improve women's access to abortion, go out bush, go to places where there are not clinics existing already. Why centre yourself in major cities where there are already existing clinics if you're trying to improve access for women? You're not. You're trying to take over the market.

Marie Stopes may not have extended services in rural and regional areas until the advent of telehealth, but in 2011 its purchase of David Grundmann's Queensland clinics did maintain existing regional services, and in the ACT in 2004 it 'saved' a clinic that served a rural constituency. Simon articulated Marie Stopes' role in sustaining services in these areas, and other potential areas, very clearly. But yes, they were seeking market power.

Rosalie also voiced a specific issue that in her view gave Marie Stopes an unfair advantage over their competitors: 'They don't have to pay taxes and we do.' As a charity, Marie Stopes does not pay income tax, and this is likely not its only advantage. It was the organisation's access to capital that enabled it to enter the market as aggressively as it did in Sydney, for example. The capacity enabled by its size, and possibly its charity status, may have played a part in its negotiations with public health institutions in WA and later Queensland—for example, Alex told me that Marie Stopes put 'staffing priority [on Perth]' and was able to 'pull people from other places to send them there … because otherwise we'll be in breach of our contract,' which would not be easy for small individual clinics to match. In turn, the contracts Marie Stopes has with public hospitals give it a small degree of economic security. Finally, Marie Stopes has the capacity to promote itself, and to promote sexual and reproductive health in general. Joseph, an O&G who had worked in public and private settings in WA, including for Marie Stopes, observed, 'They have certainly made very public where they are—what they do—they advertise quite a lot in the medical journals'. Simon added women's magazines, conferences, training settings, and research as places where Marie Stopes has a public presence. This visibility is good for challenging abortion stigma—and enhances Marie Stopes' profile.

Several interviewees commented on the high cost of abortion at Marie Stopes clinics. At the time of writing, its prices for medical and surgical services were higher than many others in the private market. While Sheelagh, who worked in the community sector in NSW, thought their prices were high, there were other providers in NSW who charged more.

Some interviewees made overall positive assessments of Marie Stopes as providers of quality care. These were more likely to be those who had worked in the public sector, but also included some private providers. Ingrid, a public hospital GP and abortion provider from SA, summed up Marie Stopes' early years:

> they have specialised in buying up the businesses of failing surgeons who are either getting too old or too cranky or too scary or don't have enough capital to upgrade their equipment. So they buy up the clinic, they completely refurbish it with brand new better equipment, they bring in all their standardised protocols, they train the staff … So they've kind of wiped out a lot of the more shonkier businesses in Australia, so good for them I say.

Looking at the private sector from the outside, Ingrid saw the value in the size of Marie Stopes as an organisation:

> they've got safe systems of work and they've got a big enough organisation that they can provide political and legal and every other kind of support to their workers … there is an administration and then a management out there that are worrying about compliance with the standards and whether the anaesthetic equipment's working this week and you know the fire alarms and all that stuff. … Whereas a private practitioner who owns their own clinic is responsible for everything and some of them are better at that than others.

Likewise, Roger appreciated the cost of these systems, including the ability 'to analyse individual performances for quality assurance.'

Like Ingrid, social worker Evie worked in a public hospital when I spoke with her in 2013, in Melbourne. She recognised that Marie Stopes has 'a right to be a business', saying, no one's paying them to be a welfare organisation. And that's what they'd say and that's understandable … the problem's not Marie Stopes, the problem is that we don't have a public health response. That's our problem.

Bunny also placed her assessment of Marie Stopes in the broader context of government failure to take responsibility for abortion services: 'It's a user pay society we're in, so why are we bagging Marie Stopes? Because they're actually the devil we need—they're providing the service.'

Marie Stopes is aware of how it has been perceived. Simon noted that 'other providers saw us as commercially aggressive when we arrived,' and Yolanda acknowledged that significant community sector organisations had been critical of Marie Stopes, some of which she found frustrating and counterproductive in relation to what she perceived as their shared purpose. She noted that the private clinics 'all disliked us immensely' in the late 2000s and early to mid-2010s. Lack of ease did not in general prevent collaboration, however, and this seems to have increased since I conducted interviews. In 2015, for example, Simon was upbeat, he thought that feelings about the organisation had changed since the early days saying, 'I think people have realised that we're not just that [commercially driven], we are about care and provision of service and providing that in the best possible way.'

An article on the online news site *Crikey* in 2022, however, suggested that complaint about Marie Stopes from private providers was current, although it also included comments from those sympathetic to the organisation's challenges.[66] Emma Boulton, who runs Clinic 66 in Sydney, which has a telehealth arm, relayed reports of long waiting times from clients who had gone to Marie Stopes. 'If you have a monopoly you can get lazy … because the business is going to come to you anyway. There's just not enough competition in Australia,' she said. She noted their dominance in the online environment. The article compared prices of Marie Stopes and other clinics in Melbourne and Sydney which were significantly cheaper.

Boulton attributed their high prices to Marie Stopes 'massive overheads'.

Differences and Debates

A third thread of tension, if not criticism, related to Marie Stopes' clinical practices and work culture in Australia. The organisation's global nature sets it apart from all other providers. Key players over the years have worked in developing countries and, as noted above, some have visited projects overseas. The association with MSI Asia Pacific also brings a global perspective, as does the sense of belonging to the MSI parent body.

Marie Stopes brought its British clinical model to Australia, adjusting it where required to fit local conditions. Simon described the UK model as 'very nurse-driven,' but this did not fit Australian health culture or the Medicare system. Simon went back to Tim Black's philosophy to explain:

> this is a procedure that should be de-medicalised, that could be done without the need for anaesthesia, and that, if the environment is de-medicalised and women's anxiety is reduced by a de-medicalised environment and by what was termed 'vocal local', which means talking to the woman and distracting her from the discomfort, the procedure could be done without the need for it to be a complicated medical procedure with anaesthesia ... They also used manual vacuum aspiration which is a simpler means of emptying the uterus.

In fact, by the time Marie Stopes opened in Australia, low-level sedation had become the norm for surgical abortions and the organisation had left behind some aspects of the de-medicalised model.

Some doctors explicitly disagreed with de-medicalisation as they perceived it, even though it had not been introduced to Australia in its purest form. This included some who worked for Marie Stopes. Aware of but not persuaded by 'the feminist' argument that a de-medicalised environment is best, Simon saw the perspective as originating in part from the illegal and clandestine history of abortion and thought that (surgical) abortions 'should be being provided to day surgery standards.' For him this was a matter of safety.

Others made specific observations about divergent clinical practices although these were also made of other private providers. Having initially been puzzled by the use of manual vacuum aspiration (MVA), Roger eventually came round on this technique, acknowledging its documented safety. MVA is common in Aotearoa New Zealand, and continues to be used at MSI Australia at the time of writing.

The other side of the discussion expressed disappointment at Marie Stopes' disinterest in de-medicalising abortion practice. Viv's background at Bessie Smyth clinic, where local anaesthesia alone had initially been the preferred feminist practice, led her to chide Marie Stopes for its lack of commitment to local anaesthesia: 'That was out the window as soon as MSI took over,' she told me. Simon admitted that the shift away from local anaesthesia was 'a little bit provider-initiated,' as well as being enabled by more refined approaches to sedation. As for their commitment to de-medicalising the environment: he laughed. Echoing Viv, he said, 'Well, it's gone out the window!'

The parameters of the debate rehearsed here have of course shifted significantly with the increasing percentage of medical abortions being performed—a phenomenon that was just emerging when most of my interviews were conducted. At the time of writing the organisation foregrounds its full accreditation against the National Safety and Quality Health Service Standards, which demand detailed protocol documents, and its compliance with other relevant professional guidelines. Roger, who prided himself on his own standards when in private practice, described Marie Stopes' protocols as 'beautiful, hefty documents on best practice and well researched.' Sheelagh pointed out the potential gap between protocols and patient experience, but this was a humorous reference to her own organisation as much as to Marie Stopes. Since 2018 Marie Stopes has worked with appointed Consumer Advisors as well as actively seeking feedback from patients.[67] In 2022 their website reported that 'Our 2020 patient satisfaction rate for all our clinics was 95%'.[68]

Differences in work culture were also noted. Working for Marie Stopes meant working for a large organisation, and this had pros and cons: for some the latter could include corporate protocols and regulations, productivity expectations, and bureaucratic distance from management. Commentary on the patient experience and work culture at Marie Stopes raised issues that could apply to any large clinic. Rosalie, for example, relayed comments from patients about 'just being rushed through,' but as WA GP Laura reflected, 'that's always a risk when you've got twenty-five people waiting for a procedure that day.' Not all patients were represented as describing the Marie Stopes experience in this way. Iona, a doctor who worked sessionally for Marie Stopes in WA, baulked at the encouragement of competitive camaraderie between different clinics around the country when this invoked particular expectations of productivity, as it sat uncomfortably with her preference for prioritising individual care needs. She was concerned about 'the whole idea that you can have [an] agenda that you're going to impose on clients ... just so paternalistic.'

Conclusion

Marie Stopes came to Australia looking for opportunities to provide sexual and reproductive health services, specifically abortion, in order to generate financial surplus for its work in developing countries. Its vasectomy work has been as significant as its abortion work in this respect. It entered a healthcare sector defined by a model of abortion provision which I describe as neoliberal. Not surprisingly, the jurisdictions in which the public hospital system has provided nearly all abortions—SA and the NT, and those where the market is small—Tasmania and the NT—are those where Marie Stopes has not established clinics. Elsewhere, Marie Stopes has become both commercially dominant in the private sector and, arguably, a stand-in for public provision at a time when public provision has been in decline.

Simon's summary of the space that Marie Stopes fills sounds like what a public health system might ideally provide: 'Marie Stopes is an organisation that's here for the long term and that's dedicated to provision of safe, accessible abortion. ... I think we can safely assume that there will always be access to abortion services.' While it may stand in for public provision, however, Marie Stopes is not a public provider. It is (mostly) not paid to offer public services, or to train an abortion-providing workforce, or to facilitate community and collegiality in the abortion sector. While it has in the past and does still provide in-house training for doctors to offer medical abortion, its approach to training for surgical procedures has been mixed, as Yolanda and Alex noted, perhaps mediated through internal tension about potential market competition. Insofar as it takes on training and supports conferences and so on, it acts out of self-interest albeit in fulfilment of its social mission. It is a private operator which has carved out space in a private market. Its healthcare provision and, perhaps more so, MS Health has enabled contribution to its overseas operations, in some years more than others. When it generates a surplus this is not from efficiencies with government funding, as in Britain, but from Medicare rebates and patient fees (for vasectomy as well as early medical abortion) and its pharmaceutical business.

It could be argued that the presence of Marie Stopes has enabled ongoing negligence by the public sector. While this is not its fault, it might be its effect. Some statements from the organisation in recent years have made this point.[69] In a neoliberal system of care it is, as Bunny put it, 'the devil we need.' It has kept a private system of abortion provision afloat when doctors and flagging clinics were unable to continue but it has also obscured the failure of the public sector in abortion provision and covered over the conditions of its own necessity. Its contracts with the WA and Queensland governments might mitigate the worst of user-pays models of care for a limited cohort of patients, but they also maintain the charity model of access, a limited version of universal health care; in the ACT its contract comes close to providing universal access.

As the dominant player in the market, without peer, Marie Stopes has arguably inhibited the development and prosperity of its potential competitors. Its consolidation of its position in Sydney and Melbourne in particular, at a time when abortion rates were starting to decline, was observed by interviewees including Davina and Simon as a disincentive to smaller players who might have newly invested in small clinics providing surgical abortion.

Marie Stopes has demonstrated the limits of the commercial sustainability of surgical services in regional areas and for patients needing abortions over 20 weeks pregnancy, and the contingent nature of the provision of financial discounts for patients—limits born of pressing financial concerns in a pandemic. Given that the regional and Maroondah clinics relied on a FIFO medical workforce that reflected the small number of doctors trained in and willing to provide abortion care, these are limits exacerbated by abortion exceptionalism. In this context, as became evident during COVID-19, as a stand-in for public provision Marie Stopes does not ensure sustainable provision of surgical services into the future.

On the plus side, and it is a big plus, MS Health's achievement in making medical abortion widely available across the country is something that the public sector could never have done and the commercial sector showed no interest in doing. Arguably it is exactly Marie Stopes' hybrid nature, as a commercial operation with significant access to capital and a social mission that provides services, that made it both plausible and possible for them to make this move.

When I interviewed Alex in late 2017, while she was working for Marie Stopes, and asked if she had concerns about the position the organisation occupied in the sector, she replied in the affirmative: 'It's just really vulnerable.' She then asked the obvious question: 'What does this mean for Australian services?' If the organisation falters, as the UK organisation did in 2016, it could not be temporarily covered for by another national provider, as occurred with BPAS in England and Wales. Should MSI Australia decide to permanently withdraw part or all of its surgical abortion services, who would step in? This is a hypothetical. The 'viability guarantee funding' the government provided to Marie Stopes in 2020 suggests that there can be a public safety net for essential services, but how this may play out in a 'post pandemic' future is of course unknown, and is unlikely to address, for example, a decision by MSI Australia to withdraw surgical services.

Marie Stopes has what I conceptualise as a double effect, both enabling and constraining. It operates in the tensions between its commercial frame and its social mission, and between its domestic mission, its management from London and its service to MSI's Asia Pacific operations, even though its contributions have been negligible in some years. These tensions are not unique. A recent report on the corporatisation of medical general practice in Australia—a related but by no means identical context—notes 'potential for tension between a doctor's responsibility towards their patient and their obligations to the company'.[70] For an NGO with MSI Australia's mission this is also a tension for Australian management, between providing quality care and managing the budget and responsibilities to the MSI parent body. In relation to the international NGO setting, the question of accountability to 'the communities in which they work' is a key paradigm of concern in the critical literature. In their discussion of accountability one author writes that given the competitive nature of the development field, agencies need to be encouraged to 'go beyond mere sharing of what has been done' to facilitate both greater accountability and the outcomes desired by the local community.[71] This suggestion can be transferred to the context in which MSI Australia works in Australia.

MSI's mission to 'bring choice to women around the world' is haunted by the colonial history of development work.[72] Is it a colonial presence in Australia? The power dynamic between two wealthy Western countries which are in some ways still metropole and outpost is not colonial in the way that a relationship between a developed and a developing country might be. The reshaping of a local ecology of health care by an organisation coming from overseas, which is far from all bad in this case, does resonate in some respects with colonial processes, but it could also just be the forces of business. The demise of the APFA, which some interviewees attributed to the effect of Marie Stopes' presence on the providers who had kept the organisation going, is salutary in this context. But organisations ebb and flow and new groupings take the place of those which fade. On the plus side, as a domestic service provider Marie Stopes' commitment to reconciliation and dealing with racism is laudable. In 2019, before COVID-19, 10 per cent of patients who accessed The Choice Fund were Aboriginal and Torres Strait Islander people, and 24 per cent were born outside Australia.[73] The effects of any downturn in the state of the fund will, however, fall most heavily on these groups of people.

The work of MSI in developing countries is beyond the scope of this chapter, but I think it is important to keep this invaluable contribution in mind when understanding Marie Stopes in Australia. It is not the work of this chapter to dissect the organisation's relationship to colonialism in that part of their work. MSI Australia's promotion of their contribution to sexual and reproductive healthcare work in our region is low-key. However, Yolanda's description of the labour of Marie Stopes midwives in the Philippines comes close to 'a romantic essentialising of the poor Third World woman'. To claim credit for the effects of the midwives' work because it wouldn't happen 'without the work we did in Australia' downplays the agency of the local women while maintaining the First World woman in the driver's seat, arguably reiterating the 'white woman's burden' to save Third World women.[74] Journalist Gina Rushton implies a similar critique in her account of lunch with 'two white women' from Marie Stopes who gave her a pamphlet explaining that their family planning services in Asia and the Pacific 'were an incredibly cost-effective "climate-change mitigation strategy" by slowing population growth and therefore lowering emissions'. Rushton notes of this logic that it is not the developing world's emissions which need most attention.[75]

MSI Australia's claim to leadership of sexual and reproductive health in Australia, in health care and in public conversation, is bold.

It is also open to contest. It raises questions of accountability, appropriate for an NGO: Who anointed it as a leader? Who reviews its priorities and changes in direction? What is its impact? And to make sense of responses to these questions, what are the unavoidable constraints with which it works? The staff who devise and deliver healthcare services and those who advocate for better law, policy and clinical care, including those who spoke with me in interview, are more than up to the job. MSI Australia the organisation is defined by the conflicting imperatives that mark its presence in Australia. In two decades it has restructured the private provision of abortion. For some, including private providers who experienced this as competition, this makes it hard to live with. In the current neoliberal model of abortion provision its position may be tenuous although should this system be reshaped by greater public commitment to ensuring adequate access, as it publicly hopes, it may enjoy a degree of certainty as is experienced under the NHS in England and Wales. Or, it may decide to entirely reconfigure its relationship to abortion service delivery.

Chapter 5

Early

The single biggest change in the experience of first trimester abortion in Australia over the last thirty years has been the growing availability of early medical abortion using mifepristone and misoprostol. Compared to a surgical procedure, early medical abortion delivers a different physical, personal and social experience for the pregnant person. It can be provided in primary healthcare settings, by GPs. Ideally, its availability offers people in Australia choice between two distinct methods of abortion. It can also reconfigure geographical restrictions to access, with great potential advantage for those outside the metropolitan centres where surgical services are concentrated. In the early 2020s, early medical abortion accounts for between 30 and 40 per cent of all abortions in Australia.[1] It is notable, however, that Australia was one of the last Western countries to make early medical abortion in its ideal pharmaceutical form legally available. Only Canada, which did not authorise mifepristone until 2015, lagged behind, although authorities in that country moved swiftly to create policies enabling its availability directly from pharmacies and via telehealth, unlike Australia.[2]

The use of traditional herbal preparations or chemicals to induce abortion has a long history among women around the world, albeit one that is increasingly forgotten in modern times.[3] Australian historians Finch and Stratton note that 'working class women at the turn of the [twentieth] century had an extraordinary amount of folk knowledge about abortion compared to today's standards'.[4] In a low-budget short feminist documentary made in South Australia in 1994, a young woman tells the story of successfully inducing her abortion by drinking a herbal tea, a method shared by her mother's midwife—a sign of this 'folk knowledge' surviving late into the twentieth century.[5] The French company Roussel Uclaf began pharmaceutical research to develop the use of anti-progesterone agents for their abortifacient properties in earnest in the early 1980s, producing what became known as RU486.[6] The drug became commercially available in France in 1988, in the UK in 1991, in Aotearoa New Zealand in 1998, and across Europe during the 1990s and 2000s. It began to be manufactured and distributed in the USA in 2000 and in China and India in 2002. The standard regimen comprises mifepristone, as RU486 has become known, which ends the pregnancy, and misoprostol (ideally taken 24–48 hours later) which causes it to be expelled from the uterus. The World Health Organization (WHO) has listed the drugs as 'essential medicines' since 2005.[7]

Feminist geographer Sidney Calkin has observed that 'Abortion access today is in the midst of a significant spatial transformation driven by medical and technological changes'.[8] This is the effect of the increased availability of early medical abortion, which is the work of feminist and pro-choice activists, health professionals, policy-makers and regulators. Innovative means of delivering the pills to people in countries where it is not legal, such as Ireland before 2018, Poland, where it is still illegal, and many South American countries, have enabled thousands who would otherwise use ineffective or unsafe methods, travel outside their country or continue an unwanted pregnancy, to access an abortion, mostly safely.[9] The benefit of medical abortion for making abortion more accessible in developing countries, both where abortion is legal and where it is not, has been emphasised since its earliest availability.

Many countries where abortion is legal see a steady increase in the proportion of medical abortion among all abortions once abortion pills are approved and made available.[10] One researcher has suggested that in European countries, the proportion of all abortions that are provided medically correlates positively with women's economic and political participation. They argue that a country's level of gender equality may shape the nature of the abortion care it provides, including which methods are made available and which are chosen.[11] Both the legal and illegal cases illustrate the claims made by feminist commentators that laud the capacity of early medical abortion to deliver patient control, autonomy and privacy.[12] Calkin concludes her article, however, with a note about responses to the potential of abortion pills in both legal and illegal settings: states either 'attempt to eradicate it from a territory entirely or to re-position it under state sanctioned medical supervision'.[13]

This chapter draws primarily from published accounts, media and activist material. None of the oral history interviews I conducted for the book took place after 2017—which was still in the early days of early medical abortion in Australia—so they do not function as an up-to-date source of comment and do not feature prominently in this chapter.

Prequel

The long delay in the formal arrival of early medical abortion to Australia belies the fact that Australian medical researchers were in contact with leading French scientists and involved in the development and trial of mifepristone from its earliest years. Opposition to their work was also evident from the early years. Dr David Healy, Professor of Obstetrics and Gynaecology at Monash University from 1990, led attempts to introduce mifepristone to Australia in the 1980s and 1990s.[14] In the 1980s he worked with Dr Étienne-Émile Baulieu, one of those who first developed the drug and who visited Australia and Aotearoa New Zealand in 1990, on the potential of RU486 for contraceptive purposes.[15] His article about new developments in the use of anti-progesterone drugs published in 1985 argued that they could 'lead to a revision of our concepts of abortion'.[16] In 1994, he ran WHO-sponsored trials of mifepristone for contraception and abortion in Melbourne and Sydney as part of a global program of trials. After questions were raised about the trials' administrative and ethical approval process, however, they were temporarily halted by the then federal Minister for Health, before being reinstated with Healy claiming that all proper processes had been followed.[17] Women involved in the trial found early medical abortion satisfactory, reporting that it provided them with 'a more active role in the process, thus allowing them to achieve a certain degree of autonomy'.[18] A call for further research on early medical abortion was included in the NHMRC report into abortion in Australia, which was being prepared at the same time as the trials were being conducted.[19]

There was an early reticence around early medical abortion from some feminists. Australians Renate Klein and Lynette Dumble and American Janice G Raymond, who were associated with FINRRAGE (Feminist International Network of Resistance to Reproductive and Genetic Engineering), published *RU486 Misconceptions, Myths and Morals* in 1991.[20] The book sought to counter the 'initial euphoria' that greeted the announcement of RU486, arguing that there was a need for a perspective not based in the vested interests of 'medical researchers, drug companies, and population control organizations'. The authors argued that the drug was untested and dangerous to women, and could, if allowed to become the dominant form of abortion, threaten the provision of surgical abortions. Klein and Dumble were among those who challenged David Healy's drug trials in 1994.[21] In contrast, longstanding abortion activist and clinic owner Jo Wainer was an early feminist enthusiast of early medical abortion.[22] She saw great value in its non-invasive nature and the heightened level of women's engagement with the process. She also foresaw the spread of abortion provision beyond clinics into the community, and predicted that this would normalise abortion, while also expressing caution about potential deficits in support for women undergoing the process, the potential ineptitude of GPs, the loss of specialist surgical skill and the withdrawal of state support for surgical abortion. On balance, however, she celebrated the advances that early medical abortion would bring in safe and dignified care for women.

The Harradine Amendment

In any case, the promise of this early period of Australian involvement in the development of early medical abortion came to an abrupt halt with the 1996 election of the Howard LNP government, although trials of mifepristone related to contraception continued in WA. The government needed the support of conservative Christian Senator Brian Harradine from Tasmania, and in return for his vote on key pieces of government legislation in its first year, it agreed to support a proposed amendment to legislation that would revise the operation of the TGA. Harradine was openly opposed to abortion, ignored research that showed the safety of mifepristone, and quoted at length from Klein, Raymond and Dumble's book. The amendment he sought required that any application to import abortifacient drugs must have the approval of the Minister for Health over and above approval from the TGA. Although the 'Harradine amendment' was opposed by the Australian Democrats (henceforth the Democrats) and some members of the Greens, and questions were raised by some ALP women, it was supported by the parliament and passed into law.[23] Not surprisingly, there were no applications to import mifepristone during the eleven-year life of the Howard government, in which two conservative men held the health portfolio for all but two years.

The period in the wake of the Harradine amendment was quiet in relation to mifepristone, but not without murmurs of the need for change. There were two papers on early medical abortion, in Austria and the USA respectively, presented at the APFA conference in 1999, and mention of the Australian situation at the 2001 conference. Articles in mainstream and left-wing media mentioned RU486 in the context of discussion about other abortion matters. In September 2000 an article in *The Age* reported on the US Food and Drug Administration's decision to approve the abortion pill and quoted a range of local spokespeople who supported making it available in Australia, including Democrat Senator Meg Lees, the AMA vice president, and Family Planning Victoria President Professor Gab Kovacs. Leading anti-abortion activist Margaret Tighe was also quoted describing RU486 as a 'human pesticide'.[24] Later that year an article in *The Bulletin* about early medical abortion reported the APFA's plans to lobby for RU486 and quoted the president Christine Healy's comment on the savings that early medical abortion would bring to Medicare, but concluded that few commentators 'expect any change in the current political climate'.[25] Early in 2001, an article in *Green Left* about the closure of the WHF clinic in Tasmania referred to the call by the coordinator of the Hobart Women's Health Centre to make RU486 available to Australian women.[26] The story coincided with the announcement that a bill to undo the Harradine amendment, sponsored by the Democrats, would be debated in the federal parliament. The Democrats' press release included statements of support from the AMA, the Doctors Reform Society, WEL and pro-choice activist Leslie Cannold.[27] The bill was defeated. Finally, in 2001, the Women's Health Committee of RANZCOG developed the college's first statement on misoprostol, including its use for abortion and affirming its suitability.[28]

Alongside these public calls for change, some doctors were responding directly to requests from patients. There is public evidence as well as hearsay to indicate that some doctors were prescribing methotrexate with misoprostol to induce abortion in the late 1990s and early 2000s. Methotrexate is an inferior but adequate alternative to mifepristone which was available in Australia for non-reproductive purposes, and could legitimately be used 'off label' to induce abortion. The 2000 article in *The Bulletin* quoted Sydney GP Geoff Brodie at length about his preparation to offer methotrexate abortions in response to 'consumer demand'. He had used the method once and was quoted saying that efforts to prevent the import of RU486 would not 'stem the tide of medical abortion'. The article noted concern from AMA Vice President Trevor Mudge that women might access the pills on the internet, indicating this possibility if not actuality at this time.[29] Nicola, who worked in the Tasmanian government at the time, told me that an obstetrician who was offering methotrexate abortions in Hobart was thought to be a significant factor in the closure of the WHF clinic there in 2001, as his practice ate into the clinic's market.

In addition to using methotrexate, some doctors were pursuing individual routes to use mifepristone. As mentioned in Chapter 3, in the early 2000s Brisbane gynaecologist Adrienne Freeman was pursuing a one-woman campaign to make medical abortion available. It was reported in a news item in 2004 that having been refused support from RANZCOG, she was seeking sponsorship from the British Royal College of Obstetricians and Gynaecologists for her plan to import RU486. She was not successful. However, while not explicitly supporting Freeman's approach, the news article concluded with a comment from Dr Angela Taft from the Public Health Association of Australia: 'The pill is an option Australian women should have'.[30]

These individual and organisational efforts came to a head in October 2005 when obstetrician Caroline de Costa published a viewpoint article in the *MJA* aptly titled 'Medical Abortion for Australian Women: It's Time'.[31] The article began with the story of a woman whose suffering in the face of lack of abortion could have been avoided had early medical abortion been available to her, detailed the properties of mifepristone and its appropriate use, confronted the forces preventing its availability in Australia, mentioned the rapid introduction of Viagra into the Australian market by way of comparison, and concluded it was time to 'face facts' and allow women to choose mifepristone. The article came when anti-abortion forces in the Australian government were on the rise. The 2004 federal election had delivered the conservative Howard government a majority in both houses of parliament and government members were vocal about their opposition to abortion.[32] De Costa attributes her decision to take action to accounts of the first five years of mifepristone in the USA which she heard in May 2005 at the annual clinical meeting of the American College of

Obstetricians and Gynaecologists in San Francisco. She returned to Australia 'determined to try to make mifepristone available'.[33] Her viewpoint article drew immediate response from parliamentarians, medical groups and organisations focused on reproductive rights, and hundreds of stories from women and colleagues about the practice of misoprostol and methotrexate-misoprostol combination abortions—enough for de Costa to conclude that 'medical abortion is currently extensively practised in Australia'.[34] After de Costa's article in October, a period of debate and media coverage ensued and a private members' bill to remove the Harradine amendment was introduced into the Senate. A Senate committee, convened in December and operating over the summer break, received '2496 submissions and 2292 additional pieces of information' and held three public hearings. Most contributors opposed the bill, but most major medical bodies and many women's health and reproductive rights groups made submissions in support.[35] The private members' bill was sponsored by a cross-party group of four female Senators, one of whom, Democrat Lyn Allison, spoke briefly to the parliament of her own abortion. It passed the parliament in February 2006. Sociologist and long-time abortion scholar and activist Rebecca Albury saw the resounding defeat of the arguments put forward by its opponents as a sign of 'the ultimate failure of the politics of shame' that had historically been deployed in relation to abortion.[36]

Interregnum

The demise of the Harradine amendment did not immediately lead to any change in the availability of early medical abortion but it did encourage doctors to become Authorised Prescribers of mifepristone.[37] This was the TGA scheme that Brisbane maverick Adrienne Freeman had been pursuing, which gave approval to named individuals to import a drug for specified uses. De Costa's joint application for Authorised Prescriber status, made with Cairns colleague gynaecologist Mike Carrette, was lodged while the Senate campaign was beginning and in April 2006 de Costa and Carrette became the first

Authorised Prescribers of mifepristone in Australia. They imported the drug from Istar, an Aotearoa New Zealand company established by a group of doctors to bring mifepristone into that country in the absence of any pharmaceutical company moving to do so. De Costa and Carrette's application, which required 'mountains of paperwork and much political negotiation', was limited to specifically defined extreme cases of need. They performed only ten abortions in their first ten months as Authorised Prescribers, for patients with severe medical conditions who had been pregnant for less than 63 days.[38] The RWH in Melbourne followed suit.[39]

Medical abortions with methotrexate continued to be offered in this period, for example at the Cairns Sexual Health Clinic, where doctors publicly documented their practice, and by Marie Stopes.[40] In the wake of de Costa and Carrette's move, however, more existing providers began to apply to become Authorised Providers, and, once authorised, to offer early medical abortion with mifepristone for ordinary first trimester abortions, also importing the drug from Aotearoa New Zealand.[41] Doctors at the PAC and other public hospitals in Adelaide led the way from 2009, and were followed by doctors at Marie Stopes from 2009. Ingrid, one of the SA GPs at the forefront of the move, recalled that Istar used the money it made from selling mifepristone to run 'two fabulous conferences as a sort of a return treat ... All the Australian doctors went across to New Zealand.' The requirement for approval from a hospital ethics committee or similar body made the application process long, arduous and slow, and meant some applications met with significant obstruction (see Chapter 3). Not surprisingly, four years after de Costa and Carrette became the first, there were only 187 Authorised Prescribers in the country, and these were mainly existing providers working in SA, Cairns and the east coast capital cities.[42]

Enter MS Health

In 2009, in the absence of any interest from pharmaceutical companies in importing mifepristone and at around the same time as their doctors were becoming Authorised Prescribers, Marie Stopes began negotiating with the TGA, seeking to become importers of the abortion pills (see Chapter 4).[43] The initial application to register mifepristone on the Australian Register of Therapeutic Goods, and misoprostol for use with mifepristone, eventually to be marketed as MS-2 Step, was deliberately modest, for use only up to 49 days (7 weeks) of pregnancy, and was approved late in August 2012. Mifepristone was also approved for termination 'for medical reasons beyond the first trimester'.[44]

The conditions imposed in the final approval were stringent: GP Simon, who worked at Marie Stopes during this period, noted that at the time the TGA was known internationally as 'a very tough and very difficult regulatory body', when compared to, for example, Aotearoa New Zealand. As well as the upper limit of 49 days of pregnancy, the TGA specified that only registered medical practitioners could prescribe the pills. Marie Stopes' application was approved on the condition that the pills would only be made available under the conditions of its Risk Management Plan (RMP), which ensured 'pharmacovigilance and risk minimisation activities'. This included 'practitioner education on the appropriate selection of women, the counselling of women, the need for patient consent, information on the risks and adverse events, and the need to follow up women who have been prescribed the medicine', and 24-hour after-care telephone service.[45] The training for medical practitioners was separate from the range of detailed relevant clinical guidelines already produced by RANZCOG, which are mentioned in the TGA's registration document. Medical practitioners, except for Fellows and diplomates of RANZCOG, had to undertake an online training session that was several hours long to become registered as prescribers. Pharmacists had to be nominated by a registered medical practitioner to dispense the pills, and also had to register. Each prescription would require an authority script from the PBS, to be obtained over the phone. The RMP included Marie Stopes' undertaking to conduct 'a post-market study that looks specifically at serious adverse events'. These conditions remain in place at the time of writing, in an illustration of Calkin's observation that where abortion is legal, governments often respond to the introduction of medical abortion by keeping it under tight control.[46]

Ingrid thought that this high level of regulatory requirement was 'because the TGA was so paranoid about abortion and anxious about the risks of abortion'. She described the indignant reaction of a senior medical colleague (not an O&G) at one of the hospitals where she worked:

> 'I'm a specialist, I can prescribe Vincristine [a powerful cancer drug] if I want. All I have to do is write out a prescription, how come I have to go to a website and register?' You know this is a layer of regulation over and above what they would do for any other drug.

In 2013 Marie Stopes launched its not-for-profit company MS Health to import and distribute the drugs. Once it was licensed by the TGA, the cost of the pills to the patient increased sixfold, from the $50 Istar had charged Authorised Prescribers to $300. This was understood to be an effect of both the large outlay that MS Health had made and the future costs of the training, support and surveillance to which its RMP was committed. However, after MS Health made an application to the Pharmaceutical Benefits Advisory Committee, in August 2013 mifepristone and misoprostol were listed on the PBS, making the pills available to those with concession cards for about $6 and to all others for about $36. Even after this dramatic drop in the cost of the pills, though, the cost of a medical abortion continued to rival—and in some cases exceed—that of a surgical abortion. Journalist Samantha Maiden wrote in December 2013 that 'four months after RU486 was listed on the PBS by former Prime Minister Julia Gillard, most women are still paying nearly $500'.[47] Maiden quotes Children by Choice's Cait Calcutt saying, '"The cost is a shock to women. It's also a shock to other health professionals as well who may be calling on behalf of their clients. They thought it would be cheaper"'. Marie Stopes explained this fee with reference to the cost of all the medical services involved, consultations and ultrasounds, plus cover for the small proportion of early medical abortion that fail (quoted as up to 10 per cent in 2013) and require a surgical abortion.

There were a number of institutional obstructions to the smooth rollout of early medical abortion in the early years. The initial limit on TGA approval only for pregnancies up to 49 days was understood to be a discouraging factor given that it left very little time for a person to identify their pregnancy, make a decision, seek an appointment, have an ultrasound where required, and be seen by a doctor. In 2015, the TGA approved the pills for use up to 69 days (9 weeks), alleviating this constraint.[48] The two drugs were then combined as a composite pack, marketed from May 2015 as MS-2 Step.[49] Medical insurers who did not initially distinguish between medical and surgical abortion also dampened any early interest on the part of doctors. Doctors who were not already providing surgical abortions and who wished to offer medical abortion faced a prohibitive $5000 annual increase in their insurance premium.[50] At the end of 2014, however, after lobbying by the relevant medical colleges, Avant—the major medical insurer of GPs in Australia—remedied this financial disincentive.[51] In addition, the requirement for the pills to be dispensed by pharmacists who, like doctors, had to register, posed challenges. Rural GPs wishing to prescribe often found difficulty locating a willing pharmacy. Even in Sydney, only half of the community pharmacists surveyed in a research study in 2014 were in support of abortion. Those not already dispensing reported a lack of knowledge and skills necessary to do what they (sometimes erroneously) thought would be required, and also described workplace dissension about offering abortion pills.[52] Finally, the law in SA, the NT and the ACT required that abortions must be provided in a hospital, which prevented the take-up of medical abortion provision by GP practices or community clinics. While public hospitals in SA expanded their services to offer medical abortion, those in the NT and ACT did not (changes in legislation in the NT in 2017, the ACT in 2018, and in SA in 2022, have since removed this obstruction). Presentations at conferences in 2014 and 2015, as well as interviews I conducted, suggest that the early uptake of early medical abortion by GPs in other jurisdictions was disappointingly slow.[53] GPs were reticent for a range of reasons, which many assumed were at least partly related to the stigma attaching to abortion providers of all types.

The arrival of telehealth abortion in Australia stood out for its potential to meet the needs of those outside metropolitan centres. The most significant development in the early years was the launch of the Tabbot Foundation in September 2015. Tabbot was established by an existing private provider, O&G Paul Hyland. It set out to offer 'an Australia-wide telephone consultation home medical termination of pregnancy service', although it was unable to serve those in SA and the territories, where abortion had to be performed in a hospital.[54] For patients with a Medicare card the cost was $250. After one week, it was reported that the foundation had been 'so overwhelmed by prospective patients it cannot meet the demand'.[55] Research into the first 18 months of Tabbot's operation indicated that the foundation had quickly grown to provide close to 1 per cent of all abortions in Australia. The study reported a high level of satisfaction among patients—a cohort which, as anticipated, was disproportionately resident outside major cities. Tabbot was 'a turning point for abortion care in Australia'.[56]

The Tabbot Foundation closed in early 2019, not for lack of demand but because of the strain on Hyland, for whom 'it was an expensive business to run and he did so at great personal cost — "I sold my house".'[57] Marie Stopes' national telehealth service had been established in 2016 and was growing. Some established NSW-based providers, including Emma Boulton's Clinic 66 and Sue Brumby's Blue Water Medical, also opened telehealth services in the wake of Tabbot's closure.[58]

The availability of early medical abortion has led to a proliferation of clinics and GP practices offering the service, some via telehealth. How many is unclear, because only some make their service publicly known, but at the time of writing, available lists of abortion providers indicate that there are over one hundred community clinics and GP practices in Queensland (nearly all along the coast), around one hundred and eighty (a good smattering offer languages other than English) in Victoria, and nineteen in Tasmania, most in Hobart or Launceston. Any GPs in SA who may be offering early medical abortion since this became possible after July 2022 are not yet advertised on the government website.[59] The number of surgical services in each of these jurisdictions is much lower than the number offering medical abortion. There are no centrally compiled lists of abortion providers in the other jurisdictions, including in NSW, the country's most populous state, so it is hard to even estimate overall numbers of prescribers. MS Health's count of registered prescribers at the end of 2022 stated 3885 nationwide—this from a possible pool of approximately 32,000 GPs and around 2000 O&Gs, or in other words roughly 12 per cent of the combined possible workforce. NSW has fewer prescribers than Victoria, despite having 20 per cent more people.[60] And not all of those who are registered will be active prescribers.

Some community-based clinics, including Aboriginal Community Controlled Health Organisations and government sexual health clinics, offer the service entirely bulk-billed: that is, at no cost to the patient. For those GPs and private clinics that provide information, prices for early medical abortion range from the costs of medication (under $10 for patients with a Health Care Card) at a GP or community clinic that bulk-bills, to from $620 at MSI Australia. Prices for telehealth also vary, widely. Clinic 66's Abortion Online offers the service for $255. MSI Australia's website states that the cost is from $325.[61] All these costs are for patients with a Medicare card. Those without pay more than twice as much. Patients with a Health Care Card receive some discount. These costs do not include the diagnostic ultrasound required before the procedure, although this is also often accessed at no cost to the patient.

It is hard to know how many abortions in Australia have been provided since abortion pills became available in Australia. A study of patients who had had abortions in the six months November 2014 to April 2015 at Marie Stopes clinics across all mainland jurisdiction except the NT and SA showed that one quarter had had early medical abortion.[62] The latest report from SA at the time of writing, for the year 2022, reported that nearly 60 per cent of all abortions in that state were early medical abortion, compared to 23.7 per cent in 2014.[63] In WA, the only other state which reports abortion numbers, the uptake was also increasing, but from a lower base, moving from 15.8 per cent in 2014 to 33 per cent in 2018 (latest report).[64] (As an early point of reference, 2014 is after abortion pills became available on the PBS but before the gestational limit was extended from 49 to 63 days.) In the NT, in the first year after law reform, which enabled medical abortion to be provided outside hospitals and the government funded Family Planning Welfare Association NT (FPWNT) to deliver medical abortion at no cost to the patient, over 72 per cent of all abortions were medical.[65] The lack of accurate figures for each jurisdiction makes it hard to identify a national figure. However, two things seem clear—there is an upward trend in the proportion of early medical abortion among all abortions, and there are differences between jurisdictions in these early years.

The COVID-19 pandemic significantly increased demand for early medical abortion, especially by telehealth. By October 2020 Marie Stopes was reporting significant uptake in demand in the first half of the year—increases of '163% in metropolitan areas, 42% in regional areas and 189% in remote areas, when compared to the same times last year'.[66] Many of the GPs and community clinics which now offer telehealth abortion may have begun to do so during the early period of COVID-19, when demand increased and the federal government provided a Medicare rebate for telehealth for the first time.

Given the highly political nature of the story of the introduction of early medical abortion in Australia, it is perhaps not surprising that both Marie Stopes and many abortion providers in the public system, who were at the forefront of its rollout, have published research in leading medical journals both about their earliest endeavours and their work since then, usually in collaboration with academic colleagues. These include doctors Caroline de Costa and her colleagues in Cairns, Ea Mulligan in Adelaide, and Marie Stopes' Philip Goldstone and colleagues.[67] Tabbot's Paul Hyland and Marie Stopes' deputy medical director Catriona Melville have also published research on patients accessing their telehealth abortion services.[68] Healthcare workers from the Gateway clinics in rural Victoria have published on their pioneering work, documenting the viability of nurse-led models in rural and regional areas.[69] This research has served to notify the medical community of the introduction of early medical abortion, comment on clinical approaches and document medical abortion's safety, efficacy and high level of patient satisfaction. Some abortion providers also continue a more direct advocacy, publishing calls for legal change and the relaxation of regulations in medical journals. Among them is Caroline de Costa, who has been tireless in this regard, keeping the politics of abortion in front of Australian medical readers.[70] The authors of these research papers demonstrate the activist mentality of many abortion providers. Their academic collaborators also work independently on understanding and promoting medical abortion, and the conclusion of one such article, that we need to 'expand the pool of both primary care and telemedicine providers', is echoed across this emerging body of work.[71] Arguably most significant for both its institutional resources and its commitment to using research to improve access to abortion, is SPHERE, the NHMRC Centre of Excellence which has a core focus on improving 'the quality of care, availability, and accessibility of medical terminations for women'.[72] It has conducted The Orient Study to investigate nurse-led delivery of medical abortion care (and LARCs), and led The Australian Contraception and Abortion Primary Care Practitioner Support Network.[73] Taken together as a body of research this work offers a history of the leadership and significant work of doctors and medical academics in promoting medical abortion in Australia.

There is still a long way to go, especially in rural areas where the provision of medical abortion could make a big difference. Not all GPs are sympathetic, and even sympathetic rural GPs are ill-informed, and few provide the service. A study of Tasmanian GPs showed that about half the participants were interested in providing medical abortion, but uncertainty around information and training, support and after-hours care were major barriers to doing so. The GPs called for greater leadership to pave the way for medical abortion.[74] Other obstructions to the wider provision of medical abortion services were also identified: the lack of a Medicare incentive to offer medical abortion, stigma, and the burden of training and administrative processes. Medicare rebates for the cost of consultation and support for the cost of tests are therefore needed. Finally, many rural women are unsupported and socially isolated while undergoing medical abortion. The capacity of telehealth to solve problems of access for those most in need—'certain rural population cohorts, especially minority, Indigenous, marginalised or socially vulnerable women'—is limited. This is especially the case when people needing abortions lack 'the personal skills and favourable circumstances to access telemedicine'.[75]

The Future of Early Medical Abortion in Australia

What is the future of early medical abortion in Australia? The sexual and reproductive health community has a clear agenda for improving access to it. I have noted above the work of SPHERE; before it was a coalition of the RWH, the Centre for Rural Sexual Health at the University of Melbourne and the FCC which promoted early medical abortion to the rural primary healthcare workforce in Victoria and supported providers. Children by Choice and state-based family planning organisations also offer training and support for doctors.[76] Several organisations have identified the legislative and regulatory changes that are needed to extend the availability of early medical abortion. The introduction of a new Medicare item number specifically for medical abortion is widely supported, as this will more adequately recognise the length of consultations involved in primary health provision.[77] MS Health lodged applications with the TGA in December 2022 to reduce the requirements that regulate early medical abortion. They sought to scrap 'registration for GPs to prescribe and for pharmacists to dispense the drugs', allow other healthcare professionals to prescribe early medical abortion, and drop the need to seek authority by telephone for every script. Medical experts were reported to be urging caution, while SPHERE described the proposed changes as 'baby steps' towards deregulation.[78] Seeking a TGA extension of the gestational limit from 63 to 70 days, which would bring Australia in line with countries like England, Wales and the USA remains an outstanding priority.[79]

One answer to the question of the future is: *nurses and midwives*. As well as removing the TGA's stipulation that only doctors can prescribe early medical abortion, this requires change to state and territory abortion laws that require doctors to perform abortions, enabling nurses to perform ultrasounds and prescribe the relevant pharmaceuticals, and reviewing the MBS to support nurse-led care.[80] These changes are necessary for the full implementation of models of the nurse- and/or midwife-led medical abortion model proposed in research and already in place in countries around the world, including the US, Canada, and many developing countries.[81] There may also be a role for Aboriginal and Torres Strait Islander Health Workers, who are mentioned in the NT, Queensland and NSW legislation, although they are an already stretched workforce.[82]

Beyond the move from doctors to nurses as the primary providers of early medical abortion, the practice of 'self-managed abortion' is being discussed vigorously in international forums. This can be defined as 'the self-sourcing of abortion medicines (mifepristone and misoprostol, or misoprostol alone) followed by self-use of the medicines including self-management of the abortion process outside of a clinical context'.[83] The term can include sourcing pills through mainstream medical sources, as well as beyond. The discussion has been prompted primarily by contexts where abortion is illegal and women use abortion pills outside of the mainstream health system. It has also been prompted by the potential of telehealth provision (legal or illegal), in which the pregnant person does not necessarily have to leave home to access abortion (although in Australia they will commonly do so in order to have an ultrasound to confirm pregnancy), the need to create safe abortion options during the pandemic, and the feminist and grassroots push to challenge the need for any kind of professional or state-mandated control over abortion. In a report on a 2018 international conference that considered the new landscape that has been enabled by early medical abortion, international abortion activist Marge Berer noted that self-managed abortion might be harm reduction when other options are unavailable, *or* self-determination and a preferred option when there are a range of services.[84]

Two cases of 'self-managed abortion' outside the medical system have come to public knowledge in Australia as a result of attention from law enforcement authorities. In 2009 in the Cairns case a family member brought the pills from Ukraine; in 2015 a Sydney a woman accessed pills from the internet. In both cases the woman, and in Cairns her male partner, faced criminal charges (see Chapter 6). There are also anecdotal accounts of women bringing pills from their countries of origin when travelling or emigrating to Australia. In 2013 Ingrid told me a story of a woman who presented to the Emergency Department at one of Adelaide's public hospitals:

> She'd had four early medical abortions with drugs that she got over the counter in India. The first two she'd had in India, then she moved here and she brought two doses with her, as her own supply of drugs ... Anyway, so then she fell pregnant in Australia, she took a dose, she had a completely uneventful medical abortion and then later she fell pregnant again, and used the last of the tablets she'd brought with her and she had a problem. It was an incomplete abortion, she had some retained products of conception. So she went to her local GP who didn't know what to do, of course, because you know this is all new to them. So her GP referred her into [the public hospital].

Ingrid was well aware that at the time, this woman could have been be reported to the police for committing an offence. Decriminalising legislation in all jurisdictions has since removed the possibility of the pregnant person being charged with abortion offences. The point here, however, is that self-managed abortion has been practised in recent years in Australia, in some instances to the satisfaction of the pregnant woman.

Berer noted of the 2018 conference that the heart of the discussion was the degree to which women can self-manage their abortions, and how much medical control should be surrendered.[85] Four years later, the debate has moved on. Research shows that with good information, support during the process and options for health care should the abortion not go to plan, self-managed abortion is safe and satisfactory. The WHO endorses this approach and in 2022 released guidelines for self-managed abortion, including how health services can support the practice.[86] Feminist groups that proactively organise around self-managed abortion, particularly in Africa and South and Central America,

> share a political belief that every person who comes to them has the capacity and right to a safe and dignified abortion informed by the values and needs most important to them ... [they signal] a wrangling of power away from medical and state-based authority that has suppressed ways of thinking about abortion.[87]

Discussion of self-managed abortion, including potentially illegal delivery of pills by international telemedicine abortion providers, is already prominent in the USA after the overturning of *Roe v Wade*.[88]

Medical Abortion – Is That All There is?

There are cautions to note in response to the almost single-minded focus on medical abortion—whether prescribed by GPs or obtained via telehealth—as the solution to the problems of poor access for people in Australia who need abortion care (I am not aware of any Australian groups actively promoting self-managed abortion outside of the health system). In 2017, in an article in the international journal *Contraception*, an international panel of providers, advocates and researchers considered the question, 'What if medical abortion becomes the main or only method of first-trimester abortion?'[89] Australia was represented by private provider and telehealth instigator Paul Hyland, who saw early medical abortion as 'the way of the future'. 'Given the choice, that's what women want', he wrote. Telehealth abortion was 'the ultimate method'. He noted 'the inevitable redundancy of surgical facilities—along with reallocation of health funding, job and skill losses, and a renewed emphasis on education and early intervention'. Hyland was the most uncritically enthusiastic among the article's contributors. In Norway, where early medical abortion was dominant, the commentator speculated about the impact of the loss of practical skills in surgical abortion. In Aotearoa New Zealand early medical abortion was about 10 per cent and the commentator concluded that for the time being 'there is no public demand for medical abortion'. She called for law reform and greater nurse involvement to make medical abortion more available. The doctor from Spain, where 75 per cent of abortions were surgical, located the question of early medical abortion squarely in the bigger issue of the need for public provision of abortion care. In this context he concluded that 'we must focus not only on the provision of medical abortion, whose expansion benefits the pharmaceutical industry above all', and urged training in all methods and choice for women. Against a history of early medical abortion in South America, where pills were first distributed illegally through underground networks, the writer from Colombia celebrated the coming lawful introduction of mifepristone in her country and concluded, 'I believe that no one method for abortion should be the only method'. The joint commentary by the authors from Brazil and Mexico located early medical abortion in the context of restrictive laws, high rates of stigma, and minimal public provision, where it had already produced a decline in abortion complications and deaths. They speculated that doctors might be more likely to provide the pills, as it enabled distance from illegality and stigma, and also noted that where and when abortion becomes legal, doctors who may not have skill in surgical procedure are well prepared to immediately start prescribing abortion pills. They imagined a future where women would be accessing medication 'without either the knowledge or intervention of anybody else'.

My extended account of this article points to the importance of historical and political context when understanding medical abortion. The technology is not neutral; it takes on different meanings depending on national and local contexts and the positions of those who speak of it.[90] Hyland's unfettered enthusiasm for the method *qua method* versus the Spanish commentator's insistence on centring public provision before thinking about method exemplifies this. On the one hand Australian and international research fairly unanimously finds that medical abortion is safe and effective, judged satisfactory by patients, and valued for its enabling of confidentiality, privacy and greater bodily autonomy. Some people value the lesser level of medicalisation and its 'natural' feel.[91] Control over when and where the abortion will take place is valued and evaluation of telemedicine is very positive.[92] Sweden, Norway, Finland and Scotland have the highest rates of early medical abortion—around or over 90 per cent of all abortions in 2019 (in 2017 for Finland). The Nordic countries allow early medical abortion to 12 weeks, Scotland only to 9 weeks. But on the other hand, if we understand that some benefits are contextual, and notwithstanding the proposed equation between gender equality and high rates of early medical abortion in any given country, these rates raise the issue of choice and access to surgical abortion. Many studies of choice of abortion method 'highlight the likely heavy influence of providers' preferences in the users' decision making process'.[93]

Apart from those who oppose abortion outright there is little diversity in the positions taken in research or political opinion in Australia about early medical abortion, although there is recognition of its limits. On the one hand, it is not yet available to all who might benefit, and on the other, it is not the solution for everyone. Telehealth abortion is celebrated, but it may not be suitable for those in most need, who may not have conditions in their homes that make self-managed abortion safe. The needs of those who lack 'privacy, safety from interference and violence from partner and/or family, not being able to give a reason to stop working, lack of safe 24-hour access to a toilet, inability to deal with the bleeding and the pain, and problems to dispose of the products of conception' are acknowledged internationally.[94] Some of the eight women who tell their abortion stories in small videos on the Australian *I had one too* website talk about the downsides of early medical abortion. One woman says she was 'completely unprepared for … the symptoms and the emotional ride', another described 'the worst pain I've ever had' and 'a lot of blood' and a third recalled 'you're on your own a little bit … the unknown is quite frightening'. Two of these would have preferred a surgical abortion.[95]

Most international and Australian commentators are cognisant of the decline in current levels of access to surgical abortions that a general shift to early medical abortion may produce. In the 2020 *Framework for Abortion Access in NSW*, Family Planning NSW and collaborators state that 'there will always be a need for surgical abortion options and healthcare professionals to be skilled in this area'.[96] In October 2020, at the height of the first year of the COVID-19 pandemic, Marie Stopes reiterated this call, particularly for second trimester abortion.[97] Proponents of self-managed abortion as the way of the future, also endorse the need for abortion care 'within formal systems'.[98]

In the neoliberal context, 'self-managed' abortion incorporating varying degrees of independence can both mean and require an individualist approach. Writing of the use of illegally obtained misoprostol in countries where abortion is legally restricted, researcher Lie-Spahn has coined the term 'reproductive neoliberalism' to refer to 'the idea that, in lieu of state-provided equitable and holistic reproductive care, women can still achieve reproductive autonomy through entrepreneurial, legal, and pharmaceutical prowess'.[99] In other words, when public and even private services are inadequate, responsibility and competency devolve to the individual, who must become 'self-managing' in order to access needed health care. The account in one Australian study of some women in rural regions who accessed telehealth abortion suggests they embodied this subject position. All had difficulty accessing information, but had the literacy and internet search skills necessary to find telehealth. One woman, like several others, found the service 'On Google basically, I did a bit of research because being around here, there was you know not much choice'. Some women had to juggle their abortion care with other commitments around work and childcare: 'Women generally reported social isolation and low levels of support'.[100] The authors of the study commented that 'personal skills and favourable circumstances' are required to access telehealth, and not all will embody the 'prowess' needed to self-manage. Lie-Spahn coins the term 'paradoxical inequity' to describe telemedicine.

Few of my interviewees spoke about the downsides of early medical abortion; however, one stood out. In 2013—that is, before early medical abortion had taken off in Australia—women's health worker June summed up most of the concerns expressed in the research and in contemporary public storytelling about early medical abortion:

> what my worry is, is if we look to RU486 as a solution we won't have the choice, there won't be surgical abortions available anymore, well there will, but they'll still be a D&C [*sic*] and only those in the know will get them. And yes there are all sorts of difficulties associated with anaesthetics and curettes and blah, blah, but if you have really skilled doctors who are skilled in providing abortions, it's actually quicker, safer … [A former senior medical colleague] was like—15 minutes, it's a minor anaesthetic, it has almost no impact unless someone's allergic, you don't wake up sick, it's over in no time, and that's actually safer for women. And his view back in the 90s was that whilst RU486 may be seen as the panacea, that it's, you know it's isolating women, you know they largely abort at home, there's a great deal of pain associated with it, and so that's why I, for me, my daughters having the choice means a choice between RU486 and a clinical or [surgical] abortion.

Choice?

The matter of choice of abortion method is unresolved. The choices of those seeking abortions must be understood in their historical and social contexts. Victorian abortion providers reported in 2015 that patients made decisions for individual pragmatic and subjective reasons, shaped in part by stigma.[101] My rough skim of available abortion services around Australia at the time of writing shows the growing (but still inadequate) availability of medical when compared to surgical services. This is to be expected but rather than reflecting peoples' preferences, the lack of surgical availability shapes them. In a later study a woman from Victoria commented 'I think the surgical felt like the easier option for me ... but [early medical abortion] was the only option I had locally.'[102] If early medical abortion is the only service on offer for several hundred kilometres, or is significantly cheaper than surgical, then choice of method is compromised, though this is not to say that early medical abortion in these cases would not be satisfactory.

I do not return here to the early 1990s technocautious, if not technophobic, views on RU486 expressed by FINRRAGE and affiliates.[103] The scientific and social scientific research since then has shown that early medical abortion is safe. This includes self-managed abortion, which many have found entirely suitable to their needs. June, whom I quoted above, might find the research findings of widespread satisfaction with early medical abortion reassuring, and the normalising shift to local GPs and telehealth—and eventually to nurses and midwives—might lead her to express fewer misgivings if interviewed today. I do, however, wish to point to the possible (unintentional) effects of the singular focus on medical abortion as the solution to the problems of abortion access in Australia. While the moves to promote early medical abortion and locate abortion services in our predominantly privately provided system of primary health care have many benefits, they should not be allowed to overshadow the ongoing need for surgical services and training in these, or demands for public health responsibility for abortion care.

There are commercial factors that may create uncertainties in the availability of early medical abortion in Australia in the future. Australia relies on imports for 90 per cent of its medicines, and this includes early medical abortion. This dependence means that Australian supplies are subject to disruptions in international market and supply chains.[104] The challenges of the COVID-19 pandemic have contributed to difficulties in some early medical abortion supply chains around the world.[105] In Australia the import of mifepristone sits with one company, MS Health, the only not-for-profit pharmaceutical company in the country; in comparison, there are seven companies that import sildenafil, the drug usually known and marketed as Viagra. It is unlikely that other companies will join the market in the near future, the decline in the number of abortions performed in Australia each year is a disincentive to this. But these matters are speculative and beyond the scope of this chapter.

I am struck by the prescience of those who observed medical abortion in Australia from its earliest days. David Healy was right in 1985 when he predicted that RU486 would reorient our ways of thinking about abortion. Jo Wainer's enthusiasm in 1990 for medical abortion's ability to return the abortion process to women's control has also been justified. On the other hand, the concerns she foresaw are still expressed—lack of support for those undergoing the process, loss of surgical skill, and the threat to state support for surgical abortions (although in most states this has hardly ever been secure to start with). Geoff Brodie's faith in 2000 that conservative efforts would not halt the inevitable arrival of mifepristone was rewarded. Over twenty years later, with early medical abortion still heavily (over)regulated by the state, nurse- and midwife-led provision is on the foreseeable horizon. Finally, I am struck by the recognition from even the most committed proponents of self-managed abortion that we need to keep in mind the ongoing need for surgical abortion, the principle of choice of method, and the public provision of services and support for all abortion care.

Chapter 6

Decriminalised

Many people would nominate decriminalisation as the most significant change in relation to abortion law and provision in Australia over the last thirty years. Legal, medical and feminist activists have been calling for it since the 1970s, and since 1990 there have been well over twenty abortion law reform bills in Australian parliaments, creating periods of heightened public debate. All but one of those that have passed into law have been pro-choice in orientation. The twenty-first century has seen decriminalisation achieved in seven out of eight jurisdictions (at the time of writing), and safe access zones (SAZs) that prohibit protest activity around abortion clinics have been introduced in all. Parliamentary debates have been covered widely in mainstream media and on social media, both playing a significant role in disseminating information and broadening the base of campaigns. Large numbers of individuals and organisations have mobilised around decriminalisation, in support and in opposition. There is no doubt that the achievement of decriminalisation has been a major victory for the pro-choice movement.

But what exactly is this decriminalisation of abortion as it has been legislated around the country? What impact has it had on the provision of abortion services—and access to them? Has it led to the removal of exceptionalising regulations? Are there issues that have been obscured by the focus on achieving decriminalisation?

Decriminalising legislation in Australia has coincided with liberalising constitutional and/or legislative changes in Ireland, Aotearoa New Zealand and Northern Ireland, and with the 'green wave' of reform in Central and South America, especially in Argentina, Mexico and Colombia.[1] As mentioned in the Introduction, the overturning of *Roe v Wade* in the US Supreme Court in 2022 captured media attention and the popular imagination concerning global abortion rights, but it does not reflect the global trend in abortion law, of which Australia is a leader. Understanding the meaning and impact of the decriminalisation of abortion in Australia therefore has international significance.[2]

My questions about abortion law draw on a long history of considering the law and law reform as focuses for social change. In 2005, feminist legal scholars Reg Graycar and Jenny Morgan published 'Law Reform: What's in It For Women?', arguing for the need to pursue law reform while also challenging and redefining 'the narrow frameworks within which these issues [related to equality for women] are debated'.[3] And US legal scholar Rachel Rebouché has noted that while 'there appears to be faith in liberal laws promising liberal access, and in restrictive laws restricting access', globally, 'empirical studies' repeatedly find that this assumption is 'unfounded' and that law and health care are not necessarily related.[4] Aileen Moreton-Robinson's 2004 observation that 'The law in Australian society is one of the key institutions through which the possessive logic of patriarchal white sovereignty operates' and that its colonial nature needs to be kept in the forefront of consideration about any claims to its progressive potential hovers over this chapter.[5]

Histories of the campaigns for decriminalisation during the twenty-first century are mostly yet to be told in detail, and I will not attempt this task here. Instead, this chapter offers a narrowly focused historical account and a critical analysis of decriminalisation and its effects, drawing on both documentary and media research and oral history interviews, although as the last of these was conducted in 2017 they are limited to discussing decriminalisation and its effects up till that point.

Abortion in Law: 1990s

In 1990, although the legal status of abortion was defined in the criminal law of each state and territory, many individuals did not know this, and the private and public services that provided abortions were fairly confident their practice was lawful.[6] In Victoria, NSW and Queensland, the legality of abortion was an effect of court rulings in cases in which well-known abortion providers were charged with performing unlawful abortions. The ruling by Justice Menhennit in the Supreme Court of Victoria in 1969 was the first and most significant of these.[7] Menhennit ruled that an abortion was lawful if the doctor believed that it was necessary to protect a woman from 'serious danger to her life or physical or mental health' and was proportionate to 'the danger being averted'. In 1972, Justice Levine made a similar ruling in a lower court in NSW, adding social and economic stress to the definition of mental health that could be invoked to make an abortion legal.[8] Fourteen years later, Justice McGuire made a similar, if more cautious, finding in Queensland.[9] In SA and the NT, the law was reformed in 1969 and 1973 respectively, but these liberal reforms put in place stricter requirements than the court rulings above, as both required two doctors to agree that a pregnancy was a risk to a woman's life or health, and that abortions be performed in hospitals. Both also set upper time limits beyond which abortion was not lawful: 28 weeks in SA (later understood as 24), 23 weeks in the NT with different criteria applied after 14 weeks. Both allowed abortion if the child would be 'seriously physically or mentally handicapped', and both included a clause which affirmed a doctor's right to conscientiously object to performing abortion. An ordinance in the ACT in 1979 also required that abortions be performed in hospitals, but this was intended to prevent the proposed opening of a private abortion clinic rather than to allow the provision of abortion care as was the case in SA and the NT. There was neither court precedent nor law reform in WA or Tasmania; in both states, abortions were performed on the implicit assumption that the Menhennit ruling would apply.[10] It is notable that states and territories with similar legal frameworks have had significantly different systems of provision.

As indicated by the doctors I quoted in Chapters 1 and 3, while the criminal law had some effect, it did not necessarily impose a dampening effect on abortion services. The ACT is the clear exception here, as it was not until 1992, when the ACT government repealed the 1979 legislation, that the way was opened for the establishment of the RHS clinic in Canberra. Nevertheless, there were regular instances in which the criminal law's capacity to determine abortion practice came to the foreground.

In 1994, for example, the *CES v Superclinics* case in NSW raised concern when the trial judge dismissed a woman's claim for negligence against a clinic because it had failed to diagnose her pregnancy, thus preventing her from having an abortion and leaving her with the costs of raising the child.[11] Justice Newman claimed that the abortion she had lost the opportunity to seek would not have been legal. The NSW Court of Appeal overruled the decision 2–1, and the matter was eventually settled out of court in October 2006, but not before the defendants had won the right to appeal to the High Court and the Catholic Church had been given leave to appear as *amicus curiae*, thus raising the unwelcome spectre of the High Court deciding NSW abortion law.

In another case, early in 1998 two doctors from one of the two private abortion clinics in Perth, WA, were arrested in relation to an abortion performed two years earlier after it was revealed that a Māori woman had taken home foetal remains after her abortion in accordance with cultural tradition.[12] Doctors in the public hospital system stopped performing abortions. This led to a rapid process of law reform—though one that stopped short of decriminalisation—in May of that year, and the dropping of charges against the doctors.[13] Similar events took place in 2001 in Hobart, when doctors at the RHH were threatened with arrest after a complaint by a fifth-year medical student who reported that doctors were providing abortions simply because 'the woman did not want to have the child'. The Director of Public Prosecutions stated, surprisingly, that the Menhennit ruling would not apply. Public hospital doctors and nurses ceased providing services and the Tasmanian parliament passed reform legislation that also stopped well short of decriminalisation but averted the arrest of the doctors.[14] Notably, neither case was initiated by a patient's complaint. Both reform Acts clarified the terms under which abortions could be lawfully reformed: the WA Act removed the possibility of prosecuting women but the Tasmanian Act did not, doctors in both jurisdictions could still be charged with a criminal offence if they did not meet the conditions under which an abortion was justified. Both Acts added extra conditions to what had been usual practice.

Also in 1998, a bill introduced by a conservative independent politician reformed abortion law in the ACT. The legislation now required, among other things, restrictive informed consent processes and for 72 hours to pass between the initial appointment and the abortion operation—both requirements drawn from the playbook of the US anti-abortion movement.[15]

The two decades since these events took place have seen significant legal change across seven of Australia's eight jurisdictions. While there are minor differences, decriminalisation in each jurisdiction has at minimum repealed aspects of the criminal law and removed the pregnant person's liability to criminal prosecution, making abortion lawful when performed by a doctor on request (except in the NT) up to a certain time in pregnancy, and in an emergency to save the pregnant person's life at any stage of pregnancy. All jurisdictions have maintained, or added, offences with respect to abortion provided by an unqualified person.

Feminist and pro-choice organisational and community mobilisation has been key in each jurisdiction, usually in the face of significant opposition from anti-abortion forces. In all cases, the major parties have given members a conscience vote and, in most, ALP, Greens and Independent MPs have comprised the bulk of votes in favour of decriminalisation.

Getting the Ball Rolling: 2002–13

Wayne Berry, then Minister for Health in the ALP government of the ACT, had both introduced the 1992 law reform that paved the way for the opening of the RHS clinic in 1994 and supported its establishment.[16] Concerned with the possible impact of the *CES v Superclinics* decision, in 1994 he also unsuccessfully introduced a bill to repeal abortion from the criminal law. It was not until 2001, when the ALP returned to government and the number of female members in the ACT Assembly increased, that Berry was able to act again. In December 2001, from the back bench, he introduced two bills to decriminalise abortion, one repealing abortion from the Crimes Act and the other repealing the 1998 Act. A new ACT campaign group, Options for Women, formed a week later. The community and parliamentary campaign culminated in September 2002 with the passing of Berry's two bills, along with a third introduced by pro-choice ALP colleague Katy Gallagher which amended the *Medical Practitioners Act 1930* to require that abortions be performed only by doctors in approved facilities and to specify that no one was obliged to perform an abortion. The Assembly voted 9 votes to 8.[17] A fourth bill, anti-abortion in intent, failed.

Two years later a campaign for decriminalisation started in Victoria, motivated partly by an upsurge of anti-abortion views in the federal government.[18] Following a meeting held at Trades Hall in November 2004, the Abortion Law Reform Association was revived under the influence of former ALP premier Joan Kirner and led by the ALP women's organisation Emily's List, with support from Women's Health Victoria, the Public Health Association of Australia and Liberty Victoria. A second campaign group, ProChoiceVic, worked closely with the YWCA.[19]

In July 2007, Candy Broad, an ALP member of the upper house, introduced a private member's bill to decriminalise abortion. Shortly afterwards, the Attorney-General requested advice from the Victorian Law Reform Commission (VLRC) on removing 'offences relating to terminations of pregnancy where performed by a qualified medical practitioner(s)', and Broad withdrew her bill. Having consulted thirty-five organisations and received over 500 submissions, the VLRC reported on its findings in May 2008. Minister for Women Maxine Morand then introduced a government bill into the lower house in August. The bill passed the parliament, unamended, in October, 47 votes to 35 in the lower house and 23 to 17 in the upper.[20]

The Victorian Act allows a doctor to 'perform an abortion on a woman' on request up to 24 weeks of pregnancy, and registered nurses or pharmacists who are appropriately qualified to supply medication to cause an abortion up to 24 weeks. A medical practitioner can perform an abortion for a woman who is more than 24 weeks pregnant if they consult with another medical practitioner and the two agree that an abortion is 'appropriate in all circumstances'. The Act requires a health practitioner who has a conscientious objection to abortion to inform the woman of such and refer her to a practitioner whom they know does not have an objection, pioneering such conditions for those who object.

Tasmania was the next state to move.[21] Its 2001 law reform required that two doctors approve an abortion, and this had proved an obstacle to access. Nicola, who worked in the Tasmanian Health Department in the 2000s, told me that it was six or seven years before the government produced material explaining the 2001 law for doctors. More than one interviewee told me that doctors in Tasmania claimed to be 'confused', but Rosalie, a GP who provided abortions in Tasmania, demurred: 'You know, I think they just don't want to.' The key organisations in relation to women's sexual and reproductive health—Family Planning Tasmania, Women's Health Tasmania and youth service The Link—periodically raised issues of inadequate access with Health Ministers in ALP governments during the 2000s, and change began when Michelle O'Byrne became Minister for Health in 2010. Unlike her predecessors, when the abortion issue was brought to her attention she expressed interest and in 2012 met with representatives from Family Planning Tasmania and Women's Health Tasmania, now joined by the Women's Legal Service.

O'Byrne's private member's bill to decriminalise passed Tasmania's lower house in April and, after consideration by a Legislative Council Government Administration committee, passed the upper house in November 2013 by 9 votes to 5 (only one

Liberal in the parliament supported the bill) and was then accepted by the lower house.[22] The Act allows a doctor to perform an abortion up to 16 weeks of pregnancy 'with the woman's consent', and after 16 weeks if another doctor—one of the two being a specialist in obstetrics and gynaecology—is consulted and both believe it is necessary for the woman's health. The initial bill had been changed after the Tasmanian branch of the AMA lobbied against the requirement that a doctor with a conscientious objection refer a patient to another doctor and the possibility of fines for not doing so, and the Act therefore states that doctors with conscientious objections must instead notify patients of 'the full range of pregnancy options'. Notably, the Tasmanian bill was the first to introduce SAZs.

Momentum Gathers: 2013–17

The pace of parliamentary activity in other jurisdictions, both pro-choice and anti-abortion, started to pick up at around the time decriminalisation was taking place in Tasmania. Conservative politicians in WA in 2012, and in NSW and SA in 2013, attempted to introduce legislation that would confer personhood status on the foetus in cases of assault on a pregnant woman that resulted in the loss of pregnancy. At the same time, John Madigan, a conservative Democratic Labour Party Senator from Victoria, proposed a bill in the federal parliament to disallow Medicare rebates for abortions performed for the purpose of sex selection, which remained in play until Madigan lost his seat in 2016.[23] It was also alleged that some Victorian doctors with conscientious objections to abortion were flouting their legal obligation to refer patients on, and a group of doctors and some politicians called for the removal of the referral requirement.[24] The state council of the Liberal Party therefore voted to revisit the 2008 law, but in the end no bill eventuated.

Elsewhere, and subsequently, the direction in Australian parliaments was increasingly pro-choice. The first successful legislative change after decriminalisation in Tasmania came in late 2015, when the ACT and Victorian parliaments legislated to create SAZs, the culmination of a long fought battle in Victoria, led by psychologist

Susie Allanson at the FCC.[25] Moves towards decriminalisation in other jurisdictions were also emerging. For example, in an interview in September 2015, abortion activist and public health advocate Priscilla talked me through the conversations about inadequate abortion services that had taken place between FPWNT and NT Health Ministers since 2012.[26] There had been no action, so at some point, a loose group of women set up the *What RU4 NT?* Facebook page to provide a focal point for activism. The campaign was anchored by the FPWNT and supported by the Public Health Association, the NT College of Midwives, CRANA (the peak body for the health workforce in remote Australia) and small, funded women's service organisations in the NT, and driven by about a dozen academics and lawyers and doctors. In November 2015 the Independent Speaker of the Legislative Assembly, Kezia Purick, introduced a private member's bill to enable access to early medical abortion. In May 2016, the Legislative Assembly voted to not even discuss it.

In 2014, prompted by concern about 'Zoe's Law'—the NSW bill to recognise foetal personhood first proposed by conservative Christian Fred Nile—Greens member of the upper house Mehreen Faruqi launched the End12 campaign to decriminalise abortion in NSW with support from a broad coalition of women's, medical and legal organisations.[27] Nile reintroduced his bill again in 2015, and the Greens commissioned opinion polling which found that 73 per cent of people in NSW supported decriminalisation. The campaign culminated in Faruqi's introduction of a bill to decriminalise abortion and add conscientious objection obligations and SAZs. Her bill was defeated 14 votes to 25 in May 2017.

In April 2016, the Supreme Court in Queensland approved an abortion for a twelve-year-old girl when doctors were reluctant to proceed without legal authority.[28] This came in the wake of the 2009 'Cairns case' in which a young woman and her male partner had been arrested on criminal charges relating to abortion. The uncertainty about the legality of medical abortion that followed the arrests led to the cessation of medical abortions by some doctors in 2009. Having declared that she would not seek to decriminalise, the then-Premier Anna Bligh (ALP) effected minor reform to ensure that the 1986 McGuire ruling extended to medical abortion.[29]

Outraged by the need for the twelve-year-old to go to court, in May 2016 Independent member of the Queensland parliament Rob Pyne introduced a private member's bill to completely repeal abortion from the criminal law, and a second to add health regulations. These were discussed by separate parliamentary committees, which received 1400 and 1200 submissions respectively. Pyne withdrew his bills in early 2017, and in June the Attorney-General Yvette D'Ath asked the Queensland Law Reform Commission (QLRC) to investigate 'modernising Queensland's laws relating to the termination of pregnancy'.

In the meantime, action had begun in SA.[30] The SA Abortion Action Coalition (*saaac*) had been formed in early 2016, prompted by longstanding conversations about the inadequacy of access to abortion services in SA, especially for people living outside metropolitan Adelaide. It recruited support from over forty women's, legal and medical organisations. The parliamentary campaign for decriminalisation began in late 2018 when Greens member Tammy Franks introduced a bill in the upper house to completely repeal all reference to abortion from the law and add SAZs. Shortly after, the Liberal government's Attorney-General, Vickie Chapman, announced that she would ask SALRI to report on 'modernising the law' in SA. The Franks bill eventually lapsed.

Dominoes Fall: 2017–21

In March 2017 the NT Assembly voted to decriminalise abortion.[31] The Country Liberal Party had been replaced in August 2016 by an ALP government and *What RU4 NT?* had kept up the lobbying pressure. Health Minister Natasha Fyles' government bill to decriminalise passed unamended, 20 votes to 4.[32] Much debate focused on Aboriginal women, especially those in remote communities, and three of the Assembly's Aboriginal members, Selena Uibo, Chancey Paech, and Ngaree Ah Kit, spoke strongly in favour of the bill, rejecting racist stereotyping of Aboriginal women.

The NT Act enabled a 'suitably qualified medical practitioner' to perform an abortion up to 14 weeks 'if' they consider it is appropriate, and from 14 to 23 weeks following a second doctor's assessment of the woman. That is, it did not establish abortion on request as all other decriminalising Acts have done. Authorised nurses, midwives, Aboriginal and Torres Strait Islander Health Workers and pharmacists are specifically mentioned as those who may assist an abortion, under a doctor's direction. Abortions no longer needed to be conducted in hospitals. Doctors with a conscientious objection were required to 'inform the woman' and refer her to a doctor without objections or to direct another health practitioner when people in these roles have conscientious objections. The new law also included SAZs.

Queensland was next.[33] While Rob Pyne's initial move had taken the pro-choice community by surprise, Pro Choice Queensland was active from the start, and a student-based group, Young Queenslanders for the Right to Choose, formed in 2016. From mid-2018 a full-time campaign organiser was based at Children by Choice and funded from a donation and some fund-raising. (This person went on to work on the campaign in NSW.)[34] Manifesting extraordinary stamina among Queensland's submission-writing community, nearly 1200 submissions were made to the QLRC's inquiry—the state's third inquiry in three years—before its report on abortion law was delivered in June 2018. The Attorney-General's government bill passed in October 2018, unamended, 50 votes to 41.[35] A medical practitioner could now perform 'a termination on a woman' on request up to 22 weeks, and after that with the agreement of another medical practitioner and if certain basic conditions were met. The Act followed the NT Act in specifying health practitioners who could assist. Doctors and others with conscientious objections were required to refer on. SAZs were established.

Then came NSW. First, in June 2018, the parliament passed a private member's bill to create SAZs.[36] Introduced into the upper house by ALP backbencher Penny Sharpe, and subsequently into the lower house by National Party member Leslie Williams, the bill passed with little opposition, and with no sign of the storm to come.[37]

The final stage of the NSW campaign for decriminalisation emerged a year later. *Our Bodies Our Choices*, the self-described 'community campaign to decriminalise abortion in NSW' had been growing since 2018.[38] The NSW Pro-Choice Alliance, 'a collective of more than 70 organisations' led by WEL, launched its campaign for reform in May 2019. Family Planning NSW and the national Human Rights Law Centre were key supporters. Independent member of the lower house Alex Greenwich, along with fourteen other sponsors including Health Minister Brad Hazzard, introduced a private members' bill to decriminalise abortion on 1 August 2019.

Several speeches in support of the bill made reference to the 2017 conviction of a woman for procuring her own abortion when 28 weeks pregnant by accessing pills over the internet at a cost of $2000, at the urging of her male partner. Some made reference to the 2006 conviction of Dr Suman Sood for performing an abortion without meeting the requirements of the Levine ruling. The Legislative Council's Standing Committee on Social Issues convened a 'short format' inquiry into the bill on the day it was introduced to the lower house. More than 13,000 submissions were received in the short period made available, and witnesses appeared at hearings over three days. The report, delivered on 20 August, recommended simply that the Council consider the bill. The bill passed the lower house in the week it was presented, 59 votes to 31, and went to the upper house later in the month where it was introduced by Penny Sharpe. Here it passed, 26 votes to 14, on 25 September. Amendments were made in both houses.[39]

The original bill took its cue from Queensland, setting an upper limit of 22 weeks and requiring agreement from two doctors after that and mentioning others who could assist, but parliamentary melee delivered a plethora of amendments. It added specific refer-ence to informed consent and watered down the requirements for doctors with conscientious objection. It also required that counselling be offered if deemed appropriate, and that a person born from an abortion be cared for. The Act declared opposition to abortions performed for sex-selection reasons (this issue had resurfaced in the federal parliament in late 2017 when SA Senator Cory Bernardi had tried but failed to revive the Madigan bill regarding the Medicare benefit).[40] Doctors were required to report terminations to the Ministry of Health within 28 days. The NSW Act was the first to use gender-neutral language to describe the person having an abortion.

While this was happening in NSW, SA campaigners were contributing to and then awaiting the report of the SALRI inquiry.[41] Nearly 3000 responses were made via a survey platform, a further 340 submissions were written, and roundtable discussions with key individuals and groups were conducted; during this time the High Court also delivered its verdict on a challenge to Tasmanian and Victorian laws, finding that SAZs were constitutionally sound.[42] SALRI reported in October 2019, but the arrival of the COVID-19 pandemic interrupted the Attorney-General's plan to introduce a bill.

Parliamentary attention resumed in September 2020 when, following the NSW pattern, ALP member Nat Cook in the lower house and the Greens' Tammy Franks in the upper house shepherded the introduction of SAZs through the parliament.[43] A private member's bill to decriminalise abortion—Chapman's, in essence—was then introduced into the upper house by Minister for Health and Wellbeing Stephen Wade and Minister for Human Services with responsibility for women Michelle Lensink. The bill passed the upper house 12 votes to 9 and then the lower house 29 to 15.[44]

The Act put in place an upper limit of 22 weeks and 6 days; after that, abortion requires the agreement of two doctors. All qualified healthcare practitioners—not only doctors—are empowered to provide early medical abortion up to 22 weeks and 6 days. The conscientious objection clause includes the requirement to refer. The existing residency clause was removed. Like NSW's, the

SA Act uses gender-neutral language. The original bill was amended, also like NSW's, requiring an offer of counselling and an obligation to care for a person born from an abortion (the conservative Queensland member of the federal lower house George Christensen announced his intention to move a bill to require life-sustaining treatment to a person so born at the same time).[45] The SA Act prohibits abortion for sex selection, lists seven 'mandatory considerations' after 22 weeks and 6 days, adds coercion in relation to abortion to existing definitions of domestic abuse in legislation about intervention orders, enables the collection of information about individual abortions, includes a lengthy section on confidentiality, and requires the minister to report to parliament annually.

Finally, with little public attention, two jurisdictions reformed their original decriminalising Acts. In 2018 a bill introduced by Greens member Caroline Le Couteur in the ACT removed the 2002 requirement that abortion be performed in 'an approved medical facility' in the case of early medical abortion.[46] The 2002 conscientious objection clause was also revised to require doctors to inform patients of their objections. In 2021, NT Health Minister Natasha Fyles replaced the existing two-stage model with the simpler requirement, following the Victorian law, that after 24 weeks two doctors must consider abortion appropriate.[47] The new law was 'a move Family Planning NT has been calling for for years'.

These 'catch-up' legislative changes challenge the view that politicians who have lived through abortion law reform are reluctant to return to the issue, a comment activist and public health advocate Louella made about Tasmanian parliamentarians and Gwen, a key abortion activist, made in WA. It could be generational change that saw SAZs established in WA—the last jurisdiction to add them—in 2021.[48] In the wake of the overturning of *Roe v Wade*, in July 2022 the WA Health Minister made an initially lukewarm commitment to reforming WA law in response to grassroots mobilisation for this change but subsequently her department established an inquiry into law reform.[49]

From a different angle, in 2021 the NSW parliament passed a version of Zoe's Law which increases penalties for causing the death of an unborn child 'due to third party criminal acts'.[50] The Attorney-General rejected criticism from pro-choice groups who saw it as a risk to abortion rights.[51] In the federal arena, Queensland conservative Senator Matt Canavan's Human Rights (Children Born Alive Protection) Bill 2022 is under consideration by a committee at the time of writing. The bill 'would introduce measures that require health practitioners to provide medical care, treatment and statistics on children born alive as a result of terminations', a legislative tactic from the US anti-abortion movement and is opposed by human rights advocates and the sexual and reproductive health community.[52]

A National Trend

This chronological account of twenty-first century decriminalising law reform identifies a clear national trend. Campaigns in Australia have been state-based, but social media, Children by Choice and other conferences, and personal networks have facilitated national connection, and some national bodies such as the Human Rights Law Centre, the online feminist campaign group Fair Agenda and abortion provider Marie Stopes, along with national and local branches of organisations like the YWCA and RANZCOG, have been prominent advocates for decriminalisation in nearly all campaigns. Some individuals have been involved in several campaigns: O&G Professor Caroline de Costa, for example, wrote submissions and/or gave evidence to the QLRC, VLRC and SALRI inquiries and the Tasmanian parliamentary committee. And the reports and debates in various parliaments have all drawn on their predecessors.

The prompts to start campaigning for decriminalisation have varied. In some cases it was specific barriers to access arising from the legislative framework; in others specific local events; and in Victoria general concern about the rise of anti-abortion action. In some cases momentum began with parliamentarians, in others with

community activists. Official inquiries were conducted in five jurisdictions. Initial unsuccessful attempts at legislative change, all but
one of which were more liberal than the bill that finally passed,
paved the way in most.

In four out of seven jurisdictions, decriminalisation has come
from private members' bills, although some sponsors have held
ministerial positions in the government of the day. These have been
more vulnerable to amendment than government bills. Female
members have voted for decriminalisation proportionately more
than their male peers, but while reform has occurred most often
under ALP governments, in all cases it has had the support of the
relevant premiers and other senior ministers. However, in most cases
parliaments have been more conservative on abortion than their
constituents. Popular support for decriminalisation sits at approximately 80 per cent, but as the numbers in the determining
parliamentary votes show, votes have rarely reached that mark.[53]

Public, media and parliamentary discussion about abortion have
manifested through a range of discursive contests; what follows is
therefore only an overview. The names of the feminist and
pro-choice activist organisations involved, and their slogans, reveal
key tropes dating back to the 1970s and 1980s, with 'choice', 'our
bodies our choice' and 'abortion as health care' predominating.
'Reproductive rights' also appears, and public opinion has been
invoked regularly, while 'access to services' is a more recent development.[54] Institutional discourses of abortion are narrower. The terms
of reference for law reform bodies have focused on the need to
'modernise' laws, although reports from these inquiries give extended
accounts of clinical practice (VLRC and SALRI), facilities (SALRI)
and 'access and availability' (QLRC), echoing what Rebouché
describes as 'the turn to public health' in deliberations by US courts
and legal and regulatory institutions, often at the behest of lawyers,
researchers, and other advocates.[55] In this context it is notable that
the needs of Aboriginal women are mentioned throughout the
QLRC report, and are the subject of a chapter in SALRI's report
which draws on submissions from Aboriginal agencies along with

other sources. The objects or purposes of the Acts of parliament that decriminalise abortion, where stated, concern the 'regulation of abortion providers' and the enabling of 'safe access' to health services (i.e., freedom from harassment at clinics).

Research into the discursive framing of parliamentary debates, nearly all of which is focused on Victoria, highlights both a range of historically familiar stereotypical and stigmatising representations of women and a respect for women's rights and their capacity as decision-makers.[56] While 'formal choice' was an assumed value for most, discussion of reasons for having an abortion, including suspicion of those designated as 'social', and representations of the woman seeking an abortion through notions of 'lack' (of education, income, security or ability to cope) were common. There was little support for ease or convenience in access to abortion while abortion 'as a decision which women agonise over' was common.[57] Law reform is posited as the answer to the problem of outmoded and ineffective law.[58] Personal storytelling about reproductive issues including miscarriage, adoption, disability and sometimes abortion by members of parliament has been a feature of all debates in the twenty-first century, from both sides of the issue, in the mainstream media and in political campaigns.[59] In the afterglow of success, much celebration focused on the understanding of abortion as a health matter, and on women's autonomy. Queensland Attorney-General Yvette D'Ath, for example, is quoted saying, 'We've done this for our mothers, our sisters, our daughters, our friends. For women who have fought long and hard for the right to autonomy over their own bodies'.[60]

I have given scant attention in this account to those who have stood in the way of decriminalisation, although their success lies primarily in adding conservative amendments to original bills such as requirements that doctors offer counselling and references to sex selection, which draw on anti-abortionist appropriations of pro-woman discourse.[61] The requirements to care for a person born from an abortion recalls the notion of foetal viability, attempts to bestow foetal personhood status, and the US trope of 'born alive'. So do the requirements around upper limits of pregnancy. And future attempts by anti-abortionists to change abortion law cannot be ruled out. An account of the anti-abortion movement, including the leadership role played by the national Australian Christian Lobby in many cases, and the presence of financial and organisational links to US groups, will therefore be an important part of the history of the campaigns for decriminalisation.[62]

Decriminalisation: A New Form of Regulation

In truth, except for the ACT no jurisdiction has completely removed abortion from the criminal law, and all have introduced requirements, either in stand-alone abortion bills or as amendments to health law, that did not previously exist. In other words, one form of legal regulation has been replaced, if not completely, by another. The decriminalising laws thus continue to make abortion an exceptional case of health care—and a mediated case of bodily autonomy.

Abortion stands alone as the only medical or surgical procedure which is specified in legislation as unlawful if performed by an unqualified person. In all jurisdictions except SA and Victoria, an 'unqualified person' is anyone other than a doctor. The SALRI report describes this law as 'the residual offence'.[63] It notes that under the authority of the *Therapeutic Goods Act 1989* (Cth), obtaining mifepristone 'outside of registered pharmacies or medical practitioners is illegal', and that 'there are existing health laws (such as holding out to be health practitioner)' and 'criminal laws (such as assault or causing harm or serious harm), to deal with unqualified persons'. While SALRI finds these 'arguably inadequate', it is unclear if anything remains that is not covered by non-abortion-specific law. While 'holding out' and assault laws do not deal with abortions provided or assisted by people who do not claim health qualification and/or where there is no harm to the pregnant person and/or they consented (as in contact sport which may result in harm), evidence of such practice is slim, if not negligible. One could ask, 'What would be the problem if such practices existed?' In any case, many submissions point out that better access to abortion services will see unregulated practices disappear.

SALRI urges that we remember the concerns about unsafe abortions from the 1960s and the VLRC and QLRC reports and individual parliamentarians refer to 'backyard abortions', an arguably anachronistic term. SALRI notes hearing 'anecdotal accounts indicating unauthorised procedures by unqualified persons'—a reference largely to early medical abortion, 'particularly in rural and regional areas'—although it acknowledges that that these accounts were contested.[64] It notes a 2007 case in Sydney and a 2013 case in the UK in which mifepristone was supplied by a Chinese medicine shop and an Ayurvedic health centre respectively, in which convictions were obtained under abortion law, along with the Cairns and Sydney cases previously discussed in which women were charged over the illegal use of abortion pills. However, the Therapeutic Goods Act would cover all these cases. The unqualified person offence would apply to someone like the young man who assisted his girlfriend in the Cairns case. It could also apply to those who assist women such as international students who abort with pills brought from their home countries.

Geographer Sydney Calkin has observed how early medical abortion is dissolving the link between the clinic, the nation state and abortion, especially when it is sourced from the internet, delivered via telehealth and by activists supplying to people in countries where abortion is severely restricted. Calkin notes, however, that 'anti-choice states' have responded with strategies to 'control the space of the clinic, the medical consultation process and the body'.[65] This describes the situation in Australia: at the moment of decriminalisation, except in SA and Victoria, any expansion in modes of access to early medical abortion was specifically headed off by confining the ability to prescribe it to doctors. If or when the TGA relaxes its requirement that MS-2 Step can only be prescribed by a doctor, the other jurisdictions will have to amend their abortion law to fully enable this economically sensible, clinically safe and patient-oriented development. And while enabling suitably qualified nurses and others to perform surgical abortions currently seems well beyond the Australian legal and medical imagination, it has long been established that these health workers can and elsewhere do practise surgical abortion safely and mainstream medical leaders in the UK have called for this.[66]

Decriminalising legislation introduced protections for conscientious objection to abortion where not previously legislated, or revised what was already in law. The legislated rights and responsibilities introduced for those with conscientious objections only repeated what was already stated in the policies and/or codes of ethics of various peak health bodies including the AMA, RANZCOG, the Nursing and Midwifery Board of Australia and the Pharmacy Board of Australia.[67] For this reason, not all pro-choice supporters endorsed legislated conscientious objection.[68] A recent global survey of studies of conscientious objection has further indicated that it restricts access to abortion services 'by creating barriers to obtaining services, and indirectly, by exacerbating pre-existing barriers to access'. This includes the practice of 'convenient objection', in which practitioners use conscientious objection as cover for other reasons to not perform abortions.[69] That 'convenient objection' is practised in Australia became apparent in research conducted in Victoria six to seven years after decriminalisation: Keogh and colleagues surveyed nineteen 'experts in abortion' and found that the conscientious objection clause had 'increased the legitimacy of "opting out" of abortion provision, and that as a consequence of this clause, whole institutions could justify not providing abortion services'.[70]

When considered together, the offence of the unqualified person and the inclusion of conscientious objection in the new decriminalising laws not only continue to exceptionalise abortion but perpetuate the problem that I identified at the beginning of Chapter 3. It is now (re)legislated in every jurisdiction bar SA and Victoria that only doctors can lawfully perform abortions, *and* that their choice not to do so on the grounds of conscientious objection is explicitly—some would argue unnecessarily—protected.

At the same time, the removal of the doctor's authority to decide if an abortion is justified up to a certain stage of pregnancy opens up space for both doctor and patient. It relieves doctors of the legal burden of assessing the worthiness of a patient's request, a change most doctors who are willing to provide abortion care will welcome.[71] Further, it implicitly affirms the pregnant person's decision-making authority, even though that authority retains special legal consideration.

This affirmation, however, is only implicit, because while the decriminalising Acts explain the conditions under which abortion can be performed lawfully, they do not give rights to the person requesting the procedure. The right to access abortion, and all health care, materialises only in the marketplace of private health care, public health policy, and the discretion of doctors. Further, the requirement for consent in the Tasmanian and NSW Acts, and in the WA Act, actively undermines the status of the person seeking an abortion. Whether or not the respective parliaments knew this, requiring consent is a strategy from the US anti-abortion repertoire, in which intrusive terms of consent are often spelled out. While it may seem counterintuitive to quibble about informed consent, given that all medical treatment already requires the patient's consent this requirement is unnecessarily exceptionalising. Finally, given that the party requiring consent is also the one setting the terms of engagement, it reinstates medical authority over abortion.[72]

The fact that all decriminalising legislation since the ACT's has specified a number of weeks of pregnancy beyond which different regulations apply both limits and, some argue, enables the provision of abortion services (I discuss this in in detail in Chapter 7). Explicitly stating the conditions under which an abortion is lawful after the upper limit clarifies the legal performance of later term abortions. But, as Erica Millar argues, upper limits continue to exceptionalise all abortions through a troubling binary divide between early and late, on request and on approval, and, implicitly, good and bad.[73]

The degree to which many of the details in the various Acts, and the new regulations that have followed, will pose snags in implementation is unknown. Notwithstanding many clauses requiring only what is already clinical best practice, the level of detail in the SA and NSW Acts in particular has the potential to induce excessive caution in practitioners and expand grounds for complaints by both patients and colleagues. For example, the SALRI report recommended against prohibition of abortions performed for reasons of sex selection, noting the absence of significant evidence of its practice in Australia, and warned of its potentially racially discriminatory implementation.[74]

If Acts of parliament are evidence of 'historically contingent values and practices',[75] then the decriminalising laws testify to the latest, at least partial, defeat of the fifty-year-old demand to end the legal exceptionalising of abortion. This mirrors the US pattern where 'the history of liberalization' has been 'accompanied by the language of exception'.[76] The Acts effect victory for doctors in relation to the historical contests over who should have authority over the pregnant body, albeit with some diminution of that authority in those who provide abortions. However, there are also gains for people who need abortions: their authority is implicitly recognised, up to an upper limit of pregnancy beyond which the law continues to stigmatise and create ambivalence. As Acts of parliament are also 'linguistic structures that can take effect only through acts of interpretation' and are 'simultaneously constantly evolving',[77] the new laws may, for example, see abortions being provided for people with later term pregnancies where this would not previously have been the case. In any case, the possibility of conservative interpretation and implementation of new laws, in local as well as state, territory or national arenas, indicates the need for constant vigilance.

Does Decriminalisation Improve Access to Abortion Care?

Except where decriminalisation has removed specific legal obstacles, such as the hospital requirements in SA, the NT and the ACT, the causal relationship between it and subsequent changes in provision is hard to determine. When determining whether decriminalisation has improved access to abortion care, we must think not only of changes to the letter of the law, but also of decriminalisation's manifestation in political culture and community awareness. The question of timing is also tricky. Changes that occur in the immediate wake of law reform, even if they could legally have taken place before decriminalisation but didn't, might be considered direct effects. But if they occur some time later, do they still count as effects of decriminalisation? Notwithstanding legal change, when has the political moment of decriminalisation passed?

For some people, decriminalisation is experienced subjectively. In 2015 Phyl, the O&G who provided abortions in public hospitals in Victoria, said to me,

> Before decriminalisation, you had to prove to me that I should grant you an abortion ... and I had to document the reasons, under the Menhennit ruling ... and so women would sit there waiting to be granted an abortion, and I could see the moment where they thought, 'All right, I've got one,' yeah. And so I feel a lot better about that interaction.

This is a meaningful change for the doctor, but if the patient doesn't know about the change or is still intimidated by medical authority, they may not experience similar release from oppressive law. Bree, the Victorian women's health worker, told me in 2013 that 'from an education perspective it has been quite an improvement in relation to being able to clearly state what their rights to abortion access are.' This clarity will apply to all states where abortion had not previously been legislated. The more material effects of decriminalisation are, however, varied.

In the ACT, the NT, SA, and Tasmania, decriminalisation removed specific legal obstructions to improving access to services. In SA and the NT these were the hospital requirement and the two-doctor rule, along with the two-month residency requirement in SA. The two-doctor rule also applied in Tasmania from 2001 and the hospital rule in the ACT between 2002 and 2018. Decriminalisation removed these for abortions under the upper limit, and single GP and telehealth provision of early medical abortion became lawful. However, doctors will not necessarily become prescribers of early medical abortion and if telehealth is not promoted, its uptake may be slowed.

In the ACT the most onerous obstructions related to the requirements of the 1998 Act. Julie worked at the RHS clinic in Canberra in a management role at the time, and explained that providing abortion care 'was actually not so much about delivering the service but making sure that we met our obligations in case they were ever scrutinised in court, because we were scrutinised a lot.' She described decriminalisation in 2002 as a 'brand new day,' but noted that it was the purchase of the clinic by Marie Stopes in 2004 that actually 'save[d] the space where women could access services in the ACT.'

The involvement of Health Minister Michelle O'Byrne in the wake of decriminalisation in Tasmania in 2013 was promising. As noted in Chapter 2, the Tasmanian Health Department funded resources to inform the public and sent information to doctors. But within six months of decriminalisation the government changed hands, and under the new conservative Liberal Minister for Health, Michael Ferguson, who held the portfolio until 2019, there was no improvement in access to affordable abortion care despite repeated promises and plans.[78] The three private clinics in Tasmania closed during this period, one after the other; this was unrelated to the law, but despite telehealth filling the gap for some, access to services plummeted. Research conducted in 2018 showed that significant uncertainty about 'indemnity, financial reward and access to medications' and adequate support and training was still getting in the way of interested GPs becoming providers of early medical abortion.[79]

In the Top End, in contrast, change was dramatic and has been sustained, as I noted in Chapter 2. While decriminalisation allowed this to happen, it was the government's decision to fund FPWNT that was central to making it happen.

There has been no research of which I am aware on the provision of early medical abortion by GPs in the ACT since the 2018 change to the law. At the time of writing, information about services on the Sexual Health and Family Planning ACT (SHFPACT) website is limited to links to Marie Stopes and the GCA clinics in the area and a note that some doctors may provide early medical abortion.[80] I have no evidence of decriminalisation having any effect on the provision of later term abortions in any of these jurisdictions (I will discuss this further in Chapter 7), and as the new law in SA was only implemented in July 2022, at the time of writing it is too soon to tell what impact decriminalisation will have on access to services. However, some public hospitals and a small handful of rural GPs in SA were already providing early medical abortion, so any change will be less dramatic than that in the NT.

As noted in Chapter 2, in both Tasmania in 2021 and the ACT in 2022, governments have announced significantly increased commitment to the public provision or funding of abortion.[81] These announcements have come some time after decriminalisation, and as public provision could have been implemented before the law reform, it is hard to attribute these moves to decriminalisation alone. In Tasmania credit must go to persistent lobbying by the key sexual, reproductive, women's and youth health services, assisted by the change in (still Liberal) Health Minister in 2019. In the ACT, Minister for Women in the ALP government Yvette Berry, the daughter of decriminalisation pioneer Wayne Berry, made the announcement.

In Victoria, Queensland and NSW, where there were originally no specific legal obstructions and where abortion services were predominantly privately provided, the impact of decriminalisation on abortion provision has been small, hard to measure or negligible. Phyl, in Victoria, was disappointed when interviewed in 2015:

> I probably thought that a little bit ... after abortion law reform, there'll be more providers willing to do this job ... But it hasn't panned out that way ... I thought that there might be more services opening at public hospitals ... That hasn't been the case.

This view was confirmed by research in 2015. Interviewees at that time in Victoria thought that since decriminalisation, 'access to public services [had] shrunk,' and they were particularly concerned about access to services for later term abortions.[82] Shifts in the private sector, including the closure of the Marie Stopes Maroondah clinic in 2021, were driven by market logics. Early medical abortion had been pioneered by Marie Stopes in Victoria before decriminalisation, its availability increased in the wake of TGA approval and its subsequent availability on the PBS, along with the educational work of key doctors and institutions, most recently SPHERE. It is possible that the growing number of GPs who offer early medical abortion may be partially an effect of decriminalisation given that some feel more comfortable in the clarified legal environment. The Victorian government now funds the comprehensive My Options website and 1800 number, providing information about providers in all areas of Victoria.

In its celebration of decriminalisation, the Queensland Government stated, 'Queensland Health will now roll out a comprehensive implementation plan for health professionals', as described in Chapter 2.[83] The government established a website offering general information with links to the Children by Choice website. (Their Abortion and Contraception Services Map, a comprehensive guide to providers across the state, was initially produced with philanthropic, not government, funding.)[84] In March 2022, news of crises in abortion access in regional Queensland prompted Rockhampton state MP Brittany Lauga to say, 'When we passed the bill it was about equality and access to health care … Little did we know we'd see a decline in the quality of health provision'.[85]

Although the Health Minister in the NSW Liberal government made no commitment to improve access in the wake of decriminalisation, NSW Health did establish an abortion information service. Information is sparse, but the site includes an 1800 number for more information (and, notably, states that referral for sex-selection abortion will not be provided).[86] In a media article in 2020, Minister Hazzard, one of the decriminalising bill's sponsors, made it clear that he had no interest in pursuing the problem of access or of committing public hospitals to providing abortions.[87]

The one unmitigated success story from the period of twenty-first century abortion law reform is the introduction in every Australian jurisdiction of SAZs around abortion clinics. Many abortion providers around the country told harrowing stories of the harassment of staff and patients before the establishment of SAZs. They have been unanimous in their positive assessment of the new laws, and Ronli Sifris and colleagues have concluded that SAZs 'are achieving their objective of protecting women's dignity, privacy, safety and wellbeing'.[88]

Conclusion

In an article in an academic law journal in 2021, Dwyer and her colleagues ask, 'Is there still a need for abortion-specific laws?' They conclude that no, there is not. Examining the existing policy and provisions of 'the modern health framework', they find that these are more than adequate to ensure the provision of 'safe, effective, appropriate and accessible abortion care, including the accountabilities of health care providers', and thus conclude that specific laws 'will almost inevitably cause unforeseen access and quality problems because they cannot allow for medical and other advances affecting abortion care'.[89] I suggest that such laws may also enable 'convenient objection' through clauses that entrench conscientious objection, and that the sex-selection sections in the SA and NSW Acts have potential racialising effects. The general effects of the ongoing exceptionalising of abortion in law are harder to predict, however, as are the possible headaches born of the potential for anti-abortion litigation and obstruction in public health settings, especially in NSW and SA where sections of the Acts born of conservative amendments could be open to interpretation.

The two decades of decriminalisation in Australia have not repealed abortion-specific laws, but they have created new regulatory frameworks based in health law for providers to navigate. Arguably, in jurisdictions that previously relied on court precedent, the most significant effect of decriminalisation *per se* has been—contrary to popular expectation—to make little or no difference to the provision of abortion services.

Decriminalisation in the ACT, the NT, SA and Tasmania has already delivered, or will make possible, what was available in the other jurisdictions: single GPs in private practice and community clinics, and telehealth, providing early medical abortion. In other words, decriminalisation in these jurisdictions has opened up the private market and/or community provision. This is not necessarily a bad thing, and immediate increased public commitment in the NT and subsequently in the ACT and Tasmania suggests that it is not thus far undermining public provision. However, the change does not flow the other way. Victoria, Queensland and NSW have not gained the commitment to public provision that has characterised provision in SA and the NT since the 1970s and has been improved since decriminalisation in the NT, the ACT and Tasmania. Nor has it solved the problems of private provision. Many abortion insiders will not have been surprised.

This is where we might identify a relationship between decriminalisation and neoliberalism. Inasmuch as market deregulation is neoliberalism's foundation value, it is consistent with decriminalisation. But in SA, the NT and Tasmania, where public provision has been or has become significant, the small size of the market and its geographical dispersion mean that private stand-alone clinics are unlikely to be established and private provision will only ever come from GPs (from mid-2023 the ACT has had publicly funded provision by private providers). This private provision in primary health care is likely to increase, but will not address the needs of those who require surgical procedures, and until Medicare remuneration for early medical abortion is increased, it will not necessarily make it more affordable to access from GPs. The entrenched system of private provision seems to carry the same drag on change as, fortunately, the history of public provision does in SA and the NT. Notably, this is a not a Liberal/ALP issue, given that a Liberal government in Tasmania has moved towards public provision and

ALP governments in Queensland and Victoria have been unable to do so systematically thus far.

Neoliberalism is also enacted in the discourse of decriminalisation through its appropriation of the concepts of choice—a key organising concept for feminist and liberal abortion politics for over fifty years, and the self-managing subject. Millar argues that in the Victorian debate pro-choice discourse assumed that 'women inevitably regulate their own abortion conduct' and will make good choices—this is not the same as a feminist notion of women exercising reproductive freedom.[90] But while choice has not been the only trope through which campaigns for decriminalisation have succeeded, unless it is constantly wedded to the concept of affordable, accessible, culturally appropriate and safe provision of services, it is a conceptual and political limit on the capacity for further change.

My final comments are speculative personal musings that go beyond the strict legal domain or the context of service provision. In the political and discursive arenas I see two lines of impact. One flows from the mobilisation of individuals, organisations, journalists, academics, sympathetic politicians and their advisors, and key bureaucrats in government departments in the service of decriminalisation. These people have become better educated about abortion and better networked than was previously the case. This education has flowed into the broader public through generally sympathetic media and social media, helping to destigmatise abortion, and this mobilisation has provided points of reference for and opportunities to engage in feminist politics and discourse. Some key organisations that worked for decriminalisation have faded, others have continued to press for better services after its achievement, and some new organisations have entered the space.

On the other side of the ledger, if improved access to services is the measure of success, the campaigns for decriminalisation have been an enormous expenditure of energy for, in some jurisdictions, little return. The notion that abortion is controversial has been further entrenched during the struggle for decriminalisation: not only anti-abortion activists and politicians but also pro-choice politicians and media sources reiterate this view, belying majority popular support for decriminalisation and Rebecca Albury's 2007 observation that Australians have a 'tolerance for the ambiguities of abortion'.[91] That abortion politics can be summed up as 'pro' and 'anti' is also reiterated by decriminalisation campaigns. Relatedly, the notion that abortion is singularly an issue of morality, as signalled by conscience votes and legislation for conscientious objection, is entrenched. These framings have the effect of obscuring and/or taking attention away from other issues such as equitable and accessible provision, and culturally appropriate services.

In relation to the law, I worry that the success of decriminalisation bolsters uncritical faith in law reform as an avenue for progressive change. I have argued that decriminalisation alone is limited, or even negligible, in terms of improving access to abortion services. However, there is more at stake here in the context of major contemporary political challenges to the legitimacy of law. Women With Disabilities Australia note the debates about abortion decriminalisation and the law reform enacted were significant for 'the *absence of criminalisation* of forced and coercive abortion ... pursuant to disability-specific law'.[92] First Nations women have argued, in the context of carceral feminist proposals for law reform to criminalise coercive control in domestic violence situations, that such reforms may harm those already disproportionately targeted by criminal law in a legal system that is often violently stacked against First Nations people.[93] In these contexts, the decriminalising abortion success story may have an ideological effect of renewing faith in law *per se* and in liberal narratives of progress while possibly obscuring law's ongoing enactment of coercion and violence. It needs to be subjected to critical analysis.

I do not disavow the change that decriminalisation brings. However, I recognise that while the many realms in which reproductive justice is contested are full of opportunities for its realisation, they are not singularly determined and are never stable. Herein lies the persistent need for ongoing activism.

Chapter 7

Late

… doing something or taking place after the expected, proper, or usual time.

—*Oxford Languages Dictionary*

Late abortions are often made out to be different from early abortions. Focusing on late abortion is a central strategy of anti-abortion activists, and explaining late abortion and defending adequate service provision for those who need it is often challenging for pro-choice advocates and commentators. And after a certain point—which varies in Australia depending on where you live—the later in pregnancy you request an abortion, the less adequately it is provided, and the greater its cost to the patient.

However, the marking of time is a social practice, and 'late' is thus a relative term. In the experience and regulation of abortion, different institutional and subjective times brush up against each other—the time of finding out you're pregnant, the (waiting) time for an appointment at the hospital or clinic or GP, the time of tests, the time of the law. These overlapping and often contesting times are, according to legal scholar Joanna N Erdman, 'ultimately struggles over ethical and political values, authority and power'.[1]

The epigraph at the top of this chapter sums up my understanding of 'late' abortions. Not only are they by most definitions a small proportion of all abortions in Australia—that is, unexpected and unusual—they are in many contexts particularly stigmatised, and thus not 'proper'. The term 'late' is frequently used to describe abortions after 20 weeks of pregnancy, partly because in all jurisdictions the outcome of any pregnancy after 20 weeks must be registered as a birth, but some seeking an abortion after 16 weeks of pregnancy will be 'too late' to access one without significant travel away from home. It can also be applied to abortions conducted after the first trimester of pregnancy. And those seeking early medical abortions after 9 weeks are currently 'too late' to use this method. So although the term has no essential meaning, it is often marked by understandings that are legal, ideological and normative, and by the closing down of options to access a service.

Some providers and pro-choice organisations eschew 'late' and use first and second trimester to describe difference in the stage of pregnancy. Others classify abortions by the number of weeks or the type of procedure.[2] I continue with 'late' to foreground its slipperiness as a term and keep questions about its meaning alive.

The number of late abortions and their proportion of all abortions when defined as after 20 weeks in Australia can be roughly estimated from data from the two states that publish annual statistics about abortion. In WA in 2018 (latest available figures) this was 1.1 per cent; for SA in the same year it was 2.1 per cent. If defined as after the first trimester it was 6.1 per cent in WA and 8.9 per cent in SA.[3]

There are a range of circumstances that lead to people presenting late for an abortion. System delay is common, and threads through other reasons for presenting late.[4] They can include legal restrictions, institutional processes, poor advice or deliberate obstruction from doctors, lack of geographically accessible services, and lack of affordability. Changed circumstances such as the sudden loss of a partner or diagnosis of severe illness or 'foetal anomaly' can lead to a late request for a termination. Some tests which will inform a decision about continuing a pregnancy cannot be conducted until late in pregnancy; some require more tests for confirmation. People outside big cities often experience system delay in accessing tests at all. The VLRC's 2008 report also noted that tests to diagnose 'foetal abnormality' were conducted later for public patients than for private ones, and were of lower quality,[5] and while some denominational hospitals which offer maternity care—mostly Catholic ones—offer foetal diagnosis, if the patient then decides to end the pregnancy they have to take the time to find a service elsewhere. It has been increasingly recognised that some people are hampered by abusive partners who obstruct their access to abortion services,[6] and more people than you would think identify symptoms of pregnancy late, or have them mis-identified by health professionals, and so if they wish to end the pregnancy must have a late abortion. Personal circumstances, including drug and alcohol dependency, depression and ambivalence and/or denial about the pregnancy, may slow decision-making and/or capacity to access health care. Finally, patients who already experience structural disadvantage in relation to health care, including residence outside big cities, poverty, homelessness, lack of access to Medicare, youth, poor access to information and racism are vulnerable to system delay. Aboriginal and Torres Strait Islander people are disproportionately represented among those who present late.[7]

The divide between late abortions sought after diagnosis of 'foetal anomaly' and those sought for what are described as 'psychosocial reasons' is regularly reiterated in both medical data and popular discourse, and pro-choice commentators tend to lean on the cases that follow a troubling foetal diagnosis, but the numbers that populate this distinction vary widely. In WA in 2018, nearly 80 per cent of abortions over 20 weeks were for foetal anomaly, but in SA in the same year only 51.1 per cent were.

The foetus and its viability are often at the centre of heightened discussions of ethics in relation to late abortion. Viability is usually understood as the point from which a foetus can live independently outside the pregnant person's uterus—a definition both framed by medical science and dependent on it, and one for which there are well-established critiques. As Erica Millar points out, biological viability is 'not universal—and is abstracted from the social, cultural and material conditions of existence', for 'there is no magic line after which preterm neonates automatically survive', and any such line depends on access to sophisticated technology.[8] Of more significance is the erasure of 'parental (and, disproportionately maternal) labour' in a biological definition of viability. Once the subjectivity of the individual pregnant person is taken into account, viability can only be defined in relation to what is socially, materially, emotionally and spiritually possible for them, and perhaps their family.

There are differences between early and late abortions, however defined, for the pregnant person and for providers. A counsellor who works with 'late women' (in her case over 18 weeks) notes the individual nature of each experience but also writes of a 'state of rush, shock, confusion, stress, there is often little time to allow for women to contemplate their experience, and any complexities in their feelings or in their decision making'.[9] She finds that 'feelings of being alone, and ashamed are even more acute'. GP abortion provider Simon, who spoke with me in 2015, commented on the multiple dimensions of difficulty for doctors who provide late abortion:

> I mean, it's technically more challenging, its aesthetically and ethically more challenging, and it's harder to get anaesthetists and nurses to work on that service as well ... it's a special, dedicated kind of person that works on those lists.[10]

I do not dismiss the ethical concerns that trouble many in relation to late abortion. My approach in this chapter is informed by Erdman's discussion of the law, in which she concludes that thinking about late abortion must be

> to spend time with, to seek to understand, and ultimately to support women who seek later termination of pregnancy ... [and] to realize the truest compassion of law in the hardest of times, when morality, health, and justice make their strongest demands.[11]

However, this chapter is not about the need some pregnant people will have for late abortions. I take this as read. Instead, it draws on documentary evidence including media coverage and articles published in medical journals, and on oral history interviews with doctors and others involved with providing late abortions, to provide a history of the provision of late abortion in Australia since 1990 and, relatedly, its status as an exceptional matter worthy of institutional regulation or proscription.

Abortions for 'psychosocial reasons' after 20 weeks have been provided in the main by a very few private clinics, and by the PAC in Adelaide and the RWH in Melbourne, while abortions after diagnoses of 'foetal abnormality' have mostly been provided by public hospitals as part of obstetric care. This distinction between 'psychosocial' and 'foetal abnormality' abortions is also one between surgical procedures performed by GP surgeons and inductions of labour performed by O&Gs, although some O&Gs also do surgical procedures, both of which involve attendance at a clinic or hospital over two or three days. Discussion of clinical approaches is outside my scope, but it should be noted that there have been changes and improvements in these over time, and that the provision of foeticide is a key issue in this context. By tracing a history of the bifurcated provision of late abortion, I hope to make it easier to see what is needed to support the person who seeks a 'late' abortion *on their terms*.

The terms 'psychosocial' and 'foetal abnormality' are commonly used to describe the two—apparently distinct—most frequent reasons for late abortions, but these embody problematic sexist and ableist assumptions about decision-making, and about the nature of foetal and human difference. I have decided to retain 'psychosocial' here but to use 'foetal anomaly', which is also common and less harsh than 'abnormality', unless quoting directly. In general, however, rather than avoiding the problematic assumptions of the terminology, I aim to highlight them, with the goal of enabling a critical relationship to their meaning.

Late Abortion in the 1990s

In 1990 only SA and the NT had legislated upper limits beyond which abortions were not legal except to save a woman's life. Only they specified the legality of abortion on the grounds of foetal anomaly; the court rulings that had liberalised law in the eastern states were silent on this matter. The NHMRC report written in the early 1990s explained that

> The maximum gestational length at which services are provided varies widely between States, regions and providers. In some hospitals and clinics, only first trimester services are generally available. Most clinics, and those hospitals which provide mid-trimester services, accept the World Health Organisation guideline (1978) that TOPs should only be undertaken after 20 weeks in cases of fetal abnormality or serious illness in the woman.[12]

SA's annual report on abortion for 1990 showed that abortions for women at 14 or more weeks of pregnancy accounted for 3 per cent of the total. Rennie Gay from SA told the 1990 Women and Surgery conference that there was a divide between 'deserving' and 'undeserving' cases based on the reason for abortion.[13] There had been no access at all for abortions after 12 weeks 'on psycho-social grounds' since June 1988, meaning that the 3 per cent were almost all for foetal anomaly. Those seeking 'early mid-trimesters' were sent to Melbourne and 'late mid-trimesters' to Sydney. As Gay predicted, the opening of the PAC in 1992 soon resolved this problem, as it initially offered surgical abortions to 18 weeks. From 1994 the PAC went to 22 weeks, with most abortions performed for psychosocial reasons.[14] By 1995 the percentage of abortions over 14 weeks in SA had increased to 6.8 per cent. Procedures were done by dilatation and evacuation (D&E) at the PAC and others at the WCH by induction of labour.[15]

Jo Wainer reported to the same conference that late abortions in Victoria were offered at the Monash Medical Centre and the

RWH.[16] Most were for foetal anomaly. Induction of labour was the only option at Monash because, Wainer stated, 'none of the staff [were] prepared to learn how to perform the more difficult D&E'. Smaller hospitals referred patients to the RWH, which performed abortions to 20 weeks and sometimes later in some foetal anomaly cases, and made special arrangements to accommodate staff sensitivities.[17] Some private clinics provided services to 16 weeks, but after that there were 'only a limited number of specialists trained and prepared to do procedures'.[18] In 1997, The Women's Clinic on Richmond Hill offered surgical abortions to 18 weeks and by early 1998 a new clinic at Maroondah, established by David and Melissa Grundmann, was performing abortions to 20 weeks.[19]

At David Grundmann's Planned Parenthood of Australia clinic in Brisbane abortions were already available up to 24 weeks, and Grundmann stated that he would go over the 24-week line when 'the circumstances [were] ... extreme'.[20] Queensland's other well-known abortion provider, Dr Peter Bayliss, stopped at 20 weeks.[21] Grundmann and his partner Dr Mark Schulberg performed abortions at both Brisbane and Maroondah, and counsellor Susan Kelly spoke and wrote publicly about her work.[22] In 1997, however, the clinic's work prompted Queensland's conservative National Party government to ask the Queensland Medical Board to conduct an inquiry into the need to regulate abortion after 20 weeks, causing concern among pro-choice activists.[23] A 1998 news item stated, 'at least 50 per cent of patients [at the Brisbane clinic] come from interstate—women desperate enough to pay up to $5000 and travel half way across the continent for an abortion'.[24] As only SA residents could access the service at the PAC, the role of national provider of late abortions for psychosocial reasons thereafter shifted to Victoria's Maroondah clinic.

In NSW, Preterm's limit was 14 weeks and Geoff Brodie's Australian Birth Control Services clinics went to 18 weeks. He told a journalist that 'you do lose staff over gestational issues'. The division between late abortions conducted for foetal anomaly and those for psychosocial reasons created tensions among the doctors, but in response to a comment about the preference of some activists in the

WA crisis of 1998 to remain silent about late abortions, Brodie said, 'The middle-ground gynies who do foetal-abnormality terminations are being dragged into the pit with the abortionists and it's about time'.[25]

In WA, prior to the 1998 law reform the KEMH had 'an informal policy' of performing abortions to 18 weeks, according to a counsellor at the hospital.[26] According to Joseph, a Perth O&G with whom I spoke in 2016, the KEMH went to 'about 20 weeks and John Charters' Zera clinic provided surgical abortions 'quite late' (but under 20 weeks) at this time. In 1998 Cheryl Davenport, the parliamentarian who led the law reform, stated that less than fifty abortions were performed after 20 weeks in 1997, and most were for foetal anomaly.[27]

There is little evidence to suggest that any late abortions for psychosocial reasons were performed during the 1990s in Tasmania, the NT or the ACT, but no reason to think that late abortions for foetal anomaly did not take place, albeit in small numbers. One case of the former came to light in Darwin in 1998.[28] Dr Henry Cho, who was the mainstay of abortion provision at Darwin's public hospital through the 1990s and 2000s, performed an abortion at the Darwin Private Hospital because of his concern for the woman's psychological health. Cho had initially indicated to staff that the woman was about 19 weeks pregnant, but later agreed that she may have been around 22 weeks. A baby was delivered following induction and lived for about 80 minutes. The only recommendations from the subsequent coroner's inquiry concerned development of protocols for the live birth of a foetus/infant after an abortion. I am not aware of any doctor in the ACT or Tasmania at this time who would have acted to meet a patient's wishes as Cho did in this way.

The APFA produced detailed standards of practice and guidelines for second trimester surgical procedures, releasing an updated version in 1998.[29] One year later, its conference became the focus of controversy, as noted above, when one of three invited guests from the US, two of whom were late abortion providers, was held up at Sydney airport by immigration officials and required to sign a statement claiming that he would not incite 'discord'.[30] Ten years later the Australian news media would cover the story of the murder of the second provider, Dr George Tiller, at church in Kansas by an anti-abortion gunman.

Hospital Committees Decide

The 1998 reform to WA's abortion law institutionalised the requirement that a hospital committee decide on a woman's request for late abortion.[31] Since then, all requests for an abortion after 19 weeks of pregnancy have been considered by two medical practitioners chosen from a ministerially appointed panel of at least six, who ascertain whether a foetal or maternal medical condition would 'in their clinical judgement' justify an abortion. If approved, the abortion must be carried out in a ministerially approved facility. Cheryl Davenport, the ALP MP who led the parliamentary process, wrote that this hospital requirement was 'designed to prevent abortions being performed by the D&X (dilatation and extraction) method' used by David Grundmann (in the US in the 1990s anti-abortionists assigned the non-medical term 'partial birth abortion' to D&X, a variation of a D&E).[32]

Between June 1998 and December 2003 there were fewer than forty abortions performed per annum in WA for women more than 20 weeks pregnant, all of which were for foetal anomaly. These comprised about 0.5 per cent of all abortions. All were done at the KEMH by inducing labour, with foeticide used after 24 weeks.[33] KEMH obstetrician Jan Dickinson's account of the decision-making process at this time reported that 'for contentious cases', more than one meeting of the committee might be required. Eleven requests were declined by the panel, seven of which were 'solely for psycho-social reasons'; it was known that one woman travelled interstate, and in all cases 'psychologic counselling and ongoing support [were] offered'.[34] In 2016, Joseph told me that 'the social work department [at the KEMH] is very good in terms of organising to go east but it's very disruptive and very expensive. They don't get any medical assistance to go there.'

Joyce, who worked in the social work department at the KEMH, told me a story about a young woman from the remote north of the state who needed an abortion. She was more than 20 weeks pregnant. Travel to Melbourne—a journey of over 6000 kilometres each way—was her only option. The story related the unjust enormity of her situation, but also the support she received from disparate sources including the ALRA fund and a Catholic priest in Melbourne who was her only contact there. Similarly, Perth GP Laura was aware of a series of events that had taken place around 2010 illustrating another kind of injustice and enormity, and courage, for both the pregnant woman and the doctors involved. The woman was a drug user and 21 weeks pregnant:

> ... she really hadn't recognised what was going on, she had no money at that stage, the ALRA had wound up and the funds had gone. So [the doctor] did something really dreadful. [They] broke the law and [they] gave her some misoprostol which was all [they] had at the time, and brought her back and ruptured her membranes at 21 weeks and then told her to go to King Edward and say that her membranes had ruptured spontaneously ...
>
> And, and it was all okay. But [the doctor] could go to gaol for that, and at the time, [the doctor's colleague] knew about it and he was happy to support [them] but they kept it very quiet.

Laura's account reflects the stories told to researchers in 2019–21 by nurses and midwives who had provided abortion care, sometimes unlawfully, for women who were experiencing gender-based violence. The authors characterise this 'transgressive practice' as mostly *'misleading the system* to get the person to the abortion'. All of them felt their actions were justified, and none were remorseful.[35]

In Victoria, another political event—the controversy in 2000 over the abortion performed for a suicidal woman who was 32 weeks pregnant at the RWH in Melbourne (see Chapter 3)—had significant consequences for the regulation of late abortions in public hospitals. Writing in 2004, Lachlan de Crespigny, one of the doctors at the centre of the episode, stated that 'it has resulted in the fears of doctors and it has encouraged development of abortion committees, making it harder for some women to obtain an abortion'.[36] For example, when the controversy became public, formal Termination Review Committees (TRCs) were established to consider requests for abortions 'at or after "viability"', at the RWH for requests after 23 weeks and at Monash for requests after 24 weeks. The Monash committee was made up solely of clinicians, but the RWH committee was chaired by a hospital management nominee who had veto power.[37]

The decriminalisation of abortion in Victoria in 2008 and the specification of the conditions under which abortion after 24 weeks could be lawfully performed removed the need for TRCs, but they persisted, often with the effect of limiting access.[38] In 2015 the refusal of the RWH's TRC to approve a request for an abortion from a woman who was 26 weeks pregnant and suicidal made the news, and an RWH doctor was quoted anonymously as saying that the hospital refused such requests on the grounds that no staff were willing to do the procedure, but that he would have been willing if asked, and that many staff were distressed when such requests were refused.[39]

In 2011–12, Kirsten Black and colleagues interviewed twenty-two abortion-providing doctors from Queensland and NSW about access to late abortion for patients with diagnoses of foetal anomaly. Most such abortions were conducted in public hospitals, many of which had clinical ethics committees. NSW state government policy required a multidisciplinary team 'to make an assessment of whether the grounds for abortion are justified'. Such teams are referred to in the literature from 2005 on and could 'include a hospital legal representative and a minister of religion'. In Queensland, at least two specialist doctors needed to approve, 'as well as the director of medical services', but this was 'less directive than the NSW Guidelines'.[40] O&G Chris, whom I interviewed in 2013, talked to me about the process at the Royal Brisbane Women's Hospital (RBWH). Requests for abortion for foetal anomaly after 22 weeks were referred to an ethics committee, and in 2013 had been performed up to 35 weeks. All but one of the doctors interviewed for the research conducted by Black and colleagues, and Chris, had also referred women interstate, mostly to Victoria.

A 2004 article about difficult ethical decisions made at the John Hunter Hospital in Newcastle, NSW, gives an unusually detailed account of such a case.[41] A woman had received a foetal diagnosis of duodenal atresia and Down syndrome at 25 weeks and requested an abortion. The obstetrician called for an Acute Clinical Ethics Service (ACES) consultation. Although ACES supported the woman's request, the CEO requested further review and the involvement of the full Institutional Clinical Ethics Committee. The committee was divided, and 'after taking advice from several different sources' the CEO refused the request. The family was informed of the decision two weeks after requesting the abortion.

I found only brief references to TRCs in other jurisdictions. Ethics committees that operated similarly to those in NSW but had been established prior to the NSW policy existed in the ACT for the small number of late abortions conducted there, and the AMA noted in 2012 that panel reviews operated in Tasmania to consider abortions after 20 weeks, while the SALRI report was told that hospitals in SA could choose to convene committees 'of medical and non-medical personnel' to decide on requests for late abortion.[42]

While some commentators noted that TRCs could both provide ethical guidance for clinicians and assume responsibility most have not seen a role for such committees in clinical decision-making.[43] Criticisms of them include that they create delay, which weighs most heavily on people from rural and remote locations. Their lack of transparency and accountability, inconsistent decision-making over time, vulnerability to the demands of conservative hospital management, and decision-making removed from those seeking late abortion are flaws noted by many. Their vulnerability to being dominated by individuals was also commonly noted, including by Joseph, who had knowledge of the WA committee and who said that when an abortion was sought for psychosocial reasons, 'if the psychiatrist felt that there was no real need from a psychiatric point of view to do it the rest of the committee could hardly argue with that.'

The legislatively mandated review of the first three years of the WA legislation reported the full gamut of complaints, including the pressure to make a decision before 20 weeks, and noted that after a refusal patients reported 'guilt and grief'.[44] It also reported concern with the inadequacy of the counselling services provided to such patients, which was offered through the hospital where the request had been denied, inappropriately it was thought. In 2017, GP Alex, who was part of the medical team at the Maroondah clinic, talked about patients who regularly came from WA:

> So those women, in good faith, go 'Well this baby's got a really serious heart problem,' go to them [the panel], and then they go, 'That's not really a good enough reason,' and so they are just, they feel absolutely dreadful that they're now then asking for a termination when these experts have told them that they shouldn't be thinking about that.

The cost of the procedure, travel and accommodation, and any arrangements necessary to leave home for several days, compounded their distress.

Only small numbers of people seeking late abortions in public (and some private) hospitals have gone before ethics committees—those over 20 weeks in WA, and over 22, 23 or 24 weeks elsewhere. But this does not mitigate the significance of the erasure of their autonomy, which is noted by most commentators. In most hospitals the patient has no right of appeal.

Decriminalised yet Exceptionalised

While no legislation since WA has mandated committees to decide on late abortions, each instance of decriminalisation—with the notable exception of the ACT—has divided pregnancy into two (or, in the NT between 2017 and 2021, three) stages in order to impose exceptional regulatory conditions on abortions conducted beyond an upper limit. Unlike processes applied by individual doctors or institutions in relation to late abortions, these legislative rules are clearly visible, and so too is some of the political decision-making behind them.

A significant part of the anti-abortion activism that motivated the decriminalisation campaign in Victoria focused on late abortion. In February 2005, Catholic Health Minister Tony Abbott supported the call for a ban on abortions after 20 weeks made by a newly constituted group of religious leaders and conservative politicians.[45] Later that year Bronwyn Pike, the self-described 'pro-choice' Victorian Health Minister in the ALP state government, expressed concern at the growing number of patients coming to the Maroondah clinic—by this point the only one in the country providing a service over 24 weeks—from interstate for late abortions. Of the 197 people who had a late abortion there for psychosocial reasons in 2004, 91 were non-Victorians, Pike noted. She proposed a mandatory cooling-off period for women seeking late abortions after 20 weeks. Abbott expressed strong support for this, labelling Victoria as 'the late-term abortion capital of Australia'. David Grundmann responded by saying, 'Good on him ... maybe more people will come and see us before it's too late'. Pike's proposal was 'scrapped'.[46]

In 2007 the Victoria government commissioned the VLRC to advise on options for abortion law reform. The VLRC replied with three models for the government to consider. Model A codified the status quo; Model B decriminalised abortion and introduced a two-stage model, before and after 24 weeks of pregnancy; and Model C removed all specific regulation of abortion.[47] The government chose Model B. In between the tabling of the VLRC report and the introduction of the government's bill, conservative Tasmanian Senator Guy Barnett introduced a bill into the federal parliament to disallow the Medicare item number which provides a rebate for second trimester abortions. The matter was referred to a committee but eventually lapsed.[48]

In the gap between Tasmanian Health Minister Michelle O'Byrne's announcement of her private member's bill to decriminalise abortion and its introduction into the parliament a month later, the upper limit it specified dropped from 24 to 16 weeks.[49] The Tasmanian AMA's submission to the government, which recommended that two doctors should approve abortion after 14 weeks and a panel review process do so after 20 weeks, had been released in between the bill's announcement and its introduction in parliament.[50] The Launceston *Examiner* wrote that O'Byrne's bill was 'softened in a bid to get it through Parliament'.[51]

As noted in the previous chapter, the 2017 Northern Territory Act divided pregnancy into three, allowing abortion between 14 and 23 weeks on the basis of two doctors' assessment, reflecting perhaps the 1973 law reform which also specified 14 and 23 weeks. In Queensland, the QLRC acknowledged the many submissions which argued for no upper limit but recommended an upper limit of 22 weeks, preferring 'a reasonable balance between concerns about the woman's autonomy and calls for additional oversight for terminations after 22 weeks'.[52] The government's bill followed this model. The NSW bill followed the Queensland Act, with the addition of a note in the section about abortion after 22 weeks stating that the treating specialist could ask for advice from 'a multi-disciplinary team or hospital advisory committee'. Later in the same year the SALRI report advised against legislating any such mechanism, cautioning that 'may' could be read by some as 'shall' and lead to mandatory committee involvement.[53]

SALRI recommended no upper limit at all for SA, or, 'in the alternative', an upper limit of 24 weeks.[54] The Attorney-General released her bill in late 2020 with an upper limit coming in at 22 weeks and 6 days, making SA the only jurisdiction in Australia where an upper limit is specified in days as well as weeks. Her bill followed the upper limit imposed by the more conservative public hospital in SA rather than the 23 weeks and 6 days limit at the PAC. On a different note, in 2021 the political force of sustained advocacy and a willing Minister in the NT saw the two-part upper limit structure of the 2017 law reform changed to the simpler limit of 24 weeks.

Notably, no amendments to reduce upper limits introduced in the parliament have been successful in changing the various decriminalising bills that passed into law in Australian parliaments between 2002 and 2021, nor in WA in 1998. In 2020 in Queensland, however, some members of the LNP opposition called for a review of abortion law, particularly in relation to upper limits.[55]

Late Abortion in the Wake of Decriminalisation

The ACT, Tasmania and the NT

Although there is no reference to weeks of pregnancy in ACT law, the availability of late abortion has been limited. The Sexual Health and Family Planning ACT website currently indicates that surgical abortion is available at the MSI clinic in Canberra up to 16 weeks, but after that time in pregnancy abortion remains relatively rare except for a handful performed for severe foetal anomaly, all by induction of labour. There is some Patient Travel Assistance Scheme support for those who must travel.[56] The situation is similar in Tasmania, where the Women's Health Tasmania Pregnancy Choices website indicates that despite abortion on request being lawful up to 16 weeks, Tasmanian public hospitals generally only provide surgical abortion to 14 weeks.[57] One private provider goes to 16 weeks. These are all publicly funded and PATS is available for those who need to travel. Angela Williamson's story of seeking an abortion in Hobart over a three-week period in 2018 is a salutary tale of how a sympathetic but uninformed GP, a single private O&G providing abortions in the second trimester with limited capacity, and the legal upper limit of 16 weeks combined to force her to Melbourne for an abortion at 17 or 18 weeks, at a cost of more than $4200.[58] In 2023 some abortions are provided in the public system up to 20 weeks at the discretion of two doctors, as required by law, one must be an O&G, and after that may be referred to a panel. After 16 weeks all abortions are conducted by induction, with foeticide. In the NT, where the legislated upper limit is 24 weeks, and after with two doctors' assessment, availability at smaller public hospitals is limited to 12 or 14 weeks but is available at the Darwin Hospital to 24 weeks although surgical procedures are limited to 20 weeks. Foeticide is offered from around 17 weeks and always done after 22 weeks. Abortions sought after 24 weeks will be considered by a panel. Some NT patients travel interstate.[59] In all of these small jurisdictions, the lack of trained and experienced staff is as significant with regard to these limits as reticence around late abortion *per se*.

Victoria

The VLRC's 2008 report noted that the RWH, Monash and the Austin Hospital provided some abortions to 20 weeks.[60] Most private clinics stopped at 14 weeks, some went to 18 weeks, and until 2010 only Maroondah went over 24 weeks. In 2013, a news report claimed that 'prevailing stigma and pressure from protest groups means few doctors are willing to undertake the procedure'. Lack of resources was blamed for the lack of service for abortions requested after 16 weeks for psychosocial reasons at the RWH, where according to a senior doctor 'demand meant they had to prioritise services based on clinical need'.[61] One study, based in interviews conducted in 2014–15, reported reduced provision over 20 weeks in the wake of decriminalisation.[62]

I spoke with Phyl, an O&G who worked at the RWH, in 2015. At that point the hospital's Choices Clinic, which provided surgical abortions, stopped at 18 weeks, and abortions after diagnosis of foetal anomaly were performed in the labour ward by induction. Seven years later, O&G Paddy Moore, who heads the RWH's Abortion and Contraception Service (the successor to the Choices Clinic), and its service coordinator Aimee Kent reported on a concerted effort to improve and extend services for late abortion at the hospital.[63] This involved those doctors undertaking the RANZCOG Advanced Training Module, the recruitment of specialist staff, the implementation of clinical improvements especially in relation to foeticide, and the staging of an all-staff consultation process across the hospital. While a termination review panel remained for cases over 24 weeks, confidence in approving requests had grown. Ongoing challenges included staff succession planning and ongoing funding support for staffing, making greater use of nursing staff and extending choice of method. The upper limit of MSI's surgical provision depends on the availability of doctors.[64]

Queensland

The 2018 QLRC report stated that most private clinics in Queensland offered surgical abortion to 14–15 weeks, private hospitals went to 19–21 weeks, and after 22 weeks abortions were only 'permitted' at particular hospitals.[65] The 2018 parliamentary committee heard that in 2016 '76 [abortions] occurred at 22 weeks gestation or later', presumably most after a diagnosis of foetal anomaly and by induction of labour.[66] Chris told me that abortions for psychosocial reasons to 20 weeks had sometimes been performed at the RBWH since the early 2000s. In Brisbane there are currently two private clinics that offer surgical abortions to 16 weeks, and the MSI Australia clinic goes to the legal limit of 22 weeks, although very young women, complex medical and psychosocial cases cannot always be accommodated. The availability of doctors at the MSI clinic who can operate to 22 weeks is stable, more so than in the other east coast states. Foeticide depends on the doctor's practice but has been offered in the past by Marie Stopes for patients who then go to a hospital for induction of labour. In public hospitals the availability of late abortion varies, depending on the skills of the doctors, the grade of hospital and conscientious objection.[67] The post-decriminalisation guidelines for termination of pregnancy make no reference to a requirement of an ethics panel after 22 weeks, nor to restrictions on hospitals.[68]

NSW

Reference to late abortion in Family Planning NSW's 2020 report is brief: 'Access varies by [Local Health District] and by hospital'.[69]

Public and private hospitals provide abortion after 20 weeks for both foetal anomaly and psychosocial reasons, presumably via induction of labour. Surgical abortions over 20 weeks are also available at 'some private clinics and Marie Stopes Australia provide surgical abortion services up to 20–22 weeks', but 'availability is limited and cost is high'. The report's table of costs indicates that the cost of an abortion in the private sector increases weekly after 12 weeks, and dramatically so after 19 weeks, to $3995 at 20 weeks and 6 days.[70]

Until the closure of Victoria's Maroondah clinic in 2021 many NSW and Queensland patients needing an abortion after 22 weeks travelled there. Marie Stopes' Philip Goldstone told the Queensland Parliamentary committee in 2018 that Maroondah was seeing about one Queensland woman over 20 weeks per fortnight.[71] Family Planning reported that the clinic cost was about $7500.[72]

SA and WA

In these two jurisdictions, government-collected statistics give reasonably accurate accounts of the incidence of late abortions. Between 2015 and 2018 those performed after 20 weeks averaged around 2.5 per cent in SA and were more or less evenly split between those for foetal anomaly and those for 'mental health' reasons.[73] Since the mid-2010s, as noted above, late abortions for psychosocial reasons have been provided at the PAC to 23 weeks and 6 days, with D&E and foeticide used for procedures after 17 weeks since 2004.[74] Prudence Flowers reported in 2020 that, in contrast to other states, there were 'multiple D&E providers at the Adelaide public clinic'. Two public hospitals also provide abortions up to 22 weeks and 6 days, albeit in a setting of ambivalent institutional culture and division among specialist doctors. Foeticide is 'not routinely offered before induction abortion'. One of the two public hospitals where late abortions were provided to 22 weeks and 6 days after a diagnosis of foetal anomaly regularly withheld information from patients about the surgical service available at the PAC, which went to 23 weeks and 6 days, and sometimes gave inaccurate information about D&E.[75] Specialised support for patients diagnosed with foetal abnormalities is strong, including through Support After Foetal Diagnosis of Abnormality, which is part of the WCH.[76] GP Lil told me that the PAC has seen an increasing number of patients with a diagnosis of foetal anomaly wanting a surgical procedure rather than induction. All late abortions performed in public hospitals and at the PAC (i.e., nearly 100 per cent) are free to the patient, but SA has not been immune to the need for patients to travel interstate or overseas when patients present after the upper limits.[77] It is too soon to measure any effects of decriminalisation on late provision.

In WA, the percentage of abortions provided over 20 weeks grew slowly during the 2000s, to 0.5 per cent in 2010, and then more steadily to 1.1 per cent in 2018.[78] This steady growth could be explained by the committee's growing leniency; this is also suggested by the growing percentage of late abortions since 2010 performed for reasons other than foetal anomaly, which has hovered around 20 per cent since 2014. Joyce, a social worker at the KEMH, talked to me in 2016 of care for late abortion patients:

> If it was a termination of pregnancy for a foetal anomaly ... some nursing staff would look after those patients, but they wouldn't look after an elective termination of pregnancy for what they call—they used to call it a social termination of pregnancy.

She said that during the mid-2010s, the KEMH did fewer and fewer second trimester terminations in-house, increasingly tendering out procedures under 20 weeks to Marie Stopes. Around 95 per cent of all abortions over 20 weeks in WA between 2010 and 2018 have been by induction. There are no recent numbers for those refused abortions after 20 weeks. GP Laura said to me in 2016, 'I haven't really sent women in to King Eddie because I think "What are the chances?" I have sent a couple of people over east.'

Summary

There are three national matters to note regarding the provision of late abortion in Australia in recent years. The ongoing precarity of the Australian late abortion workforce and tensions among doctors is a significant theme.

The stories of doctors presented here include those who deliberately obstruct patient pathways, who are supportive but ignorant of pathways to a service, who advocate for their patients and become distressed when a service cannot be found and who are willing to provide a service in a hospital but not asked to do so, plus those few stalwarts who keep late abortion services going. There are also doctors who sit in formal judgement on people requesting a late abortion, sometimes denying the request. There have been tensions between GP surgeons and O&Gs, and among specialists in hospitals. The male 'mavericks' in private practice who were the early public face of late abortion have given way to a less visible group of predominantly female clinical and researcher 'champions' in the public sector and RANZCOG. Providers of surgical services past 14 weeks are still mostly located in the private sector, except in Adelaide and Melbourne, and all are located in capital cities. The number of O&Gs who will provide late abortions by induction after a diagnosis of foetal anomaly is greater than that of GP surgeons working in private clinics. And while skill at performing foeticide is less common, induction of labour is standard obstetric practice—but many, such as those in Catholic hospitals, will not provide the service.

The experiences of doctors who work in hospital O&G departments, where abortion provision can be marginalised, differs from those of doctors in private clinics. One SA O&G interviewed by Flowers described herself as 'self-taught', and reported that she and others kept 'a very low profile', wanting 'to do the right thing by the patients' but not to 'attract attention to themselves'.[79] In contrast, Chris, the O&G from the RBWH, had seen change in the twenty-first century that was enabled by persistent advocacy and discussion led by doctors in the department:

In the last decade we have increased the gestation, reduced their requirements for termination of pregnancy in terms of allowing it to be for maternal psychosocial problems, but on the downside we have increased the paperwork, the number of doctors who have to sign off the process involved has become a bit more complicated.

Paddy Moore and her colleagues' success in extending and improving late abortion services at the RWH through a process of cultural change also shows the potential of, and need for, 'clinical champions and strong advocacy'.[80]

When I asked Lil about her career plans for the next five to ten years, her immediate reply was: 'make sure that there's succession planning, that there's people who can take over and provide this work [at the PAC]'. Lil had learned in 'an apprentice-ship type model' from the doctor who had worked from the early 1990s to improve methods for late surgical procedures at the PAC. She confirmed Flowers' observation that SA providers of late abor-tions 'seemed particularly focused on the international community of abortion providers, attending the NAF conferences in North America or visiting international sites that provide later abortion care'.[81]

For budding O&G providers, participation in the RANZCOG Advanced Training Module includes demonstration of 'knowledge and understanding of' D&E procedures for patients at 14–18 weeks of pregnancy, and involvement in at least 5 D&E procedures at 16 weeks, although this last is optional. The program also includes learning outcomes in abortion advocacy.[82] This is seeding a new generation of late abortion champions. Most recently RANZCOG has stated that it is developing a Certificate in Sexual Reproductive Health to encourage abortion provision.[83]

The need for interstate travel to access a late abortion has been a constant for small numbers of patients in the last thirty years and it has not gone away. Given the distance from WA to Melbourne, the financial burden for those travelling east is the highest, and as Alex noted, the emotional burden for those refused by a committee of medical experts is particularly gruelling. Travelling to access late abortion is the norm for people in Tasmania, the ACT and the NT, and has been recorded for every other state except Victoria. And intrastate travel is required for most people living in rural, regional or remote locations who need a late abortion, which in many respects is no different from travelling interstate.

The final matter is the significance of the closure of the Maroondah clinic in Melbourne. Established in 1998 by David Grundmann, Maroondah was subsequently owned and operated by Grundmann's partner Mark Schulberg. From 2010 until 2012, Schulberg operated with Marie Stopes; from then the clinic was operated solely by the NGO.[84] It saw patients from around the country, and a handful from the Asia-Pacific region. By the mid-2000s it was performing late abortions for patients over 24 weeks; however, following a clinical incident Marie Stopes pulled back to an upper limit of 24 weeks on the basis of clinical safety, and concern expressed from MSI in London, a decision Yolanda, who was privy to Marie Stopes management at the time, said in 2017 was met with dismay by Victorian sexual health advocates.

Many accounts testify to the quality of care provided at Maroondah, although the matters I discussed in Chapter 4 about unprofessional and criminal conduct by some doctors there before 2013 must be acknowledged. So too must the clinic's inability to accommodate patients overnight once the procedure had been instigated. Many patients spent the night before the surgical procedure in a local motel. Sydney activist Viv, who was associated with the All Options referral service in the early 2000s, recalled:

> ... [Schulberg's] nurse unit manager, she was a lovely woman ... she was an older woman and had been through the '60s backyard abortion days ... she was completely authorised by him to give reduced fees and I could get on the phone to her and get the cost cut down massively or them just accepting the Medicare bulk billing, even though

it was going be like a four-day procedure. And we would be putting in the cost of the return train trip.

GP Alex, who worked as a FIFO doctor there from 2013, recalled in 2017 that the transition from Schulberg's regime to Marie Stopes' had been rocky. New arrangements included changes in governance, new policies and procedures, new equipment, and the employment of anaesthetists who were Fellows of their college.[85] Eventually, however, staffing stabilised, management was happier and Alex was comfortable saying to me, 'It's been really good.' Angela Williamson, who travelled from Tasmania, described the clinic in 2018, writing: 'It's discreet. It makes sense. It feels right. I'm no longer being judged. I'm safe'. The staff were 'amazing'.[86]

As in all private clinics, fees at Maroondah increased with weeks of pregnancy. Patients were required to pay half the cost of the procedure before being given an appointment, and the remainder on the first day. Travel and accommodation costs, including for a support person in some cases, were extra.[87] Some patients had funding support. Alex recalled, 'We sometimes see some from Darwin who are funded by Darwin Hospital, Cairns Sexual Health fund a few people, we had somebody from Tasmania who had some sort of funding recently as well.' But in general, the clinic didn't tend to see patients 'who are desperate but haven't got money.'

I asked Alex in 2016 if they thought the clinic made money: 'I don't know. I can't see how it could. The expenses are high.' In any case, in the context of the challenges of COVID-19, the clinic closed in early 2021. As noted, some Marie Stopes clinics in other states provide abortions for psychosocial reasons to 22 weeks, and the RWH in Melbourne can offer some late abortions for psychosocial reasons, but not always for patients outside Victoria or those on temporary visas, and the pressure of increased demand is felt. Some WA patients are travelling to Brisbane to the MSI clinic there but there remains a gap in late abortion provision.[88]

Late Thinking

There is more to public and community understanding of late abortion than is aired in debates around law reform and/or when anti-abortion actors attempt to limit or obstruct it. The survey of public opinion conducted by Lachlan de Crespigny and colleagues in 2008 showed that those who supported late abortion without qualification and those for whom it 'depend[ed] on the circumstances' totalled 69 per cent for second trimester abortion and 48 per cent for third trimester.[89] When Monica Cations and colleagues surveyed opinion in SA in 2019, 63 per cent supported it in all circumstances, and a further 21 per cent 'when the woman and her health care team decide it is necessary'.[90] While the question is clearly key, there is evidence that public attitudes to late abortion have become more liberal in the last decades.

This is reflected in the public positions of the major relevant medical organisations and law reform bodies. RANZCOG's 2019 statement on 'Late Termination of Pregnancy', first endorsed in 2016, begins by saying that 'The College recognises special circumstances where late abortion (beyond 20 weeks of gestation) may be regarded by the managing clinicians and the patient as the most appropriate option in the particular circumstance'.[91] AMA South Australia's submission to SALRI stated that 'A pregnant individual should be able to decide their own best course of action, regardless of gestation'.[92] The VLRC's Model C and SALRI's own preferred position proposed a model of reform that included no reference to gestational stage at all, and this position was also put forward by many who supported decriminalisation. My suggested narrative of the increasing liberal thinking in medical and legal positions is checked, however, by Erica Millar's critical assessment of the three law reform bodies' reports on abortion. She argues that their approaches 'reified the presentation of abortion as, primarily, a medical or intractable moral issue ... [rendering] later abortion meaningful through the norm of foetal viability'.[93]

Of equal interest and significance is the representation of late abortion in popular culture and news media. Stories of women who have had late abortions have appeared in mainstream media throughout the period 1990–2022, although neither frequently nor regularly, often in the context of decriminalisation.[94] During the SA campaign for decriminalisation, in 2021 a double-page newspaper story featured two couples who had had a diagnosis of foetal anomaly. One chose abortion; the other chose to go to full term.[95] Screen representations of late abortions are relatively new. *After Tiller* is a 2013 documentary about the four remaining private providers of third trimester surgical abortions in the US following the murder of George Tiller. Maddie Parry's 2015 *Inside the Clinic* features interviews with patients and staff at Maroondah. The award-winning one-woman play *19 Weeks*, written by Emily Steel and based on her own experience of an abortion at 19 weeks after a foetal diagnosis of Down syndrome, first played in Adelaide in 2017, toured nationally in 2018 and was made into a film which premiered in 2023. Julia Hales' documentary *The Upside*, which is presented by Hales who has Down syndrome, screened on ABC television in 2020. It raises awareness about and normalises people with Down syndrome, and includes an extended discussion of the approximately 90 per cent of people who decide to end a pregnancy following a diagnosis of Down syndrome and an interview with a woman who took that path.

Frequently, late abortion patients are defended and humanised via references to diagnosis of foetal anomaly, rendering the abortion 'tragic' because the pregnancy was initially wanted. This reproduces a long history of eugenically inflected pro-natal discourse that recuperates abortion to moral virtue by celebrating the desirability of (usually white) maternity which must 'tragically' be sacrificed because of the undesirability of disability.[96] Disability advocates for people with Down syndrome and writers who draw on critical disability studies challenge the ways in which both the approaches of health professionals and much pro-choice and feminist discourse regarding prenatal tests and late abortion are built on 'stereotypes of people with disabilities, or parenting people with disabilities'.[97] Down Syndrome Australia's submission to the Disability Royal

Commission stated that once presented with a diagnosis of Down syndrome, 'families are often pressured to make a decision to terminate even when this goes against their personal beliefs', and reported both 'negative language' and a lack of support from medical professionals. The submission noted that many representations of life with a child with Down syndrome are 'at odds with research findings and the experience of most families', and describes these circumstances as 'another form of violence, abuse and neglect within the health system for people with disabilities and their families'.[98] A similar argument is made by Intersex Human Rights Australia who challenge the elimination of 'the diversity of human existence' when foetal intersex variations are identified and eliminated in IVF and by abortion.[99]

Conclusion

The legacy of historical meaning that has framed abortion through dominant cultural representations of gender and the pregnant body, amplified by the anti-abortion movement's focus on late abortion, weighs particularly heavily on those who need late abortions and those who provide them. Legal exceptionalising, patient autonomy being overridden by medical authority and the assumption that a pregnant person must and will become a mother, or parent, are all intensified in relation to late abortion. If the hierarchy of deserving and undeserving in relation to late abortion has a particular bent, it is that being deserving comes at the cost of throwing people with disability and other anomalies under the bus.

The challenges around gaining access to late abortion services are also familiar. They can be hard to find, the sustainability of the workforce is precarious, and having money and the capacity to travel may mean the difference between getting the abortion you want and having to unwillingly continue a pregnancy. The capacity to choose which method of abortion you will access depends on system issues that map onto the reason for the abortion. For those deciding on abortion following a diagnosis of foetal anomaly, a surgical service will not always be offered—certainly not after 20 weeks—and the provision of foeticide for abortion by induction is uneven. And while late surgical abortions in private clinics are usually free of the bureaucracy and sometimes judgement that can accompany late abortions in hospitals, they are expensive.

As I noted in the Introduction there are differences for the pregnant person who has and the provider who delivers a late abortion. Experience of these differences is an effect of the surrounding cultural, social, legal, clinical and institutional environments. A well-trained, experienced and supported doctor will think and feel differently about their practice of late abortion than one who does not have these advantages. And the experience of each person who seeks a late abortion will vary at every point along their journey depending on the particularity of their embodied experience and the degree of autonomy, support and decision-making power they enjoy.

The ways in which some differences are understood must be challenged. The paths by which certain numbers found their way into the Acts that decriminalised abortion make it evident that the six different numbers dotted along a spectrum from 0 to 24 weeks—seven if we include the NT's legislation between 2017 and 2021—that distinguish between early and late abortions in Australian jurisdictions are neither clinical nor ethical ones. They are political numbers alone.

The distinction between psychosocial reasons for requesting a late abortion and foetal anomaly reasons is also a cultural, social and political artefact. The routinisation of prenatal testing and the cultural environments in which these are offered and considered are as much value-laden environments as they are sites of pure scientific truth, and patients' responses to tests that show foetal anomaly are determined by individual and family differences, which may be spiritual, religious and/or ethical, and by their social and institutional contexts, as critiques by disability advocates make clear. For this reason, we should think of all decisions to seek a late abortion as being prompted by psychosocial considerations—better described as subjective considerations—and as being no less 'justifiable' because of this.

Ethical discussion about late abortions may be intensified, but as in all discussion of the ethics of abortion, the question is really 'Whose ethics apply?'. The later in pregnancy a person seeks an abortion—particularly after the upper limit that determines access in their immediate environment—the more their status as an ethical subject diminishes and becomes secondary to the ethical and legal authority of the law, doctors, committees and/or hospital managements, or to their socio-economic status. The very lack of accessibility to late abortion embodies an ethical stance. The need of the pregnant person is not a priority. They will have to pay.

The last 'truth' of late abortions in Australia that I wish to unsettle concerns their proportion of all abortions conducted in Australia, and is facilitated by contemplation of the difference between the WA and SA figures for 2018 that I noted at the start of this chapter. This is the difference between an environment defined by legal and committee-driven restrictions (WA) and one in which publicly provided abortions have been available for psychosocial and foetal reasons, to almost 24 weeks and 23 weeks respectively (SA). The WA figure of 1.1 per cent in 2018, which represents eighty-three abortions, also reflects the exclusion of those residents who accessed abortion services interstate. If WA enjoyed the same access to abortions after 20 weeks as SA, by rough calculation the number of abortions performed there would have been 158. And this determination of proportion based on the limits on what is accessible in each state of course applies across the country. Pro-choice advocates should be prepared to state that improving access to late abortion may lead to a growth in the number, and their proportion of all abortions, performed.

The distinction between early and late abortions in Australia has solidified since 2008. Of the five pieces of successful abortion law reform nationwide between 1990 and 2008—three in the ACT, one in WA and one in Tasmania—only one introduced an upper limit. The self-evidently anti-abortion law in the ACT in 1998 did not introduce an upper limit. After Victoria introduced an upper limit in 2008, every other jurisdiction followed suit, and until the NT in

2021 all have come in under the Victorian limit of 24 weeks. It would appear that anti-abortion activism, conservativism particularly among doctors, and parliamentary decision-making that proposes or accepts the need for upper limits have opened up a flank from which the idea that it is legitimate and necessary to divide the time of pregnancy has been promulgated.

It has been claimed that introducing upper limits into the law of those jurisdictions where they had not previously existed—i.e., all but SA and the NT—means that the conditions of late abortion's legality are now clearly defined. This invites the question of whether decriminalisation has seen any increase in or improvement of the accessibility of late abortions. The answer is mixed, but mostly no. In the smaller jurisdictions, the lack of health resources in general for procedures for which demand is small may outweigh abortion-specific considerations, and at the time of writing it is too soon to tell what will happen in SA. The moves towards the expansion and improvement of late abortion services in hospitals in Queensland and Victoria started, respectively, well before decriminalisation and some time after. And I have found no detailed discussion of this matter in NSW. However, the decline in surgical services around the country in general as early medical abortion expands as a proportion of all abortions conducted could have a flow-on effect for late abortion in terms of there being a smaller pool of private providers with the necessary surgical skill available even for early pregnancies. The closure of Maroondah, which was unrelated to decriminalisation, has meant a contraction in access for those outside Victoria, even if only for a small number of patients.

As I write, however, there are positive signs. The RANZCOG program to train specialists in sexual and reproductive health care, though still in its infancy, is a flickering light on the horizon. And the historical and current ongoing provision of and improvement in services at the RBWH in Queensland, the RWH in Victoria and the PAC in SA—and possibly, more quietly, elsewhere too—is encouraging. If decriminalisation gathers energy in WA, it is possible that the current, restrictive 20-week system there may be relaxed. The surgical provision of late abortions in private clinics also seems to be holding, and hospitals, private providers and health policy-makers know that the adequate provision of late abortion is supported in law and in public opinion, although I see little sign that the claims of people with disability are being heeded in terms of how such services are represented.

In an ideal world, structural features and system delays that lead to people seeking late abortions would be addressed. In the last part of our interview in 2017, Lil said of 'the second trimester people' that they are often 'at either end of their reproductive lives.' She noted 'other confounding factors, drug, alcohol, often—and so I don't think those things are going away any time soon.' Prenatal testing is also a constant, as are the dilemmas it produces. The fact that only a small number of people need late abortions is no reason to allow governments, hospitals and the medical profession to deny them reproductive justice.

Conclusion

As I approached the final stages of writing this book, the US Supreme Court overturned the 1973 *Roe v Wade* ruling that had given the right to abortion constitutional protection. The rally held in Adelaide to protest the overturning of *Roe* attracted around 5000 people, predominantly young, displaying all manner of creative homemade placards. It was a high-energy affair. It took place just one week before SA's decriminalisation legislation would finally, after sixteen months of delay while government regulations to accompany it were drawn up, be implemented. One of the speakers mentioned this at the rally, and a cheer went up, but it paled in comparison to the outrage at *Roe*'s defeat in the Supreme Court. I understand that it's hard to get excited about regulations, and many have credited the response to *Roe* with enlivening pro-choice action in Australia, but I found myself wishing that the crowd's passion was focused as much on the conditions under which abortion is available in Australia as it was on events in the US, and how these need to be, and can be, changed.

Access to high quality abortion services in Australia is by many metrics good—for those who are well informed, have cash to hand and entitlement to Medicare. Living in a capital city is a bonus. But the system of neoliberal abortion fails many. Often summarised as a 'postcode lottery', it is not chance that determines who will have easy access to a service. Based on the economics and geography of access alone, the system creates reproductive injustice for about one-third of all people who have an abortion, and for all those who have no choice but to continue an unwanted pregnancy. These are often people who are already severely marginalised by poverty, geography, isolation, youth, lack of internet literacy or connection, lack of Medicare entitlement, violent and coercive relationships, racism, ableism, homophobia and transphobia, and by abortion's own internal 'other': presenting 'late'. My hope is that this book will increase readers' awareness of how the system works and contextualise the change that is needed to make access to abortion care more affordable, accessible and culturally appropriate. The change from criminal law to legislated regulation through health law in Australia needs to be better understood, and so do the ways in which anti-abortion ideas can be promoted through ostensibly pro-choice discourse. The battle for affordable, accessible and appropriate abortion care in Australia is far from over.

It is not that there's no longer any need for discussion and analysis of politics, law and ethics. But public discussion and scholarly analysis have to date not sufficiently attended to the system of abortion provision. What I hope this book shows is that politics, law and ethics are important not only because they bear on the abstract right to have an abortion, but because they are embedded in the macro- and micropolitics of service provision.

I wrote in the Introduction about the 'rationalities of government' that create the conditions under which abortion services are provided, and referred to what political theorists Rose and Miller have described as the 'vast array of petty managers of social and subjective existence' who embody and implement these rationalities.[1] The book is full of stories of such petty managers, who have taken it upon themselves to determine the conditions of abortion provision. (I reserve the term here for those who repeat the historic pattern of resistance to reproductive rights). To identify the rationalities of government and the ways they are contested and changed, however, let us return to the three main players in the healthcare system in Australia – the state, doctors and the private market.[2]

The state has overlapped with the market and the professions to shape the meaning and provision of abortion federally through Medicare, the TGA and the PBS, and at state and territory level through law and the criminal justice system, the regulation of clinics and health care in general, PATS schemes, and the provision of abortion care in public hospitals and public-funded community healthcare clinics. In the last thirty years the state has moved in multiple directions. The continuation of the Medicare rebate has made private services affordable for many, and this must be noted, although there are calls for a more adequate rebate for early medical abortion. The TGA and PBS have enabled the widespread introduction of early medical abortion, albeit through an exceptionalising regulatory system that renders it unnecessarily surveilled and constrained on ideological, not clinical, grounds. The states and territories have wound back the criminalisation of abortion, although in every case also instituting new forms of regulation through health law. While decriminalisation may have put an end to the threat of criminal prosecution of people who seek abortions and doctors who perform them, abortion continues to be legally exceptionalised and there may be as yet unknown traps in the new regulatory frameworks it has delivered.

Notwithstanding small growths in public commitment to the provision of abortion in some jurisdictions and more significant implementation of change and improvement in others the national rate of the public provision of abortion services is probably not much better now than it was in 1990, if at all. The devolution of care to early medical abortion in primary care and the contracting of private clinics by public hospitals complicates this measurement but even so public provision is shamefully low. Decriminalisation has made little difference overall, and the least difference in the most populous states. At the policy, hospital and public clinic level, the pronatalist rationality that Janet Holmes à Court explained in 1989—that women seeking abortions are exceptions, other to those who have a genuine call on hospital care and other to birthing women, that they place an unjustified burden on the hospital and that doctors cannot be made to perform abortions—is still present. Holmes à Court saw no problem with the policy of referring women to a private service where they would be treated at their own expense. The intensified discussion of motherhood and abortion through the prism of white supremacy during the Howard years revived the whiteness of this pronatalism.[3] In this rationality, abortion is the problem. But of course, while it is underpinned by disapproval of white women refusing motherhood, it is those who are socially and economically most removed from white middle-class privilege who have the most difficulty accessing abortion care.

This kind of pronatalist thinking may be widely countered by popular pro-choice sentiment, but it continues as an expression of government thinking. Why have most public hospitals and public health clinics not provided abortion services over the last thirty years? Because governments have not expected them to provide; hospital managements have not expected O&G departments to provide; and doctors who have not expected to provide abortion care have not been confronted with any other expectations or requirements—except, from time to time, by patients.

In SA and the NT public provision was the norm in 1990, and in 1992 Adelaide's PAC became a unique and horizon-expanding model of public provision. The persistence of this public care, and its improvement in the immediate wake of decriminalisation in the NT, must be appreciated. But even here public provision has not solved all problems, especially for those in rural, regional and remote areas, and the challenges of resourcing and restructuring in the public sector, which can fall disproportionately on abortion provision, cannot be ignored. As GP Ingrid told me of the public system in SA, 'abortion has a lot of friends, there are feminists dotted all over the place who actually do want to help and support and if you can find them, you can toggle together a service, but it's always very contingent.' Even in jurisdictions and individual hospitals where public provision of abortion is entrenched, it has always at least partially rested on key individuals who advocate for and promote the expectation that abortion care is not only health care but a public responsibility.

We may be at a turning point with respect to public policy and public provision but this history of the last thirty years presents a system of abortion provision overseen by the state which has created reproductive injustice for many. The commitment of the state to reproductive rights has been half-hearted. The status of those who seek abortion services as *citizens* is highly variable; many struggle to exercise the right to health care that should be their entitlement or to experience a sense of belonging to a community that provides for its members. Those without Medicare entitlement are mostly literally excluded (except, from mid-2023, in the ACT).

The book has also introduced readers to *the doctors* who for the last thirty years have provided abortion services in Australia. Nurses, midwives and Aboriginal and Torres Strait Islander Health Workers may be notionally poised to displace doctors as the future of abortion provision in primary health care, but there's a lot of legislation and regulation to unpick and training to provide to these workforces before this materialises. In the meantime, the medical profession's exclusive authority over the practice of abortion and, after varying upper limits, over the decision to allow abortion remains intact.

A lot has changed in the last thirty years in doctors' relationship to abortion. Providers are more likely to be women than they were in the 1990s, and so are those leading the development of provision in public hospitals, in the medical bodies and in public debate. The image of publicly identified abortion-providing doctors has changed, with the male 'mavericks' and 'cowboys' who had experienced the illegal era or been trained by doctors who had, and who were at the forefront of the growth of services in the 1990s, giving way to 'women's docs' like Caroline de Costa, the PAC's Ea Mulligan, the RWH's Paddy Moore, and Uniting Church leader Carol Portmann to name only a few. MSI Australia's Philip Goldstone and Catriona Melville also lead and the doctors who have run clinics for twenty or thirty years or more in WA, Queensland, the ACT, NSW and Victoria, and others who have kept services alive over long periods in public hospitals, should also be acknowledged. Increasingly, abortion-providing doctors are delivering quality care, and there are few complaints from patients. In a media interview in 2019 Moore commented on generational change among an 'increasing number of junior doctors [who] see abortions as "bread and butter medicine"'. Her own experience of change means that 'she no longer finds it difficult to talk about what she does'.[4] These doctors are supported by a robust body of medical research that supports clinical practice. These are encouraging signs of change.

The book has also introduced a range of doctors who fit the label of 'petty managers', including those—found most consequentially in rural areas—GPs who oppose abortion and have refused to assist at all (behaviour which is now unlawful), those in public hospitals who attempt to obstruct provision, those who have provided one form of abortion but withheld information about other kinds, those who have assisted in procedures but refused to sign forms, those who do not require their students to learn about abortion, and those who sit on ethics committees and Termination Review Panels to judge whether a patient's request for an abortion will be granted. The low rates of GPs registering to become prescribers of early medical abortion is the most material evidence we have of the medical profession's ongoing reticence around providing abortion care. Most doctors are pro-choice, and the reticent majority may simply be uncertain, or too busy to register, but in any case, they enjoy cultural immunity from any expectation that they will do so.

At the institutional level, the persistently uneven training for medical students remains a barrier to the creation of a sustainable abortion-providing workforce. Although RANZCOG is taking steps to address this problem, given that most providers of surgical abortions are GPs and that it is this group who, it is hoped, will increasingly be prescribing early medical abortion, it is undergraduate medical students in universities and teaching hospitals, and existing GPs, that most need to be prepared to provide it. And the arguably unnecessary legislative specification of the doctor's right to not perform an abortion, which is supported by all relevant medical bodies, can operate as a form of convenient as well as conscientious objection.

The status of those who seek abortion as *patients* thus remains mixed. Once a person has found an abortion provider they will usually be in good hands, although some will not experience culturally appropriate care, but the journey to get there is often fraught, especially when there is no local GP to assist, or no local provider, or no doctor able or willing to perform late abortions. In any case, the authority of the patient's status is trumped by that of doctors, who have historically chosen to perform or not perform abortions, to refer or not refer, with impunity. That is, the medical profession's relationship to reproductive rights is on its own terms.

The *private healthcare market* is where abortion services have been and still are predominantly provided. For the private clinics, and MSI Australia inasmuch it is a private provider, this means that profit-making rationality prevails, which explains the historical scarcity of clinics in small markets. The economics of provision are also key for GPs in private practice, where practice managers calculate whether and how they can receive adequate remuneration for early medical abortion. Over the last thirty years criminalisation, professional isolation, workforce shortages, protesters and associated security costs, insurance issues and stigma-related difficulties have all been imposts on the private provision of abortion that other small private healthcare businesses have not faced.

The apparent increase in the abortion rate during the 1990s and its decline in the twenty-first century, which was accompanied by an expansion and then contraction in the number of clinics, saw major change in the private sector. Since 2000, Marie Stopes reconfigured the sector, attaining clear market dominance, if not the monopoly that some describe. Marie Stopes' successful application to the TGA to import mifepristone and its listing by the PBS in 2013 have likewise reconfigured the nature of the services being provided, opening up opportunities for small-scale provision but putting pressure on surgical services in the face of declining demand and upgraded standards for day hospitals. More recently, COVID-19 accelerated a turn to telehealth abortion. It is debatable whether privately provided abortion has become more affordable over the last thirty years. It probably has not. Competition may have diminished as Marie Stopes grew, but its competitive edge and growth have been the product not of lower prices but of its size.

Private providers and GPs exist outside of the institutionalised cultural imperatives that encourage government and community sector practices of cultural inclusion and acknowledgement of diversity (although MSI Australia is a leader in this context), but historically they are less likely to produce abortion stigma than the public sector. However, while the private sector welcomes its patients, the status the neoliberal system of provision in Australia bestows on those who need abortions is that of *consumer*. Notwithstanding the efforts of private providers who can and have bulk-billed or prioritised affordability, as in all areas of consumption, choice is there for those who can pay. For those who cannot pay, who find it hard to access information, who reside a long way from a service, or for whom abortion services are culturally unsafe or unintelligible, it is only marginally accessible.

A fourth player of abortion care provision in Australia also needs to be identified. This is the non-government or community sector (which although government funded has operated through a distinct rationality). Children by Choice, family planning organisations and women's community health centres have all been crucially important over the years as sources of information about abortion, and in some instances of counselling and professional training. Some state family planning organisations have become abortion providers, as have some Aboriginal Community Controlled Health Organisations. These organisations have also been leaders in advocating for abortion services, as has Marie Stopes. A fifth player could also be identified, at a stretch—the community activists and organisations, and healthcare workers in their own unpaid time, who have mobilised both for law reform and to connect with others, build community and support the cause. In this group the neoliberal delegation of responsibility to the individual (the champions) cross-fertilises the tradition of political activism.

While this book has not been about the people who seek abortions, they have been its touchstone, and I hope I have shown that while they are subject to the market, medical knowledge and the clinical and social authority of doctors, not to mention the inadequacies of the public health system, they are not passive recipients. Robbie's story of the Cairns woman whose determination to use methotrexate, with or without medical supervision, nudged the sexual health clinic into providing early medical abortion stands out, but the book also relates many other instances in which people needing abortions have put pressure on healthcare services. People with economic and cultural privilege may exercise this agency with more ease, but desperately poor and marginalised people have also persisted.

The book rests on the principle that 'abortion care is health care'. The degree to which this notion has traction reflects the achievements of activists and advocates and healthcare providers and researchers over thirty years. This principle defines the problem as the adequacy of access to good-quality, safe and affordable services. While the need for culturally appropriate services—for Indigenous people, people with disabilities and LGBTIQ people, for example— is on the agenda, it has been slower to gain recognition.

Like any principle, 'abortion care is health care' is historically and geographically specific, and can arguably have the effect of re-centring the medicalisation of abortion to the detriment of other principles such as human rights, bodily autonomy and self-determination, and reproductive justice. It is therefore important to keep an open mind and pay attention to times and places where 'abortion care is health care' might limit the apprehension of constraint, or of new horizons. As an alternative, however, I am reluctant to embrace the idea of 'self-managed abortion', for example, as an organising principle in countries where abortion is legal, because while accessing abortion pills through telehealth, through the internet or directly from a pharmacy in the same way as emergency contraception will suit many, the notion of the self-managing responsible self is too close to the neoliberal imagining of the subject—the independent individual who is responsible for themselves—for my comfort. In the context of an existing system of neoliberal abortion, the 'self-managed' abortion risks becoming the only option, rather than the preferred one.

At the start of this book I asked, 'What should be our priorities for change?' While I hope that it has stimulated critical thinking in response to this question, the book is not a vehicle for policy direction, or for activist or advocacy strategy. Documents from academic researchers, key NGOs and activist organisations, and government inquiries have provided and will continue to provide good and detailed answers. For my money, federal and state government responsibility for universal access to abortion care, the elimination of exceptionalising laws and regulations, increased public provision, more and better training for doctors and all healthcare workers, and unleashing the potential of nurses, midwives and Aboriginal and Torres Strait Islander Health Workers to provide abortion care makes a good list of starting points. Grounding our thinking in the needs of those seeking abortions who have been most marginalised by the current system of care is paramount, and this means creating services that are culturally appropriate for all and sensitive to histories of trauma, as well as economically and geographically accessible, at whatever stage of pregnancy.

Finally, we must remain aware that *abortion* —especially when represented as too many, or too late, or for the wrong reasons, or too controversial—*is not the problem*. Access to safe and affordable and culturally appropriate abortion care is not the only requirement for reproductive justice but it is necessary. The story I told at the end of the Introduction related how, some forty years ago, an abortion clinic enabled my friend's future. Since then, many abortion providers and related professionals and advocates have enabled the desired futures of many others who have sought abortions, if unevenly across structures of marginalisation, and not without significant difficulties. Knowing this history not only gives a sense of where we have come from, and who has gone before. It can be part of imagining a collective future where providing abortion care is a responsibility of the state and of all those involved in relevant health care, and where holding government, the professions and the market to account does not fall only to the committed few.

Notes

Introduction

1   Catherine Armitage, 'Abortion: The New Debate', *The Weekend Australian*, 17–19 December 1994, 25.
2   Barbara Baird, 'Maternity, Whiteness and National Identity'.
3   Kerry Arabena, 'Preachers, Policies and Power'.
4   Catherine Kevin and Karen Agutter, 'Failing "Abyan", "Golestan" and "the Estonian Mother"'.
5   Elizabeth Tilley, Jan Walmsley, Sarah Earle and Dorothy Atkinson, '"The Silence is Roaring"'.
6   Baird, 'Maternity, Whiteness and National Identity'.
7   Ibid.
8   Erica Millar, *Happy Abortions*.
9   Rebecca Albury, 'Too Many, Too Late and the Adoption Alternative', 3.
10 Sarah M Cameron and Ian McAllister, *Trends in Australian Political Opinion*, 117.
11 Barbara Baird, 'The Futures of Abortion'.
12 For example, see the special issue of *Health and Human Rights Journal* in June 2017.
13 Children by Choice, 'Abortion Rates in Australia'.
14 Lindsay Krassnitzer, 'The Public Health Sector and Medicare'.
15 See the National Aboriginal Community Controlled Health Organisations publications.
16 Krassnitzer, 'The Public Health Sector', 32.
17 Department of Health, *Victorian Women's Sexual and Reproductive Health Plan 2022–30*.
18 Australian Government Department of Health, *National Women's Health Strategy 2020–2030*, 24.
19 See Paul Lancaster, Jishan Huang and Elvis Pedisich, *Australia's Mothers and Babies 1991* and subsequent Australian Institute of Health and Welfare reports.
20 Melissa Graham, Hayley McKenzie, Greer Lawrence and Ruth Klein, 'Women's Reproductive Choices in Australia', 342–6.
21 Larissa Behrendt, Chris Cunneen and Terri Libesman, *Indigenous Legal Relations in Australia*; Leticia Funston and Sigrid Herring, 'When Will the Stolen Generations End?'.
22 Susan Goodwin and Kate Huppatz, *The Good Mother*.
23 Belinda Barnett, The Perinatal Is Political.

24   Alfredo Saad-Filno and Deborah Johnston, *Neoliberalism: A Critical Reader*.
25   Eileen Willis, Louise Reynolds and Trudy Rudge, 'Understanding the Australian Health Care System'.
26   Carol Johnson, *Governing Change*.
27   Marian Sawer, *The Ethical State?*.
28   Chris Miller and Lionel Orchard, *Australian Public Policy*.
29   Emily Baker, 'Launceston Abortion Centre to Close', *The Examiner*, 11 May 2016; Rhiana Witson, 'Tasmania Still Without a Low-Cost Abortion Facility as Premier Is Challenged on "See Your GP" Advice', *ABC News*, 7 November 2018.
30   Mridula Shankar, Kirsten I Black, Philip Goldstone, Safeera Hussainy, Danielle Mazza, Kerry Petersen, Jayne Lucke and Angela Taft, 'Access, Equity and Costs of Induced Abortion Services in Australia'.
31   Peter Miller and Nikolas Rose, *Governing the Present*.
32   Rosalind Gill and Christina Scharff, *New Femininities*.
33   Rebecca Stringer, *Knowing Victims*.
34   Joanne Baker, 'The Ideology of Choice'.
35   Kate Gleeson, 'The Limits of "Choice"'.
36   *The Sydney Morning Herald*, 'Abortion Couple Not Aware That They Broke the Law', 19 September 2009.
37   Rebecca Albury, *The Politics of Reproduction*, 19–24.
38   Millar, *Happy Abortions*.
39   Lynette Finch, *The Classing Gaze*.
40   Margaret Simons, 'Duty of Care'.
41   Wendy Brown, 'American Nightmare'.
42   Marion Maddox, *God Under Howard*.
43   Barbara Baird, 'Abortion Politics During the Howard Years'.
44   Margie Ripper, 'Abortion: The Shift in Stigmatisation'.
45   Melinda Tankard Reist, *Giving Sorrow Words*.
46   Baird, 'Maternity, Whiteness and National Identity', 202–03.
47   *AM*, 'Dana Vale Focuses on Muslims in RU486 Debate', radio program, *ABC Radio*, 14 February 2006.
48   Giovanni Torre, 'NT Aboriginal Justice Agreement Director Shines Light on Systemic Racism at Inquest into Killing of Kumanjayi Walker', *National Indigenous Times*, 6 March 2023.
49   Stefania Siedlecky and Diana Wyndham, *Populate and Perish*.
50   Caroline de Moel-Mandel, Melissa Graham and Ann Taket, 'Expert Consensus on a Nurse-Led Model of Medication Abortion Provision in Regional and Rural Victoria, Australia'.
51   Susie Allanson, *Murder on His Mind*.
52   Susie Allanson with Lizzie O'Shea, *Empowering Women*.
53   Carol Bacchi and Susan Goodwin, *Poststructural Policy Analysis*.
54   Miller and Rose, *Governing the Present*.
55   Ibid., 4, 5.
56   Loretta J Ross, 'Reproductive Justice as Intersectional Feminist Activism'.
57   The Flinders University Social and Behavioural Research Ethics Committee approved the oral history project on 7 March 2013 (no. 5958).
58   Robert Perks and Alistair Thomson (eds), *The Oral History Reader*.
59   For example, see Elizabeth Price, Leah S Sharman, Heather A Douglas, Nicola Sheeran and Genevieve A Dingle, 'Experiences of Reproductive Coercion in Queensland women'.
60   For example, see Angela J Taft, Mridula Shankar, Kirsten I Black, Danielle Mazza,

Safeera Hussainy, and Jayne C Lucke, 'Unintended and Unwanted Pregnancy in Australia'.

61 Julia McQuillan, Arthur L Griel and Karina M Shreffler, 'Pregnancy Intentions Among Women Who Do Not Try'.

62 Marian K Pitts, Murray Couch, Hunter Mulcare, Samantha Croy and Anne Mitchell, 'Transgender People in Australia and New Zealand'.

63 Willis, Reynolds and Rudge, 'Understanding the Australian Health Care System'.

Chapter 1 Neoliberal

1 NHMRC, *An Information Paper on Termination of Pregnancy in Australia*, 3–5; see also Lyndall Ryan, Margie Ripper and Barbara Buttfield, *We Women Decide*, 15–28. All reference to numbers of clinics and public and private hospital provision in this section are from these documents. Details added from other sources are acknowledged.

2 For works on health and neoliberalism, see Fran Baum, *The New Public Health*; Judith M Dwyer, 'Australian Health System Restructuring', 6; Gwendolyn Gray Jamieson, *Reaching for Health*, 266–9.

3 Rachel K Jones, Elizabeth Witwer and Jenna Jerman, *Abortion Incidence and Service Availability in the United States, 2017*; Rachel Jones, Ushma D Upadhyay and Tracy Weitz, 'At What Cost?'; Johanna Schoen, *Abortion After Roe*.

4 Patricia A Lohr, Jonathon Lord and Sam Rowlands, 'How Would Decriminalisation Affect Women's Health?', 47; Sally Sheldon, Gayle Davis, Jane O'Neill and Clare Parker, *The Abortion Act (1967)*, 116–118.

5 Alison McCulloch, *Fighting to Choose*.

6 Jo Wainer, 'Abortion as an Indicator of the Value of Women'.

7 Allanson with O'Shea, *Empowering Women*.

8 Susan Treloar, Emmi Snyder and Charles Kerr, 'Effect of a New Service on Women's Abortion Experience', 418.

9 Alison Anderson, 'The Abortion Struggle in Queensland', 8.

10 Siedlecky and Wyndham, *Populate and Perish*, 91.

11 Judy Petroechevsky, 'The Story of Children by Choice'.

12 Stephanie Grayston, 'Changing Attitudes and Services'.

13 Annabelle Chan et al., *Pregnancy Outcome in South Australia 1990*, Pregnancy Outcome Unit, Department of Human Services, Adelaide, 1991. There are two annual reports on South Australian abortion statistics – Pregnancy Outcome in South Australia and the report of the South Australian Abortion Reporting Committee. Recent reports are available online at Pregnancy Outcome Statistics, Wellbeing SA. Earlier reports are cited by author and are available on request from the department.

14 See Rosemary Pringle, *Sex and Medicine*, 69–96.

15 Carol Nader and David Wroe, 'Late Abortion: The Doctor's Defence', *The Age*, 14 October 2005.

16 Amanda Bryan, 'Shy of Retiring'.

17 Gynaecare; Clinic 66.

18 Blue Water Medical.

19 Margaret Kirkby, Discussion Paper.

20 Lee Barker, 'Establishing a Women's Controlled Abortion Clinic'.

21 L Hemmings, 'Medical Abortion in Tasmania'.

22 Baird, 'The Futures of Abortion'.

23 Leslie Cannold and Cait Calcutt, 'The Australian Pro-Choice Movement', 57.

24   NHMRC, *An Information Paper*.

25   Ibid., 55.

26   Petroechevsky, 'The Story of Children by Choice'.

27   Kirkby, Discussion Paper.

28   Ibid., 4.

29   Sheldon, Davis, O'Neill and Parker, *The Abortion Act (1967)*, 46, 116–18.

30   Bryan, 'Shy of Retiring'; Harriet Alexander, 'Oldest Sydney Abortion Clinic Closes its Doors', *The Sydney Morning Herald*, 3 September 2015.

31   Barbara Baird, 'Medical Abortion in Australia'.

32   Alexander, 'Oldest Sydney Abortion Clinic Closes its Doors'; see also Matt Smith, 'Fears Raised as One of Hobart's Two Abortion Clinic Closes', *The Mercury*, 19 July 2014.

33   NHMRC, *An Information Paper*, 20–1.

34   Ibid., 56.

35   See Children by Choice, 'Our History'.

36   Gynaecology Centres Australia.

37   See Louise A Keogh, Lyle C Gurrin and Patricia Moore, 'Estimating the Abortion Rate in Australia'.

38   *ABC News*, 'WA Government "Overlooked" Midland Abortion Clinic Issue', 12 June 2014.

39   Marie Stopes Australia, *Impact Report 2019*, 26.

40   Jacqueline Murdoch, Kirsten Thompson and Suzanne Belton, 'Rapid Uptake of Early Medical Abortions in the Northern Territory'.

41   Eileen Willis, Louise Reynolds and Trudy Rudge, 'Understanding the Australian Health Care System', 7–8; Fran Collyer, Karen Willis and Helen Keleher, 'The Private Health Sector and Private Health Insurance', 46–48.

42   Sandra G Downing, Colette Cashman and Darren B Russell, 'Ten Years On'.

43   Jane E Tomnay, Lauren Coelli, Ange Davidson, Alana Hulme-Chambers, Catherine Orr and Jane S Hocking, 'Providing Accessible Medical Abortion Services in a Victorian Rural Community'.

44   For links to the websites of the various state family planning organisations, see the Family Planning Alliance Australia website. Abortion provision by ACCHOs in NSW is uneven (Family Planning New South Wales, Women's Health NSW and Chair of Sexual and Reproductive Health Special Interest Group of RANZCOG, *Framework for Abortion Access in NSW*, 7).

45   Tomnay et al., 'Providing Accessible Medical Abortion Services', 179.

46   MS Health, Dispenser and Prescriber Program, December 2022 Update.

47   Paul Hyland, Elizabeth G Raymond and Erica Chong, 'A Direct-to-Patient Telemedicine Abortion Service in Australia'.

48   Rachel Clun, '"We Need to Be Able to Look After These Women": New Tele-Abortion Service to "Fill Gap" in Abortion Access', *The Sydney Morning Herald*, 25 October 2019.

49   Marie Stopes Australia, *Situational Report: Sexual and Reproductive Health Rights in Australia*, 5.

50   See Ryan, Ripper and Buttfield, *We Women Decide*, 159.

51   NHMRC, *An Information Paper*, 56; Brooke Calo, 'The Violence of Misinformation', 10–19.

52   *Report To The Minister For Health on the Review of Provisions of The Health Act 1911*, 56–9.

53   Sexual Health Quarters, 'Unintended Pregnancy'.

54   Lydia Mainey, Catherine O'Mullan and Kerry Reid-Searl, 'Unfit for Purpose'.

55 Barbara Baird and Erica Millar, 'More Than Stigma'.
56 1800 My Options.
57 Family Planning NSW, Talkline; NSW Government, Pregnancy Choices Helpline.
58 Susie Allanson, 'Pregnancy/Abortion Counselling'.
59 Annabelle Chan, Joan Scott, Anh-Minh Nguyen and Rosemary Keane, *Pregnancy Outcome in South Australia 2001,* 39; See Wellbeing SA, Pregnancy Outcome Statistics, for South Australian Abortion Reporting Committee, *Annual Report for the Year 2021,* 4.
60 Keogh, Gurrin and Moore, 'Estimating the Abortion Rate'.
61 Danielle Mazza, Cathy J Watson, Angela Taft, Jayne Lucke, Kevin McGeechan, Marion Haas, Kathleen McNamee, M Epi, Jeffrey F Peipert and Kirsten I Black, 'Increasing Long-Acting Reversible Contraceptives'; Luke E Grzeskowiak, Helen Calabretto, Natalie Amos, Danielle Mazza and Jenni Ilomaki, 'Changes in Use of Hormonal Long-acting Reversible Contraceptive Methods in Australia Between 2006 and 2018'.
62 Shankar et al., 'Access, Equity and Costs'.
63 See Wellbeing SA for South Australian Abortion Reporting Committee, *Annual Report for the Year 2018,* 9; M Galrao, M Hutchinson and A Joyce, *Induced Abortions in Western Australia 2016–2018,* 25–6.
64 NT Termination of Pregnancy Law Reform, 12 Month Interpretive Report.
65 Baker, 'Launceston Abortion Centre to Close'; Witson, 'Tasmania Still Without a Low-Cost Abortion Facility'.
66 David Johnston, 'Englehardt Street Clinic Closure After Recent NSW Government Decision to Create Exclusion Zones', *The Border Mail,* 14 September 2018.
67 Lily Nothling, 'With Closure of Marie Stopes Clinics, Regional Women Seeking an Abortion Will Now Find It Even Tougher', *ABC News,* 31 August 2021; Ange Lavoipierre and Stephen Smiley, 'Abortion and Reproductive Health Clinics Struggling with Stigma and Rising Costs', *ABC News,* 13 July 2021.
68 Marie Stopes Australia, *Situational Report.*
69 For decline in the period 1998–9 to 2002–3, see Parliament of Australia, *Research Brief: How Many Abortions are There in Australia?,* 7.
70 Louise A Keogh, Danielle Newton, Christine Bayly, Kelly McNamee, Anne Hardiman, Angela C Webster and Marie M Bismark, 'Intended and Unintended Consequences of Abortion Law Reform', 119.
71 QLRC (Queensland Law Reform Commission), *Review of Termination of Pregnancy Laws,* 37–8; Marie Stopes Australia, *Impact Report 2019*; Rob Inglis, 'Surgical Abortions to be Provided in Launceston and North-West Public Hospitals', *The Mercury,* 26 August 2021; Yvette Berry and Rachel Stephen-Smith, 'Canberrans to Have Free Access to Safe Abortion Services'.
72 Trish Hayes, Chanel Keane and Suzanne Hurley, 'Counselling "Late Women"'.
73 RANZCOG, 'Abortion'.
74 'About', SPHERE.
75 Josh Taylor, 'Australian Abortion and Contraceptive Provider's Ads Banned by Google', *The Guardian,* 15 December 2022.
76 Family Planning NSW et al., *Framework for Abortion Access in NSW,* 3.
77 Sally Sheldon, 'The Decriminalisation of Abortion', 363.
78 Lee Barker, 'Who Wields the Scalpel?', 91.
79 Simons, 'Duty of Care'.
80 Donna Wyatt and Katie Hughes, 'When Discourse Defies Belief'; Kirsty McLaren, 'The Emotional Imperative of the Visual'.
81 For Rockhampton and Adelaide, see Ryan et al., *We Women Decide,* 58–63, 71–86;

for Hobart, see Alison Ribbon, 'Abortion Clinic Site Row', *The Mercury*, 11 March 2002.

82   Rebecca Dean and Susie Allanson, 'Abortion in Australia'.

83   Allanson, *Murder on His Mind*.

84   Richard Yallop, 'Killing May Herald Arrival of US-style Violence', *The Australian*, 17 July 2001, 2.

85   NHMRC, *An Information Paper*.

86   Ibid., 7–9.

87   Kirkby, Discussion Paper, 2.

88   Shankar et al., 'Access, Equity and Costs', 4.

89   Arabena, 'Preachers, Policies and Power'; Trish Hayes, 'Reproductive Coercion and the Australian State'; Shankar et al., 'Access, Equity and Costs', 4; Multicultural Centre for Women's Health, *Data Report: The Sexual and Reproductive Health 2021*; Wendy Bacon, Pamela Curr, Carmen Lawrence, Julie Macken and Claire O'Connor, *Protection Denied, Abuse Condoned*, 8; Caroline de Costa, 'Medical Abortion for Australian Women'.

90   Arabena, 'Preachers, Policies and Power', 88–9; see also Sarah L Larkins, R Priscilla Page, Kathryn S Panaretto, Melvina Mitchell, Valerie Alberts, Suzanne McGinty and P Craig Veitch, 'The Transformative Potential of Young Motherhood', 553.

91   NHMRC, *An Information Paper*, 3, 14.

92   For detailed information on costs in NSW in 2020, see Family Planning NSW et al., *Framework for Abortion Access in NSW*, 8, and Caroline de Moel-Mandel and Julia M Shelley, 'The Legal and Non-Legal Barriers to Abortion Access in Australia', 114. Both give costs only as a range.

93   Children by Choice, 'How Much Does an Abortion Cost?'; Marie Stopes, 'Abortion Services'; Clinic 66, 'Abortion Online'.

94   NHMRC, *An Information Paper*, 7; Arabena, 'Preachers, Policies and Power', 88 n. 2.

95   Services Australia.

96   Susan Maury, 'Poverty in Australia in 2020'.

97   Family Planning NSW et al., *Framework for Abortion Access in NSW*, 8–9.

98   Selena Utting, Susan Stark and Nicola Sheeran, 'Hidden Women', slide 9.

99   Family Planning NSW et al., *Framework for Abortion Access in NSW*, 7.

100   For example, see Dundi Mitchell, María Nugent and Veronica Arbon, '"Shame and Blame"'; Zelalem B Mengesha, Janette Perz, Tinashe Dune and Jane Ussher, 'Refugee and Migrant Women's Engagement with Sexual and Reproductive Health Care in Australia'; Janet Kelly and Yoni Luxford, 'Yaitya Tirka Madlanna Warratinna'.

101   Murdoch, Thompson and Belton, 'Rapid Uptake of Early Medical Abortions', 974.

102   Mariyam Suha, Linda Murray, Deborah Warr, Jasmin Chen, Karen Block, Adele Murdolo, Regina Quiazon, Erin Davis and Cathy Vaughan, 'Reproductive Coercion as a Form of Family Violence', 7.

103   SPHERE, *2019–2021 Achievement Report*, 15.

104   Women With Disabilities Australia, *WWDA Submission on Sexual and Reproductive Rights of Women and Girls With Disability*, 11, 14.

105   Katja Mikhailovich and Kerry Arabena, 'Evaluating an Indigenous Sexual Health Peer Education Project'.

106   Family Planning NSW et al., *Framework for Abortion Access in NSW*.

Chapter 2 Public

1   NHMRC, *Information Paper*.
2   See Lancaster, Huang and Pedisich, *Australia's Mothers and Babies 1991*, and subsequent reports.
3   Shankar et al., 'Access, Equity and Costs', 3–4.
4   Philip Goldstone and Catriona Melville from Marie Stopes Australia, Paul Hyland who established the Tabbot Foundation, and Susie Allanson from the Fertility Control Clinic are notable exceptions.
5   Quoted in Justine Landis-Hanley, 'Choice Recognition', *The Saturday Paper*, 7–13 March 2020, 4.
6   Women's Electoral Lobby, Report to the Chairperson, Committee on the Elimination of Discrimination against Women (CEDAW), 5.
7   Gray Jamieson, *Reaching for Health*, 215, 245–54.
8   Suzanne Franzway, Dianne Court and RW Connell, *Staking a Claim*, 134.
9   Gray Jamieson, *Reaching for Health*, 250, 266.
10 Department of Community Services and Health, *National Women's Health Policy*, 29.
11 Working Party to Examine the Adequacy of Existing Services for Termination of Pregnancy and South Australian Health Commission, *Report of the Working Party*.
12 Louise Sampson, 'Australian Capital Territory Report'; Barker, 'Establishing a Women's Controlled Abortion Clinic'.
13 Barbara Baird, *I Had One Too*.
14 Ryan, Ripper and Buttfield, *We Women Decide*.
15 NHMRC, *An Information Paper*.
16 Ryan, Ripper and Buttfield, *We Women Decide*, x–xi; NHMRC, *An Information Paper*, 10–11.
17 Elizabeth Evatt, Felix Arnott and Anne Deveson, *Royal Commission into Human Relationships, Final Report, Volume 3*, 252–4.
18 Baird, 'Abortion Politics During the Howard Years'.
19 Margie Ripper and Lyndall Ryan, 'The Role of the "Withdrawal Method"', 313–18.
20 Michael Pusey, *Economic Rationalism in Canberra*, 9.
21 Hester Eisenstein, *Inside Agitators*, 184–203.
22 Sandy Edwards, Sue McKinnon, Jane Tassie and Vicki Toovey, 'Women's Health Centres – Survival and Future in a New Political Era', 42.
23 NHMRC, *An Information Paper*, 4. No figure was provided for the ACT.
24 Janet McCalman, *Sex and Suffering*.
25 VLRC, *Law of Abortion, Final Report*, 34–5.
26 Key Centre for Women's Health in Society, The University of Melbourne, Royal Women's Hospital, Family Planning Victoria, and Women's Health Victoria, *Abortion in Victoria. Where Are We?*.
27 Kirsten Black, Jane Fisher and Sonya Grover, 'Public Hospital Pregnancy Termination Services', 526.
28 VLRC, *Law of Abortion*, 34; Black, Fisher and Grover, 'Public Hospital Pregnancy Termination Services'.
29 Kerry Smith, 'Royal Women's Hospital Cuts Abortion Service', *Green Left*, 28 June 2018.
30 All figures are from the annual *Pregnancy Outcome in South Australia* reports produced by the Pregnancy Outcome Unit of SA Health and its predecessor and successor departments. See Wellbeing SA.
31 *David and Will*, 'Pregnancy Termination Concerns', radio program, presented by David Penberthy and Will Goodings, *5AA*, 19 July 2019.

32   For example, BR Pridmore and DG Chambers, 'Uterine Perforation During
      Surgical Abortion'; Ea C Mulligan, 'Striving For Excellence in Abortion Services';
      Dennis G Chambers, Ea C Mulligan, Anthony R Laver, Brownyn W Keller, Jane K
      Baird and Wye Y Herbert, 'Comparison of Four Perioperative Misoprostol
      Regimens'.

33   John Williams, David Plater, Anita Brunacci, Sarah Kapadia and Melissa Oxlad,
      Abortion: A Review of South Australian Law and Practice, 211–42.

34   Ea Mulligan and Hayley Messenger, 'Mifepristone in South Australia'.

35   Williams, Plater, Brunacci, Kapadia and Ozlad, *Abortion: A Review*.

36   Leah MacLennan, 'Central Adelaide Local Health Network Is a "Failing
      Organisation"', Administrators Tell Inquiry', *ABC News*, 11 February 2019.

37   Rebecca de Girolamo, 'Abortion Laws in South Australia: Why Is It Still a Crime?',
      Adelaide Now, 16 February 2019.

38   Suzanne Belton and Karen Dempsey, Termination of Pregnancy', 11; Carolyn
      Nickson, Julia Shelley and Anthony Smith, 'Use of Interstate Services for the
      Termination of Pregnancy in Australia'.

39   Suzanne Belton, Caroline de Costa and Andrea Whittaker, 'Termination of
      Pregnancy'.

40   Murdoch, Thompson and Belton, 'Rapid Uptake of Early Medical Abortions';
      Suzanne Belton, Georgia McQueen and Edwina Ali, 'Impact of Legislative Change
      on Waiting Time'.

41   Lauren Roberts, 'NT Abortion Waiting Times Decrease in Public Hospitals after
      2017 Law Reform', *ABC News*, 17 January, 2020.

42   Caroline de Costa, Darren B Russell, Naomi R de Costa, Michael Carrette and
      Heather M McNamee, 'Early Medical Abortion in Cairns, Queensland'.

43   Caroline de Costa, 'Early Medical Abortion in Australia'.

44   Anonymous, 'Just When You Thought It Was Safe …', 29.

45   Black, Fisher and Grover, 'Public Hospital Pregnancy Termination Services'.

46   The letter is appended to the Women's Electoral Lobby's Report to the Chairperson,
      CEDAW.

47   Ruth Greble, 'Western Australian Report'.

48   Aleisha Orr, 'Call to Dump Anti-Abortion Health Provider', *WAtoday*, 16 April
      2012.

49   Stephanie Dalzell, 'Final Steps Towards Private Abortion Services In Midland, Perth',
      ABC News; Estimates and Finance Operations Committee, *Question on Notice
      Supplementary Information*.

50   Annika Blau, 'In Good Faith', Background Briefing, *ABC RN*, 3 December 2022.

51   Galrao, Hutchinson and Joyce, *Induced Abortions in Western Australia 2016–2018*, 41.

52   A Cawley, 'Submission to the Inquiry into Therapeutic Goods Amendment'.

53   Baird, 'The Futures of Abortion'.

54   John Eddington, 'Conquering the Last Frontier'.

55   Barbara Baird, 'Tales of Mobility'; Adam Holmes, 'Fifteen Calls in Five Days: Barriers
      to Accessing Abortion in Bendigo Laid Bare', *The Courier*, 3 June 2017.

56   Caroline M de Costa, Darren B Russell and Michael Carrette, 'Views and Practices
      of Induced Abortion'.

57   Justine Landis-Hanley, 'Doctors Crippled by Religious Backlash', *Saturday Paper,* 29
      February–6 March 2020, 1.

58   Keogh et al., 'Intended and Unintended Consequences'.

59   Ben Smee, 'Queensland's Abortion Law Change Improved Access but "Postcode
      Lottery" Remains', *The Guardian*, 6 August 2019; Steven Miles, 'Abortion Legal in
      Queensland', Media Statement.

60 Smee, 'Queensland's Abortion Law Change'.
61 Personal communication with Pamela Doherty, 24 February 2020.
62 Personal communication with Kari Vallury, 29 March 2023.
63 NSW Health, For Health Professionals and Considering an Abortion; NSW Government, *Policy Directive*.
64 The current version is Queensland Government, Maternity and Neonatal Clinical Guideline Supplement.
65 QLRC, *Review of Termination of Pregnancy Laws*, 35–8.
66 Personal communication with Pamela Doherty, April 2016.
67 Department of Health and Human Services, Victoria State Government, *Women's Sexual and Reproductive Health*.
68 1800 My Options.
69 Department of Health and Human Services, Victoria State Government, *Victorian Women's Sexual and Reproductive Health Plan 2022–30*.
70 Dana Anderson, 'Tasmanian Public Hospitals to Offer Surgical Abortions', *The Examiner*, 26 August 2021; Women's Health Tasmania, Pregnancy Choices Information; personal communication with Jo Flanagan, 15 November 2022.
71 Romy Gilbert, 'ACT Government to Cover Abortion Costs From Next Year', *nine. com.au*, 4 August 2022; Tahlia Roy, 'ACT Becomes First Jurisdiction to Offer Free Abortions as Canberra Patients Shed Light on Troubling Experiences', *ABC News*, 20 April 2023.
72 Personal communication with Tim Bavinton, 11 April 2023; Women's Health Matters, *Recommendations Paper: Publicly Funded Abortion for the ACT*.
73 Amy Greenbank, 'Labor Promises Free Abortions, Pushes to Decriminalise Procedure in Federal Election Pitch', *ABC News*, 6 March 2019.
74 Gray Jamieson, *Reaching for Health*, 271–3.
75 Australian Government Department of Health, *National Women's Health Strategy 2020–2030*, 23.
76 Bonney Corbin, 'Abortion Access Is an Issue in Australia. Ministers For Women Can End Postcode Lottery', *The Canberra Times*, 19 July 2022.
77 Dana Daniel, 'Labor Women's Caucus Leader Vows to Push for Equal, Affordable Access to Abortion', *The Sydney Morning Herald*, 27 July 2022.
78 Rachel Withers, 'Culture Cowards'.
79 Benita Kolovos, 'From Sex Activist to Progressive Trailblazer: Fiona Patten's Remarkable Rise to Influence', *The Guardian*, 18 September 2022.
80 Georgia Hitch, 'Greens to Set up Senate Inquiry into Abortion, Contraception Access in Australia', *ABC News*, 28 September 2022; Tahlia Roy, 'Inquiry into Abortion Services in the ACT Regions Hears Many Find It Difficult to Access That Form of Healthcare', *ABC News*, 29 October 2022; Department of Health, Government of Western Australia, Abortion Legislation: Proposal for Reform in Western Australia.
81 Family Planning NSW et al., *Framework for Abortion Access in NSW*, 4.
82 Arabena, 'Preachers, Policies and Power'.
83 Anonymous, 'Just When You Thought It Was Safe …'

Chapter 3 Doctors

1 Sally Sheldon, *Beyond Control*.
2 Barbara Brookes, *Abortion in England 1900–1967*; Carole E Joffe, *Doctors of Conscience*; Siedlecky and Wyndham, *Populate and Perish*, 65–101.
3 Ibid., 78–101.

4   Sheldon, *Beyond Control*.

5   Ibid., 54 (italics in original).

6   Ellie Lee, Sally Sheldon and Jan Macvarish, 'The 1967 Abortion Act Fifty Years On'.

7   Kerry Petersen, *Abortion Regimes*, 49–65.

8   Siedlecky and Wyndham, *Populate and Perish*, 79–93.

9   Baird, 'The Futures of Abortion'.

10   Barbara Buttfield and Katrina Allen, 'Can Education Influence the Shortage of Doctors Willing To Provide Abortion Services'.

11   Samantha Clavant, 'Women's Right To Choose – Political Barriers and Challenges', 99.

12   Wainer, 'Abortion as an Indicator of Women's Value', 109.

13   Brian Peat, 'Intra-operative Ultra-sound for Improved Safety in Training in Termination of Pregnancy'.

14   McCalman, *Sex and Suffering*, 337–9.

15   NHMRC, *An Information Paper*, 56; Ryan, Ripper and Buttfield, *We Women Decide*, 205–6.

16   Ryan, Ripper and Buttfield, *We Women Decide*, 33, 30–9.

17   Petersen, *Abortion Regimes*, 101.

18   Ibid., 72–9. For medical positions in the 1967 UK debate, see Sheelagh McGuinness and Michael Thomson, 'Medicine and Abortion Law'.

19   Australian Medical Association, 'Reproductive Health and Reproductive Technology Position Statement'.

20   Sarah E Romans-Clarkson, 'Psychological Sequelae of Induced Abortion'.

21   Petersen, *Abortion Regimes*, 86, 87.

22   Mulligan, 'Striving for Excellence in Abortion Services'.

23   Leisa Scott, 'Born to Dissent', *The Australian Magazine*, 20–21 May 1995, 10–14.

24   Julia Haldane, '"And Aint I a Woman": Repeal Don't Reform Abortion Laws', *Green Left*, no. 507, September 2002.

25   David Grundmann, Abortion and the Law, 5.

26   Pringle, *Sex and Medicine*, 63; see Caroline de Costa, *The Women's Doc*, 85.

27   For the establishment of the PAS in 1975 and the role of Kloss, see McCalman, *Sex and Suffering*, 337–9.

28   Ryan, Ripper and Buttfield, *We Women Decide*, 91–163.

29   Sarah Connors, 'What Do Consumers of Termination of Pregnancy Want?'; see also Petersen, *Abortion Regimes*, 88.

30   Ryan, Ripper and Buttfield, *We Women Decide*, 102.

31   Carol Shand and Margaret Sparrow, The Value and Future of Abortion Provider Organisations.

32   Ripper, 'Abortion: The Shift in Stigmatisation', 72–3.

33   Ibid., 75.

34   Baird, 'The Futures of Abortion'.

35   Shannon Buckley and Angela Luvera, 'Doctors Charged For Performing Abortion', *Green Left*, no. 306, 18 February 1998.

36   Chip Le Grand, 'Doctors in Limbo on Abortions', *The Australian*, 9–10 May 1998, 13.

37   Alison Ribbon, 'Free Vote Vow on Abortion', *The Mercury*, 6 December 2001, 1–2; Shauna McGlone, 'Letter to the Editor', *The Mercury*, 7 December 2001, 18; Alison Ribbon, 'Doctor's Abortion Support', *The Mercury*, 8 December 2001, 2.

38   Paul Gerber, 'Late-term Abortion'.

39   Lachlan J de Crespigny and Julian Savulescu, 'Abortion'.

40   Baird, 'Abortion Politics During the Howard Years', 245–61.

41   de Crespigny and Savulescu, 'Abortion'.

42   de Costa, 'Medical Abortion for Australian Women', 378–80.
43   Thanks to Abby Sesterka, who surveyed 80+ key medical journals 1990–2017 for me, looking for articles about abortion written by Australian authors. The number increased markedly from 2004 onwards. This applies to the *MJA* and the *Australian and New Zealand Journal of Obstetrics and Gynaecology*. The articles are too numerous to list, but abortion-providing doctors Ea Mulligan, Dennis Chambers, Jan Dickinson, Darren Russell, Paul Hyland, Philip Goldstone and Catriona Melville, among others, as well as de Costa and de Crespigny, have all published numerous articles.
44   RANZCOG, 'Mifepristone (RU486) Statement C-Gyn 14'; RANZCOG, 'Termination of Pregnancy Statement C-Gyn 17'.
45   de Costa, *The Women's Doc*, 253–8.
46   de Costa et al., 'Early Medical Abortion in Cairns'; de Costa, *The Women's Doc*, 253–8.
47   de Costa et al., 'Early Medical Abortion in Cairns', 172.
48   Petersen, *Abortion Regimes*, 49–65.
49   de Costa et al., 'Early Medical Abortion in Cairns'; see subsequent articles by Sandra Downing, Caroline de Costa and Collette Cashman and colleagues.
50   Mulligan and Messenger, 'Mifepristone in South Australia', 342–5.
51   Ibid.
52   Leisa Scott, 'A Bitter Pill', *Courier Mail Weekend*, QW, 14–18, 2010.
53   *Sydney Morning Herald*, 'Doctor Defies Ban on Abortion Pill', 7 August 2004.
54   de Costa, *The Women's Doc*, 253.
55   Supreme Court of Queensland, *Medical Board of Queensland v Freeman* [2010] QCA 93.
56   *The Sunday Mail (QLD)*, 'Brisbane Doctor Adrienne Freeman To Launch DIY Abortion Guide', 1 August 2010.
57   *news.com*, 'Dr Adrienne Freeman Found Guilty', 25 July 2012.
58   Scott, 'A Bitter Pill'.
59   Anne O'Rourke, Suzanne Belton and Ea Mulligan, 'Medical Abortion in Australia', 236; Geesche Jacobsen, 'Abortion Doctor Escapes Jail', *The Sydney Morning Herald*, 31 October 2006.
60   These have been presented at Public Health Association of Australia and Association of Sexual Health Medicine conferences, among others, as well as at Children by Choice.
61   MS Health, Dispenser and Prescriber Program, December 2022 Update.
62   Kemal Atlay, 'National "Cut-Price" Postal Abortion Service to Close'.
63   Hyland, Raymond and Chong, 'A Direct-to-patient Telemedicine Abortion Service in Australia', 335–40.
64   Gina Rushton, 'A Postal Abortion Service That Sent RU486 to Thousands of Women Is Shutting Down', *Buzzfeed News*, 21 March 2019.
65   Family Planning NSW et al., *Framework for Abortion Access in NSW*, 7; Marie Stopes Australia, *Situational Report: Sexual and Reproductive Rights in Australia*,.
66   VLRC, *Law Of Abortion*, 48.
67   Jennifer Beattie, '"Gatekeepers" of Abortion in Australia', 223.
68   Hon Chuen Cheng and Caroline de Costa, 'Abortion Education in Australian Medical Schools', 796.
69   Prudence Flowers, *Late Termination of Pregnancy*, 73.
70   Family Planning NSW et al., *Framework for Abortion Access in NSW*, 16; RANZCOG, 'Pathways to FRANZCOG'.
71   Ibid., 10.

72   Victorian Clinical Network For Abortion And Contraception Care, https://
      medicine.unimelb.edu.au/cersh/engage/clinical-network; Royal Women's Hospital,
      https://www.thewomens.org.au/Health-Professionals/Clinical-Education-Training/
      Abortion-And-Contraception-Education-Training.
73   SPHERE, *2019–2021 Achievement Report*.
74   See 'Welcome to Healthed', https://www.healthed.com.au/.
75   Family Planning NSW et al., *Framework for Abortion Access*, 16, 19; see also Kirsten
      Black and Helen Paterson, 'A Focus on Sexual and Reproductive Health Is Central
      to Achieving RANZCOG's Goal of Excellence in Women's Health Care', 18–20,
      19.
76   VLRC *Law Of Abortion*; QLRC *Review of Termination of Pregnancy Laws*; Williams,
      Plater, Brunacci, Kapadia and Ozlad, *Abortion: A Review*.
77   For example, see Australian Medical Association (South Australia), 'AMA(SA)
      Submission to the South Australian Law Reform Institute (SALRI)'; AMA,
      'Conscientious Objection'.
78   Louise Anne Keogh, Lynn Gillam, Marie Bismark, Kathleen McNamee, Amy
      Webster, Christine Bayly and Danielle Newton, 'Conscientious Objection to
      Abortion', 2.
79   RANZCOG, 'Late Abortion'.
80   Abortion is relatively normalised in RANZCOG's *O&G Magazine* via mention in
      many contexts; for example, celebration of leading O&Gs, presidential addresses and
      so on, as well as in focused articles. Editorials in 2015 and 2019 supported better
      access to abortion.
81   Caroline de Costa and Heather Douglas, 'Abortion Law in Australia'.
82   Caroline de Costa, *RU-486*; Caroline de Costa, *Never, Ever, Again*; de Costa, *The
      Women's Doc*.
83   Doreen Rosenthal, Heather J Rowe, Shelley Mallett, Annarella Hardiman and
      Maggie Kirkman, *Understanding Women's Experiences of Unplanned Pregnancy and
      Abortion, Final Report*, 16–17; Alana Hulme-Chambers, Meredith Temple-Smith,
      Ange Davidson, Lauren Coelli, Catherine Orr and Jane E Tomnay, 'Australian
      Women's Experiences of a Rural Medical Termination of Pregnancy Service'; Sarah
      Ireland, Suzanne Belton and Frances Doran, '"I Didn't Feel Judged"'. The exception
      was a study that focused on patients' experience of criminalisation, Kathryn J
      LaRoche, LL Wynn, and Angel Foster, '"We Have to Make Sure You Meet Certain
      Criteria"'. For popular culture, see Louise Swinn, *Choice Words*; I Had One Too.
84   Heather Douglas, Kirsten Black and Caroline de Costa, 'Manufacturing Mental
      Illness (and Lawful Abortion)', 568, 575.
85   Asvini K Subasinghe, Seema Deb and Danielle Mazza, 'Primary Care Providers'
      Knowledge, Attitudes and Practices of Medical Abortion'.
86   Angela J Dawson, Rachel Nicolls, Deborah Bateson, Anna Doab, Jane Estoesta, Ann
      Brassil and Elizabeth A Sullivan, 'Medical Termination of Pregnancy in General
      Practice in Australia', 1.
87   Hulme-Chambers, Temple-Smith, Davidson, Coelli, Orr and Tomnay, 'Australian
      Women's Experiences'.
88   Frances Doran and Julie Hornibrook, 'Rural New South Wales Women's Access to
      Abortion Services'.
89   de Costa, Russell and Carrette, 'Views and Practices of Induced Abortion among
      Australian Fellows and Specialist Trainees of the Royal Australian and New Zealand
      College of Obstetricians and Gynaecologists'.
90   Hon Chuen Cheng, Kirsten Black, Cindy Woods and Caroline de Costa, 'Views and
      Practices of Induced Abortion among Australian Fellows and Trainees of The Royal

Australian and New Zealand College of Obstetricians and Gynaecologists'.

91   Williams, Plater, Brunacci, Kapadia and Ozlad, *Abortion: A Review*, 377–8; VLRC, *Law of Abortion*, 47, 114.

92   Carol Nader, 'Controversial Abortion Case That Brought A Doctor Years Of Anguish', *The Age*, 13 December 2007.

93   Millar, *Happy Abortions*, 37.

94   Deirdre Niamh Duffy, Claire Pierson, Caroline Myerscough, Diane Urquhart and Lindsey Earner-Byrne, 'Abortion, Emotions, and Health Provision', 15, 16.

95   Douglas, Black and de Costa, 'Manufacturing Mental Illness'.

96   Davina mentions the arrest of Drs Bayliss and Cullen after a raid of the Greenslopes clinic in Brisbane in 1986: see Petersen, *Abortion Regimes*, 138–9. The FCC in Melbourne had previously been raided by Federal Police in 1981, see Allanson with O'Shea, *Empowering Women*, 39.

97   Allanson with O'Shea, *Empowering Women*, 199; see also Ronli Sifris, Tania Penovic and Caroline Henckels, 'Advancing Reproductive Rights Through Legal Reform'.

98   Petersen, *Abortion Regimes*, 87.

99   Cheng et al., 'Views and Practices', 294.

100 Judith Nash, 'GP Bias Clouds Termination Advice'.

101 See Millar, *Happy Abortions*, 3.

102 Nikolas Rose, *Powers of Freedom*, 166.

103 Keogh et al., 'Intended and Unintended Consequences', 22.

104 Tomnay et al., 'Providing Accessible Medical Abortion Services', 175–180; de Moel-Mandel et al., 'Expert Consensus'; Lohr et al., 'How Would Decriminalisation Affect Women's Health?', 52.

105 Marge Berer, 'Telemedicine and Self-Managed Abortion'.

Chapter 4 Marie Stopes

1   For example, see Erik Munroe, Brandan Hayes and Julia Taft, 'Private-sector Social Franchising to Accelerate Family Planning Access, Choice, and Quality', 196; Michael Mutua, 'Kenya's Marie Stopes Ban'.

2   I use the terms 'developing' and 'developed' to describe countries elsewhere described as First World and Third World, or the Global North and the Global South. In this preference, I am following the lead of the UN while acknowledging that all these systems of categorisation have flaws.

3   Liz Ford, 'Marie Stopes Charity Changes Name In Break With Campaigner's View On Eugenics', *The Guardian*, 17 November 2020.

4   For a brief overview of provision in the UK, see Sheldon, Davis, O'Neill and Parker, *The Abortion Act 1967*, 115–124.

5   Aziz Choudry and Dip Kapoor, 'Introduction', 1.

6   Nancy Fraser, 'Feminism, Capitalism and the Cunning of History'; INCITE! Women of Color (eds), *The Revolution Will Not Be Funded*.

7   Sarah Maddison and Richard Denniss, 'Democratic Constraint and Embrace'; Catherine McDonald and Sara Charlesworth, 'Outsourcing and the Australian Nonprofit Sector'.

8   Choudry and Kapoor, 'Introduction', 1.

9   Katrina Erny-Albrecht and Petra Bywood, 'Corporatisation of General Practice: Impact and Implications'; Hal Swerissen, Stephen Duckett and Greg Moran, 'Mapping Primary Care in Australia'.

10   MSI Reproductive Choices, 'Our History'.

11   MSI Reproductive Choices, *Australian Strategic Plan 2021–2023*, 3.

12   Helen Axby, Abortion in the UK.

13   Dates for clinic purchase and closure, and financial information not otherwise referenced, were provided in a personal communication with Jamal Hakim, 5 September 2022.

14   Grayston, 'Changing Attitudes and Services', 247–8.

15   Dalzell, 'Final Steps Towards Private Abortion Services'.

16   Sheldon, Davis, O'Neill and Parker, *The Abortion Act (1967)*, 117; see also Axby, Abortion in the UK.

17   Kirkby, Discussion Paper.

18   See 'The Sood Abortion Trial', *Law Report with Damien Carrick*, radio program, *ABC RN*, 8 August 2006.

19   Carol Nader, 'Cancer Drug Used for Abortion', *The Sydney Morning Herald*, 4 July 2006.

20   Carol Nader, 'Cancer Drug To Be Used By Abortion Clinic', *The Age*, 15 June 2007.

21   Personal communication with Jamal Hakim, 5 September 2022.

22   LinkedIn profile of Maria Deveson Crabbe.

23   Caroline M de Costa, Kirsten I Black, and Darren B Russell, 'Medical Abortion'.

24   Julie Mundy, LaTrobe University, https://scholars.latrobe.edu.au/jmundy; LinkedIn profile of Suzanne Dvorak.

25   Philip Goldstone's presentations at Marie Stopes' *Reshaping Abortion Care in Australia* Webinar (29 November 2021) covered much of this story.

26   Samantha Donovan, 'Death May Spark Backlash Against Abortion Drug', *The World Today*, radio program, *ABC RN*, 19 March 2012.

27   Personal communication with Jamal Hakim, 17 February 2022.

28   Stephanie Peatling, 'Health Group Gets Green Light To Import Abortion Drug Into Australia', *The Sydney Morning Herald*, 30 August 2012.

29   Samantha Maiden, 'High Price of a Woman's Right to Choose', *The Advertiser*, 7 December 2013.

30   Julia Medew, 'Board Finds Doctor Guilty of Unprofessional Conduct', *The Sydney Morning Herald*, 19 March 2009.

31   Julia Medew, 'Doctor Struck Off Medical Register', *The Age*, 25 May 2013.

32   Paul Millar and Nino Bucci, 'Woman Dies After Abortion Clinic Visit', *The Age*, 21 December 2011; Michale Bachelard, 'Woman Tells of Late Abortion Horror', *The Age*, 23 October 2011.

33   Eliza Elliott (Lander and Rogers), 'General Practitioner Reprimanded for Unprofessional Conduct in Late Stage Pregnancy Termination'; Audrey Jamieson, Coroner, Coroner's Court of Melbourne, 'Finding into Death with Inquest Court'.

34   Donald Peat, 'Govt to Fund More Pregnancy Counselling', *PM,* radio program, *ABC RN*, 2 March 2006.

35   Dana Hovig, William and Flora Hewlett Foundation 2022, https://hewlett.org/people/dana-hovig/; LinkedIn profile of Simon Cooke.

36   LinkedIn profile of Michelle Thompson, CEO, Marie Stopes Australia, MSA.

37   MSI Australia, 'Support The Australian Choice Fund'.

38   Marie Stopes Australia, *Impact Report 2019*, 28–9.

39   Marie Stopes Australia, *Situational Report*, 9; Marie Stopes Australia, *Impact Report 2020*, 13; Marie Stopes Australia, *Pre-Budget Submission 2021–2022*.

40   Personal communication with Jamal Hakim, 17 February 2022.

41   Personal communication with Jamal Hakim, 5 September 2022.

42   Marie Stopes Australia, *Hidden Forces.*

43   Marie Stopes Australia, University of Queensland's Pro Bono Centre, SPHERE, and ASHM, *Nurse-Led Termination of Pregnancy in Australia*; Marie Stopes Australia,

University of Queensland's Pro Bono Centre, and Australian Women Against Violence Alliance, *Safe Access Zones in Australia*.

44   Marie Stopes Australia, *Impact Report 2019*, 7, 30; see also MSI Reproductive Choices, *Australian Strategic Plan 2021–2023*, 12.

45   MSI Australia, 'Apology for Forced Medical Procedures Linked to Colonisation and Racism in Australia'.

46   Marie Stopes Australia, *Impact Report 2019*, 26.

47   Michelle Thompson, 'Marie Stopes Australia Wants More Attention on Women's Sexual Health', *The Sydney Morning Herald*, 2 February 2018.

48   MSI Australia, 'Our Leadership'.

49   Marie Stopes Australia, 'Big Changes in a New Strategy Coming'; see LinkedIn profiles of Cate Grindlay and Ashley Hogarty.

50   Rachael Wong, 'A Better Cause Than Marie Stopes', *Spectator Australia*, 29 September 2017.

51   Sarah Boseley, 'Marie Stopes Suspends Some Abortion Services Over Safety Issues', *The Guardian*, 20 August 2016; Sheldon, Davis, O'Neill and Parker, *The Abortion Act (1967)*, 109–150.

52   Laura Silver, 'This Abortion Clinic Denies Claims It Has Rewarded Staff for Encouraging Terminations', *BuzzFeed News*, 21 October 2017.

53   Lauren Weymouth, 'Regulator Criticises Marie Stopes over £434,000 CEO Salary', *Charity Times*, 20 December 2019.

54   Stacy Banwell, 'Gender, North–South Relations', 8.

55   Deborah Bateson, Patricia A Lohr, Wendy V Norman, Caroline Moreau, Kristina Gemzell-Danielsson, Paul D Blumenthal, Lesley Hoggart, Hang-Wun Raymond Li, Abigail RA Aiken and Kirsten I Black. 'The Impact of COVID-19 on Contraception and Abortion Care Policy and Practice', 241–3.

56   Marie Stopes Australia, *Situational Report*, 20, 4, 4–12.

57   Figures are drawn from the annual Special Purpose Aggregated Financial Statements of 'Marie Stopes International (Australian Branch) and MS Health Pty Ltd Aggregated Group', which are available on the website of the Australian Charities and Not-for-profits Commission for 2014–2020, https://www.acnc.gov.au/charity/charities/26eb5b5d-3aaf-e811-a963-000d3ad24077/documents.

58   Personal communication with Jamal Hakim, 5 September 2022.

59   MSI Australia, 'Managing Director of MSI Australia Set to Move on Following a Decade of Reform'.

60   Marie Stopes Australia, *Impact Report 2020*, 9.

61   MSI Reproductive Choices, *Australian Strategic Plan 2021–2023*, 3.

62   Amber Schultz, 'The Right Choice: What Does the Future Hold for Australia's Largest Abortion Provider', *Crikey*, 14 July 2022.

63   Caroline M de Costa and Michael Carrette, 'Early Medical Abortion'; Suzanne Belton, Ea Mulligan, Felicity Gerry, Paul Hyland and Virginia Skinner, 'Mifepristone by Prescription'.

64   MSI Reproductive Choices, *MSI 2030*, 3.

65   Personal communication with Jamal Hakim, 17 February 2022.

66   Schultz, 'The Right Choice'.

67   Marie Stopes Australia, *Impact Report 2018*.

68   MSI Australia, 'MSI Australia Clinical Standards'.

69   MSI Reproductive Choices, *Australian Strategic Plan 2021–2023*, 3.

70   Erny-Albrecht and Bywood, 'Corporatisation of General Practice', 3.

71   Szporluk, Michael, 'A Framework for Understanding Accountability of International NGOs and Global Good Governance', 340, 359.

72   Jane Haggis and Susanne Schech, 'Meaning Well and Global Good Manners'.
73   Marie Stopes Australia, *Impact Report 2019*, 28.
74   Haggis and Schech, 'Meaning Well and Global Good Manners', 392, 392–3, 388.
75   Gina Rushton, *The Most Important Job in the World*, 88–9.

Chapter 5 Early

1   In 2017–2018 about 23 per cent of all abortions in Australia were early medical abortions. I presume this percentage has increased but my figure is an estimate. See Louise A Keogh, Lyle C Gurrin and Patricia Moore, 'Estimating the Abortion Rate in Australia'.
2   Berer, 'Telemedicine and Self-Managed Abortion'; Andrea Carson, Martha Paynter, Wendy V Norman, Sarah Munro, Josette Roussel, Sheila Dunn, Denise Bryant-Lukosius, Stephanie Begun and Ruth Martin-Misener, 'Optimizing the Nursing Role in Abortion Care.'
3   Londa Schiebinger, 'West Indian Abortifacients and the Making of Ignorance'; Jessica Marcotte, 'The Agnotology of Abortion'.
4   Lyn Finch and Jon Stratton, 'The Australian Working Class and the Practice of Abortion 1880–1939', 56.
5   *A Womb of Her Own: Four Women's Experiences of Abortion*, VHS tape, (dir. Catherine Gough-Brady).
6   André Ulmann, 'The Development of Mifepristone'; de Costa, *RU-486*, 25–36.
7   World Health Organization, *Abortion Care Guideline*.
8   Sydney Calkin, 'Towards a Political Geography of Abortion', 22.
9   Sally Sheldon, 'How Can a State Control Swallowing?'; Michelle Oberman, *Her Body, Our Laws.*
10   Susheela Singh, Lisa Remez, Gilda Sedgh, Lorraine Kwok and Tsuyoshi Onda, *Abortion Worldwide 2017*, 24.
11   Céline Miani, 'Medical Abortion Ratios and Gender Equality in Europe', 226.
12   Marge Berer and Lesley Hoggart, 'Medical Abortion Pills Have the Potential to Change Everything About Abortion'; Joanna N Erdman, Kinga Jelinska and Susan Yanow, 'Understandings of Self-Managed Abortion as Health Inequity'.
13   Calkin, 'Towards a Political Geography of Abortion', 28.
14   *Monash University*, 'Vale Professor David Healy', 30 May 2012, https://www.monash.edu/news/articles/vale-professor-david-healy.
15   Lynette K Nieman, Teresa M Choate, George P Chrousos, David L Healy, Martin Morin, David Renquist, George R Merriam, Irving M Spitz, C Wayne Bardin, Etienne-Emile Baulieu, and D Lynne Loriaux, 'The Progesterone Antagonist RU 486'; Renate Klein, Janice G Raymond and Lynette J Dumble, *RU 486.*
16   David L Healy and Hamish M Fraser, 'The Antiprogesterones Are Coming', 580.
17   David Healy and Amanda J Evans, 'Mifepristone and Emergency Contraception'.
18   Pam M Mamers, Amanda J Evans, David L Healy, Anna L Lavelle, Sandra M Bell, and Jen R Rusden, 'Women's Satisfaction with Medical Abortion with RU486'.
19   NHMRC, *An Information Paper*, 21.
20   Klein, Raymond and Dumble, *RU486.*
21   Ibid., 7, xxxiv.
22   Jo Wainer, 'The Social Impact of RU 486'.
23   de Costa, *RU 486*, 86, 95, 92, 90–4.
24   Mary-Anne Toy, 'Abortion Pill Ban to Stay in Australia', *The Age*, 30 September 2000, 3.
25   Melissa Sweet, 'The Abortion Choices', *The Bulletin*, 31 October 2001, 44.

26 Anthea Stutter, 'Non-Profit Clinic Closes', *Green Left*, no. 440, 14 March 2001.

27 Australian Democrats, 'Democrats Move to Undo Harradine Block on RU486'.

28 RANZCOG, 'The Use of Misoprostol in Obstetrics and Gynaecology'.

29 Sweet, 'The Abortion Choices', 44.

30 *The Sydney Morning Herald*, 'Doctor Defies Ban on Abortion Pill'.

31 de Costa, 'Medical Abortion for Australian Women'.

32 Baird, 'Abortion Politics During the Howard Years', 245–61.

33 de Costa, *RU486*, 96–106.

34 de Costa, 'Early Medical Abortion in Australia'.

35 Commonwealth of Australia, *Inquiry into Therapeutic Goods Amendment (Repeal of Ministerial Responsibility for Approval of RU486) Bill 2005*.

36 Rebecca Albury, 'Too Many, Too Late and the Adoption Alternative'.

37 The account here of de Costa's actions comes from *The Women's Doc*, 249–58.

38 de Costa et al., 'Early Medical Abortion in Cairns', 171–3.

39 Carol Nader, 'Royal Women's Bids for Abortion Drug Approval', *The Age*, 11 December 2006.

40 de Costa et al., 'Early Medical Abortion in Cairns', 172.

41 Mulligan and Messenger, 'Mifepristone in South Australia'.

42 Therapeutic Goods Administration, *Registration of Medicines*.

43 de Costa, Black and Russell, 'Medical Abortion', 248.

44 Therapeutic Goods Administration, *Registration of Medicines*.

45 Ibid.

46 Calkin, 'Towards a Political Geography of Abortion', 22.

47 Maiden, 'High Price of a Woman's Right to Choose'.

48 Cate Swannell, 'Medical Abortion Access Extended'.

49 Therapeutic Goods Administration, *Australian Public Assessment Report for mifepristone / misoprostol*.

50 Maiden, 'High Price of a Woman's Right to Choose'.

51 Avant Media, 'Category of Cover Changed For GPs Involved in Medical Termination of Pregnancy'.

52 Rebekah Yeaun Lee, Rebekah Moles and Betty Chaar, 'Mifepristone (RU486) in Australian Pharmacies'.

53 S Robertson, L Edney, M Wheeler, T Hunter, and D Bateson, Access to Medical Abortion; P Doherty, The GP Connection, I; P Moore and K Stephens, Can We Decentralise Abortion Services in Victoria?.

54 The Tabbot Foundation.

55 Amy Corderoy, 'Tabbot Foundation Phone Abortion Service Seeks Extra Help Due to Overwhelming Demand', *The Sydney Morning Herald*, 30 September 2015.

56 Hyland, Raymond and Chong, 'A Direct-to-patient Telemedicine Abortion Service in Australia'.

57 Gina Rushton, 'A Postal Abortion Service That Sent RU486 to Thousands Of Women Is Shutting Down', *Buzzfeed News*, 21 March 2019.

58 Blue Water Medical, 'At Home Abortion'; Clinic 66, Abortion Online.

59 Children by Choice, 'Queensland Abortion Providers'; 1800 My Options, 'Find a Service'; Women's Health Tasmania, 'Pregnancy Choices Information'; SA Health, 'Unplanned Pregnancy Services'.

60 MS Health, *Dispenser and Provider Program Update 2022*.

61 Clinic 66, 'Abortion Online'; Marie Stopes Australia, 'Medical Abortion'; Family Planning NSW, Women's Health NSW and Chair of Sexual and Reproductive Health Special Interest Group of RANZCOG.

62 Shankar et al., 'Access, Equity and Costs', 309–14.

63   *Pregnancy Outcome Statistics*, Wellbeing SA.
64   Galrao, Hutchinson and Joyce, *Induced Abortions in Western Australia 2016–2018*.
65   Murdoch, Thompson and Belton, 'Rapid Uptake of Early Medical Abortions'.
66   Marie Stopes Australia, *Situational Report*, 5.
67   For example, see de Costa et al., 'Early Medical Abortion in Cairns'; Mulligan and Messenger, 'Mifepristone in South Australia'; Philip Goldstone, Jill Michelson and Eve Williamson, 'Early Medical Abortion Using Low-dose Mifepristone Followed by Buccal Misoprostol'; Philip Goldstone, Jill Michelson and Eve Williamson, 'Effectiveness of Early Medical Abortion'; Philip Goldstone, Clara Walker and Katherine Hawtin, 'Efficacy and Safety of Mifepristone–Buccal Misoprostol'.
68   For example, see Hyland, Raymond and Chong, 'A Direct-to-patient Telemedicine Abortion Service in Australia'; Terri-Ann Thompson, Jane W Seymour, Catriona Melville, Zara Khan, Danielle Mazza and Daniel Grossman, 'An Observational Study of Patient Experiences'.
69   For example, see Tomnay et al., 'Providing Accessible Medical Abortion Services'; Hulme-Chambers, Temple-Smith, Davidson, Coelli, Orr and Tomnay, 'Australian Women's Experiences'. On telehealth, see Thompson et al., 'An Observational Study'.
70   For more recent research, see de Costa, Black and Russell, 'Medical Abortion: It Is Time'. De Costa's books *The Women's Doc* and *RU 486*, written for popular readership, evidence her political engagement.
71   Kathryn J LaRoche, LL Wynn, and Angel M Foster, '"We've Got Rights and Yet We Don't Have Access"', 260; on GPs, see Angela J Dawson, Rachel Nicolls, Deborah Bateson, Anna Doab, Jane Estoesta, Ann Brassil and Elizabeth A Sullivan, 'Medical Termination of Pregnancy in General Practice in Australia'; Deb, Subasinghe and Mazza, 'Providing Medical Abortion in General Practice'; on nurse-led models, see de Moel-Mandel, Graham, and Taket, 'Expert Consensus', 380.
72   SPHERE, 'Abortion'.
73   SPHERE, 'The Orient Study'; SPHERE, 'Partnership Project: The AusCAPPS Project'.
74   Kathryn Ogden, Emily Ingram, Joanna Levis, Georgia Roberts and Iain Robertson, 'Termination of Pregnancy in Tasmania'.
75   Ireland, Belton and Doran, '"I Didn't Feel Judged"', 55; LaRoche, Wynn and Foster, '"We've Got Rights"'.
76   Family Planning NSW et al., *Framework for Abortion Access in NSW*, 10.
77   LaRoche, Wynn and Foster, '"We've Got Rights"', 259–60.
78   Nell Garaets, 'The Game-changing Plan to Cut Barriers to Medical Abortion', *The Sydney Morning Herald*, 16 January 2023; Esther Linder, 'Access all areas', *The Saturday Paper*, 25 February – 3 March 2023, 8.
79   Personal communication with Jamal Hakim, 17 February 2022.
80   Marie Stopes, *Situational Report*, 15–17.
81   Carson et al., 'Optimizing the Nursing Role in Abortion Care'; Lydia Mainey, 'Empower Nurses to Improve Abortion Care'.
82   Alyson Wright, Karl Briscoe and Ray Lovett, 'A National Profile of Aboriginal and Torres Strait Islander Health Workers'.
83   Erdman, Jelinska and Yanow, 'Understandings of Self-Managed Abortion', 13.
84   Marge Berer, 'Reconceptualizing Safe Abortion'.
85   Ibid.
86   Joanna Erdman 'Put Abortion Pills into Peoples' Hands'; World Health Organization, *Abortion Care Guideline*.
87   Erdman, Jelinska and Yanow, 'Understandings of Self-Managed Abortion,' 16.

88 Spencer Kimball, 'Women in States That Ban Abortion Will Still Be Able to Get Abortion Pills Online From Overseas', *CNBC*, 27 June 2022.

89 Kevin Sunde Oppegaard, Margaret Sparrow, Paul Hyland, Francisca García, Cristina Villarreal, Aníbal Faúndes, Laura Miranda and Marge Berer, 'What if Medical Abortion Becomes the Main or Only Method of First-trimester Abortion?', 82–5.

90 Adele Clarke and Theresa Montini, 'The Many Faces of RU486'.

91 Elizabeth G Raymond, Caitlin Shannon, Mark A Weaver, and Beverly Winikoff, 'First-trimester Medical Abortion with Mifepristone 200 mg and Misoprostol'; Marge Berer, 'Medical Abortion'.

92 M Endler, A Lavelanet, A Cleeve, B Ganatra, R Gomperts, and K Gemzell-Danielsson, 'Telemedicine for Medical Abortion'.

93 Miani, 'Medical Abortion Ratios', 219, 225.

94 Berer, 'Telemedicine and Self-Managed Abortion'.

95 I Had One Too.

96 Family Planning NSW, Women's Health NSW and Chair of Sexual and Reproductive Health Special Interest Group of RANZCOG, *Framework for Abortion Access in NSW*, 11, 12.

97 Marie Stopes, *Situational Report*, 16.

98 Erdman, Jelinska and Yanow, 'Understandings of Self-Managed Abortion', 17.

99 Cecelia Brun Lie-Spahn, *The Pharmocratics of Misoprostol*, viii.

100 Ireland, Belton, and Doran, 'I Didn't Feel Judged', 49–56.

101 Danielle Newton, Chris Bayly, Kathleen McNamee, Annarella Hardiman, Marie Bismark, Amy Webster, and Louise Keogh. 'How Do Women Seeking Abortion Choose Between Surgical and Medical Abortion?'

102 LaRoche, Wynn and Foster, 'We've Got Rights', 259.

103 Klein, Raymond and Dumble, *RU 486*.

104 Philip Coorey, 'Australia Dangerously Dependent on Medical Imports', *Australian Financial Review*, 18 February 2020.

105 Ghazaleh Samandari, Nathalie Kapp, Christopher Hamon and Alison Campbell, 'Challenges in the Abortion Supply Chain'.

Chapter 6 Decriminalised

1 Sydney Calkin, 'One Year On, It's Clear That the New Irish Abortion Services Have Serious Limitations'; Sally Sheldon, Jane O'Neill, Clare Parker and Gayle Davis, '"Too Much, Too Indigestible, Too Fast?"'; *BBC News*, 'New Zealand Passes Law Decriminalising Abortion', 18 March 2020; Megan Janetsky, 'Colombia Decriminalises Abortion Following Regional "Green Wave"', *Al Jazeera*, 22 February 2022.

2 Marge Berer and Lesley Hoggart, 'Progress Toward Decriminalization'.

3 Reg Graycar and Jenny Morgan, 'Law Reform', 419.

4 Rachel Rebouché, 'A Functionalist Approach to Comparative Abortion Law', 101.

5 Aileen Moreton-Robinson, 'The Possessive Logic of Patriarchal White Sovereignty'.

6 This summary is drawn from: Siedlecky and Wyndham, *Populate and Perish*, 78–101; Ryan, Ripper and Buttfield, *We Women Decide*, 15–28.

7 *R v Davidson* [1969] VR 667, 672.

8 *R v Wald* (1972) 3 DCR (NSW) 25, 29.

9 *R v Bayliss and Cullen* (1986) 8 Qld Lawyer Reps 8.

10 Grayston, 'Changing Attitudes and Services'.

11 *CES and Anor v Superclinics (Australia) Pty Ltd and Ors* (1995) 38 NSWLR 47; Reg Graycar and Jenny Morgan, 'Unnatural Rejection of Womanhood and Motherhood',

323.

12   Details of events in WA, Tasmania and the ACT are drawn from Baird, 'The Futures of Abortion' and Cannold and Calcutt, 'The Australian Pro-Choice Movement'.

13   *Acts Amendment (Abortion) Act 1998 (No. 15 of 1998)* (WA).

14   *Criminal Code Amendment Act (No. 2) of 2001* (Tas).

15   Mary Ziegler, *After Roe*.

16   This account is drawn from Wayne Berry, Decriminalising Abortion in the ACT.

17   *Crimes (Abolition of Offence of Abortion) Act 2002* (ACT); *Medical Practitioners (Maternal Health) Amendment Act 2002* (ACT).

18   Baird, 'Abortion Politics in the Howard Years'.

19   This account of Victorian reform is based on Alissar El-Murr, 'Representing the Problem of Abortion'; Jenny Morgan, 'Abortion Law Reform'; Allanson with O'Shea, *Empowering Women*, 99–119; VLRC, *Law of Abortion*; *Abortion Law Reform Act 2008* (Vic).

20   *Abortion Law Reform Act 2008* (Vic).

21   This account of Tasmanian reform is based on interviews with Louella, Petra and Nicola; Charis Palmer, 'Tasmania to Amend Law to Decriminalise Abortion'; Calla Wahlquist, 'Abortion Law Backdown', *The Examiner*, 11 April 2013; Stephen Smiley, 'Tasmanian Parliament Decriminalises Abortion', *ABC News*, 21 November 2013; Ronli Sifris, 'Tasmania's Reproductive Health (Access to Terminations) Act 2013'.

22   *Reproductive Health (Access to Terminations) Act 2013* (Tas).

23   Anne O'Rourke, 'A Legal and Political Assessment of Challenges to Abortion Laws, 22–7, 27–33.

24   Henrietta Cook, 'Abortion Law Changes Eyed as Dr Mark Hobart Probed', *The Age*, 7 November 2013; Heather Ewart, 'Dropped Charges Raise Abortion Questions in Victoria', *7.30 Report*, television program, ABC Television, 3 December 2013.

25   Ronli Sifris, 'State By State'; Allanson with O'Shea, *Empowering Women*.

26   This account of the early NT campaign is based on interview with Priscilla; *WhatRU4nt*, Facebook page; Suzanne Belton, 'NT Politicians Put on Notice over Abortion Law Reform', *Croakey Health Media*, 31 May 2016.

27   This account of the End12 reform is based on Mehreen Faruqi, 'End12'; Human Rights Law Centre, 'NSW Votes Down Bill to Modernise Abortion Law'.

28   This account of the Cairns case and Pyne bills is based on de Costa, *The Women's Doc*, 259–62; *ABC News*, 'Bligh Not Taking Abortion Laws to Parliament', 25 August 2009; Meredith Griffiths, 'Abortion Laws "Ambiguous, Outdated" In Qld, NSW, Doctors Argue', *ABC News*, 10 October 2016; Felicity Caldwell, 'Qld Abortion Bill: Pyne Hails Victory Over Committee Split', *Brisbane Times*, 17 February 2017.

29   Gabrielle Dunlevy, 'Abortion Law Changes a "Settled Matter": Premier', *Brisbane Times*, 25 August 2009.

30   This account of the move to decriminalisation in SA is based on *saaac* (South Australian Abortion Action Coalition); Williams, Plater, Brunacci, Kapadia and Ozlad, *Abortion: A Review*.

31   Helen Davidson, 'Abortion Decriminalised in Northern Territory After Long Campaign', *The Guardian*, 22 March 2017.

32   *Termination of Pregnancy Law Reform Act 2017 (No. 7 of 2017)* (NT).

33   This account of the move to decriminalisation in Queensland is based on QLRC, *Review of Termination of Pregnancy Laws*; Pro Choice Qld, Facebook.

34   Personal communication with Daile Kelleher, 3 April 2023.

35   *Termination of Pregnancy Act 2018* (Qld).

36   *Public Health Amendment (Safe Access to Reproductive Health Clinics) Act 2018 (No. 26 of 2018)* (NSW).

37   Michael McGowan, 'NSW Passes Law to Establish Safe Access Zones', *The Guardian*, 8 June 2018.

38   This account of the move to decriminalisation in NSW is based on Our Bodies Our Choices, https://www.oboc.com.au; Human Rights Law Centre, 'NSW Decriminalisation Campaign Launches'; Angelique Lu and Sarah Thomas, 'Abortion Bill in NSW Set to Change Laws Dating Back to 1900', *ABC News*, 28 July 2019; Michaela Whitbourn, 'Sydney Woman Prosecuted for Taking Abortion Drug', *The Sydney Morning Herald*, 14 August 2017; Kate Gleeson, 'The Other Abortion Myth'; *ABC News*, 'Abortion Bill Leads to Late Night Debate at NSW Parliament after Heated Clashes', 6 August 2019; Australian Associated Press, 'Abortion Decriminalised in NSW after Marathon Debate', *The Guardian*, 26 September 2019; Legislative Council Standing Committee on Social Issues, *Reproductive Health Care Reform Bill 2019 [Provisions] Report 55*.

39   *Abortion Law Reform Act 2019 No. 11* (NSW).

40   O'Rourke, 'A Legal and Political Assessment', 27–33.

41   Williams, Plater, Brunacci, Kapadia and Ozlad, *Abortion: A Review*.

42   Caroline Henckels, Ronli Sifris and Tania Penovic, 'High Court Delivers Landmark Ruling Validating Abortion Clinic "Safe Access Zones"'.

43   *Health Care (Safe Access) Amendment Act 2020* (SA).

44   *Termination of Pregnancy Act 2021* (SA).

45   Paul Karp, 'George Christensen's "Nonsensical" Proposal Could Penalise Doctors up to $440,000', *The Guardian*, 23 February 2021.

46   *Health (Improving Abortion Access) Amendment Act 2018* (ACT); *nine.com.au*, 'ACT To Get Increased Access to Abortion', 19 September 2018.

47   *Termination of Pregnancy Law Reform Legislation Amendment Act 2021* (NT); Isaac Nowroozi, 'Abortion Laws Are Set To Be Reformed, Making it Easier to Terminate Later Term Pregnancies', *ABC News*, 21 October 2021.

48   *Public Health Amendment (Safe Access Zones) Act 2021* (WA).

49   Rebecca Trigger, 'Women Who Made Abortion Legal in Australia Say Now Is the Time for Further Reform', *ABC News*, 4 July 2022; Department of Health, Government of Western Australia, *Abortion Legislation: Proposal for Reform in Western Australia*.

50   Crimes Legislation Amendment (Loss of Foetus) Bill 2021 (NSW).

51   Danuta Kozaki, 'NSW Passes Zoe's Law to Impose Harsher Penalties for the Death of an Unborn Baby', *ABC News*, 20 November 2021.

52   Australian Lawyers for Human Rights, 'Human Rights Experts Warn against US-style Politicisation of Reproductive Rights in Australia'.

53   O'Rourke, 'A Legal and Political Assessment', 165–7.

54   Zoe Keys, Media Discourses of Abortion Law Reform.

55   Rachel Rebouché, 'The Public Health Turn in Reproductive Rights', 1355.

56   El-Murr, 'Representing the Problem of Abortion'; Morgan, 'Abortion Law Reform'; Anne O'Rourke, 'The Discourse of Abortion Law Debate in Australia'; Keys, Media Discourses of Abortion Law Reform.

57   Millar, *Happy Abortions*, 113–35.

58   El Murr, 'Representing the Problem of Abortion'.

59   Barbara Baird, 'Unforgetting'.

60   Queensland Government, 'Palaszczuk Government Delivers Historic Abortion Laws'.

61   Erica Millar, 'Mourned Choices and Grievable Lives'.

62   Tania Penovic, 'The Fall of Roe v Wade'.

63   Williams, Plater, Brunacci, Kapadia and Ozlad, *Abortion: A Review*, 145–59.

64   Ibid., 148.

65   Calkin, 'Towards a Political Geography of Abortion', 26–7.

66   Marge Berer, 'Provision of Abortion by Mid-level Providers'; Dennis Campbell, 'Make Access to Abortion Easier, UK's Top Gynaecologist Demands', *The Guardian*, 2 October 2017.

67   These are noted in QLRC, *Review of Termination of Pregnancy Laws*, 117, and Williams, Plater, Brunacci, Kapadia and Ozlad, *Abortion: A Review*, 360–1.

68   For discussion of this position, see Williams, Plater, Brunacci, Kapadia and Ozlad, *Abortion: A Review*, 363–5, 380–90.

69   Jasmine Meredith Davis, Casey Michelle Haining and Louise Anne Keogh, 'A Narrative Literature Review of the Impact of Conscientious Objection', 2202, 2198.

70   Keogh et al., 'Intended and Unintended Consequences', 22.

71   This observation is made of the providers in the UK in Lee, Sheldon and Macvarish, 'The 1967 Abortion Act'.

72   See Baird, 'The Futures of Abortion'.

73   Erica Millar, 'Maintaining Exceptionality', 439–58, 455.

74   Williams, Plater, Brunacci, Kapadia and Ozlad, *Abortion: A Review*, 320–31.

75   Sheldon, Davis, O'Neill and Parker, *The Abortion Act (1967)*, 264.

76   Claire McKinney, 'A Good Abortion is a Tragic Abortion', 269.

77   Ibid.

78   Ellen Coulter, 'No Timeframe for Abortion Provider to Do Terminations in Tasmania, as Women Face "Hodge-Podge" of a System', *ABC News*, 6 March 2019.

79   Ogden et al., 'Termination of Pregnancy in Tasmania'.

80   SHFPACT, 'Unplanned Pregnancy Counselling Services'.

81   Anderson, 'Tasmanian Public Hospitals to Offer Surgical Abortions'; Gilbert, 'ACT Government to Cover Abortion Costs'.

82   Keogh et al., 'Intended and Unintended Consequences'.

83   Queensland Government, 'Palaszczuk Government Delivers Historic Abortion Laws'.

84   Queensland Government, 'Termination of Pregnancy'; personal communication with Daile Kelleher, 3 April 2023.

85   Matt Wordsworth, 'Amid a Shortfall of Abortion Services for Women in Regional Queensland, Questions of Equality Are Raised', *ABC News*, 12 March 2022.

86   NSW Health, 'Pregnancy Choices Helpline'.

87   Quoted in Landis-Hanley, 'Choice Recognition', 4.

88   Sifris, Penovic and Henkels, 'Advancing Reproductive Rights', 1086.

89   Judith Dwyer, Mark Rankin, Margie Ripper and Monica Cations, 'Is There Still a Need for Abortion-Specific Laws?', 147, 148

90   Millar, *Happy Abortions*, 135.

91   Albury, 'Too Many, Too Late'.

92   Women With Disabilities Australia (WWDA), *WWDA Submission on Sexual and Reproductive Rights*, 25 [original emphasis].

93   Chelsea Watego, Alissa Macoun, David Singh and Elizabeth Strakosch, 'Carceral Feminism and Coercive Control'.

Chapter 7 Late

1   Joanna N Erdman, 'Theorizing Time in Abortion Law and Human Rights', 30.

2   Flowers, *Late Termination of Pregnancy*, 12.

3   Galrao, Hutchinson and Joyce, *Induced Abortions in Western Australia*; South Australian Abortion Reporting Committee, *Annual Report for the Year 2018*, 30, 8–9.

4   Hayes, Keane and Hurley, 'Counselling "Late Women"'.

5   VLRC, *Law of Abortion*, 42.

6   Marie Stopes Australia, *Hidden Forces.*

7   Arabena, 'Preachers, Policies and Power'.

8   Millar, 'Maintaining Exceptionality', 450.

9   Hayes, Kean and Hurley, 'Counselling "Late Women"', 4.

10   See also Kirsten I Black, Heather Douglas and Caroline de Costa, 'Women's Access to Abortion after 20 Weeks' Gestation for Fetal Chromosomal Abnormalities', 145.

11   Erdman, 'Theorizing Time', 37.

12   NHMRC, *An Information Paper*, 8.

13   Rennie Gay, 'Mid-Trimester Abortion in South Australia', 100.

14   DG Chambers, RJ Willcourt, AR Laver, JK Baird, and WY Herbert, 'Comparison of Dilapan-s and Laminaria for Cervical Priming', 347.

15   Jodie Dodd, Lauri O'Brien and Judy Coffey, 'Misoprostol for Second and Third Trimester Termination of Pregnancy'.

16   Wainer, 'Abortion as an Indicator of the Value of Women'.

17   Adrian McGregor, 'This Man is on the Frontier of Australian Abortion Practice. Now He, Like Many Other Practitioners, Is Under Threat', *The Weekend Australian Review*, 26–27 July 1997, 4.

18   Clavant, 'Women's Right to Choose', 95.

19   Mark Jones, 'Clinical Issues in Mid Trimester Abortion'; Julie-Anne Davies, 'This Foetus is 24 Weeks Old. These Doctors Are Prepared to Abort It', *Saturday Age News Extra*, 25 April 1998, 4.

20   Ibid.

21   McGregor, 'This Man Is on the Frontier', 4.

22   Susan Kelly, 'Mid Trimester Counselling'.

23   McGregor, 'This Man Is on the Frontier', 1.

24   Davies, 'This Foetus is 24 Weeks Old', 4.

25   Ibid., 5.

26   Bonnie Travers, Choice/No Choice?, 125.

27   Cheryl Davenport, 'Achieving Abortion Law Reform in Western Australia', 303.

28   Greg Cavanaugh, Coroner, Coroner's Court of Darwin, *Inquest into the Death of Jessica Jane *******.*

29   Abortion Providers Federation of Australia, *Standards of Practice and Guidelines for Member Facilities*, 9–10.

30   Baird, 'Abortion Politics', 251.

31   *Acts Amendment (Abortion) Act 1998, (No. 15 of 1998)* (WA).

32   Davenport, 'Achieving Abortion Law Reform in Western Australia', 304.

33   *Report to the Minister for Health*; Jan E Dickinson, 'Late Pregnancy Termination Within a Legislated Medical Environment', 338.

34   Ibid., 338, 340.

35   Lydia Mainey, Catherine O'Mullan and Kerry Reid-Searl, 'Working With or Against the System', 8–9, original emphasis.

36   Lachlan de Crespigny, F Chervenak, PA Coquel, Y Ville and L McCullough, 'Practicing Prenatal Diagnosis Within the Law', 492.

37   Nicole L Woodrow, 'Termination Review Committees', 34–7.

38   Black, Douglas and de Costa, 'Women's Access to Abortion after 20 Weeks', 147.

39   Julie Medew, 'Royal Women's Hospital Refuses Request for Abortion Of 26-Week-Old Foetus', *theage.com.au*, 23 October 2015.

40   Black, Douglas and de Costa, 'Women's Access to Abortion after 20 Weeks', 145; see also David Ellwood, 'Late Terminations of Pregnancy'.

41   Andrew W Gill, Peter Saul, John McPhee and Ian Kerridge, 'Acute Clinical Ethics Consultation', 204–6.
42   Ellwood, 'Late Terminations of Pregnancy'; Australian Medical Association Tasmania, 'Submission to the Tasmanian Government on the Law Governing Termination of Pregnancy', 2; Williams, Plater, Brunacci, Kapadia and Ozlad, *Abortion: A Review*, 224.
43   Woodrow, 'Termination Review Committees'; Black, Douglas and de Costa, 'Women's Access to Abortion after 20 Weeks'; Lachlan de Crespigny, 'Australian Abortion Laws'; Ellwood, 'Late Terminations of Pregnancy'.
44   *Report to the Minister for Health*, 22–23.
45   Natasha Robinson and Samantha Maiden, 'Male Pollies Risk Abortion "Backlash"', *The Weekend Australian,* 5–6 February 2005, 7; Natasha Robinson, 'Fears Raised Over Clinics', *The Weekend Australian,* 5–6 February 2005, 7.
46   Nader and Wroe, 'Late Abortion: The Doctor's Defence'; *The Age,* 'State in Rethink on Late Abortion', 25 October 2005.
47   VLRC, *Law of Abortion*, 87–93.
48   Commonwealth of Australia, *Item 16525 in Part 3 of Schedule 1.*
49   *ABC News*, 'Move to Allow Easier Access to Abortions', 8 March 2023.
50   Australian Medical Association Tasmania, 'Submission to the Tasmanian Government', 2.
51   Wahlquist, 'Abortion Law Backdown'.
52   QLRC, *Review of Termination of Pregnancy Laws*, 101.
53   Williams, Plater, Brunacci, Kapadia and Ozlad, *Abortion: A Review*, 241–2.
54   Ibid., 28.
55   Ben Smee, 'Queensland Election: LNP Tries to Keep Anti-Abortion Push out of Sight', *The Guardian*, 17 October 2020.
56   Ellwood, 'Late Terminations of Pregnancy'; SHFPACT, Unplanned Pregnancy Counselling Service; personal communication with Tim Bavinton, 11 April 2023.
57   Personal communication with Jo Flanagan, 17 November 2022.
58   Angela Williamson, 'The Apple Isle'.
59   Personal communication with Robyn Wardle, 23 November 2022.
60   VLRC, *Law of Abortion*, 34–7.
61   Jill Stark, 'Hospitals Clamp Down on Abortions', *theage.com.au*, 24 March 2013.
62   Keogh et al., 'Intended and Unintended Consequences', 22.
63   Paddy Moore and Aimee Kent, 'Equality of Access to Late Gestation Abortion in Victoria'.
64   Personal communication with Bonney Corbin, 19 November 2022.
65   QLRC, *Review of Termination of Pregnancy Laws*, 42.
66   56th Parliament Health, Communities, Disability Services and Domestic and Family Violence Prevention Committee, *Termination of Pregnancy Bill 2018, Report No. 11*, 26.
67   Personal communication with Bonney Corbin, 19 November 2022; personal communication with Daile Kelleher, 3 April 2023.
68   Queensland Health, *Queensland Clinical Guidelines*.
69   Family Planning NSW et al., *Framework for Abortion Access in NSW*, 7.
70   Ibid., 6–7.
71   56th Parliament Health, Communities, Disability Services and Domestic and Family Violence Prevention Committee, *Termination of Pregnancy Bill 2018*, 23.
72   Family Planning NSW et al., *Framework for Abortion Access in NSW,* 7.
73   *Pregnancy Outcome Statistics*, Wellbeing SA.
74   Dennis Chambers, Ea C Mulligan, Anthony R Laver, Bronwyn W Keller, Jane K Baird and WY Herbert, 'Comparison of Dilapan–s and Laminaria'.
75   Flowers, *Late Termination of Pregnancy*, 67, 68–72, 66–72.

76 Support After Fetal Diagnosis of Abnormality.

77 Flowers, *Late Termination of Pregnancy*, 73.

78 J Straton, K Godman, V Gee, and Q Hu, *Induced Abortion in Western Australia 1999–2005*; M Hutchinson and T Ballestas, *Induced Abortions in Western Australia 2013–2015*; Galrao, Hutchinson and Joyce, *Induced Abortions in Western Australia 2016–2018*.

79 Flowers, *Late Termination of Pregnancy*, 72.

80 Moore and Kent, 'Equality of Access'.

81 Flowers, *Late Termination of Pregnancy*, 67.

82 RANZCOG, 'RANZCOG Advanced Training Module: Sexuality and Reproductive Health, Contraception and Abortion'.

83 RANZCOG, Senate Inquiry into Abortion Access.

84 Jamieson, 'Finding into Death with Inquest', 18.

85 Ibid., 28.

86 Williamson, 'The Apple Isle', 38.

87 Family Planning NSW et al., *Framework for Abortion Access in NSW*, 7.

88 Personal communication with Bonney Corbin, 19 November 2022.

89 Lachlan J de Crespigny, Dominic J Wilkinson, Thomas Douglas, Mark Textor and Julian Savulescu, 'Australian Attitudes to Early and Late Abortion', 11–12.

90 Monica Cations, Margie Ripper and Judith Dwyer, 'Majority Support for Access to Abortion Care', 351.

91 RANZCOG, 'Late Abortion', 2.

92 Australian Medical Association (South Australia), AMA(SA) Submission to the South Australian Law Reform Institute (SALRI).

93 Millar, 'Maintaining Exceptionality', 454.

94 For example, see Davies, 'This Foetus is 24 Weeks Old', for detailed accounts of the stories of Amanda and Polly; in the lead-up to the NSW decriminalisation debate see Gina Rushton, '"It Makes Us Sound Like We're Monsters": What Having a Second-Trimester Abortion Actually Involves', *BuzzFeed*, 18 July 2019.

95 *Adelaide Now*, 'Late-term Abortion: It Was Our Toughest Choice', 25 Feb 2021.

96 McKinney, 'A Good Abortion is a Tragic Abortion'.

97 Alison Piepmeier, 'The Inadequacy of "Choice"'; Women With Disabilities Australia (WWDA), *WWDA Submission on Sexual and Reproductive Rights*.

98 Down Syndrome Australia, 'Submission to Disability Royal Commission Health Issues Paper', 8–9.

99 Morgan Carpenter, Statement on Intersex and Abortion Law Reform.

Conclusion

1 Miller and Rose, *Governing the Present*, 5.

2 Willis, Reynolds and Rudge, 'Understanding the Australian Health Care System'.

3 Baird, 'Maternity, Whiteness and National Identity'.

4 Judith Ireland, '"No One Approaches This Lightly": Leading Gynaecologist Speaks About Abortions', *The Sydney Morning Herald*, 15 September 2009.

Bibliography

Oral History Interviews (all names are pseudonyms)
Alex, GP abortion provider, December 2017, Adelaide
Anna, activist and academic, April 2013, Adelaide
Bunny, social worker, September 2016, Sydney (by Skype)
Chris, O&G abortion provider, April 2013, Brisbane
Davina, GP abortion provider, Melbourne, July 2015
Dorothy, activist, April 2013, Cairns
Evie, social worker, April 2013, Melbourne
Geri, sexual health nurse and manager, September 2015, Darwin
Gwen, activist, April 2016, Perth
Ingrid, GP abortion provider, June 2013, Adelaide
Joseph, O&G abortion provider, April 2016, Perth
Joyce, social worker, April 2016, Perth
Julie, manager, July 2015, Melbourne
June and Bree, women's health workers (interviewed together), April 2013, Melbourne
Laura and Iona, GP abortion providers (interviewed together), April 2016, Perth
Lil, GP abortion provider, December 2017, Adelaide
Louella, activist and public health practitioner, April 2013, Melbourne
Marilyn, public health practitioner, May 2016, Adelaide
Max, academic, September 2016, Sydney (by Skype)
Nic, GP abortion provider, April 2016, Perth
Nicola, Department of Health public servant, June 2013, Hobart
Petra, women's and reproductive and sexual health worker, January 2017, Hobart
Phyl, O&G abortion provider, July 2015, Melbourne
Priscilla, abortion activist and public health practitioner, September 2015, Darwin
Ralph, O&G abortion provider, August 2015, Adelaide
Robbie, sexual and reproductive health doctor, April 2013, Cairns
Roger, GP abortion provider, April 2015, Sydney
Rosalie, GP abortion provider, July 2013, Melbourne
Rowena, counsellor, April 2013, Melbourne
Sally, manager, April 2013, Adelaide
Sheelagh, sexual and reproductive health doctor, April 2015, Sydney
Simon, GP abortion provider, April 2015, Sydney

Viv, activist and women's health worker, April 2015, Sydney
Yolanda, manager, December 2017, Melbourne

Legislation and Legal Cases

Abortion Law Reform Act 2008 (Vic)
Abortion Law Reform Act 2019 No 11 (NSW)
Acts Amendment (Abortion) Act 1998 (No. 15 of 1998) (WA)
CES and Anor v Superclinics (Australia) Pty Ltd and Ors (1995) 38 NSWLR 47
Crimes (Abolition of Offence of Abortion) Act 2002 (ACT)
Crimes Legislation Amendment (Loss of Foetus) Bill 2021 (NSW)
Criminal Code Amendment Act 2001 (No. 2 of 2001) (Tas)
Health Care (Safe Access) Amendment Act 2020 (SA)
Health (Improving Abortion Access) Amendment Act 2018 (ACT)
Medical Practitioners (Maternal Health) Amendment Act 2002 (ACT)
Public Health Amendment (Safe Access to Reproductive Health Clinics) Act 2018 (No. 26 of 2018) (NSW)
Public Health Amendment (Safe Access Zones) Act 2021 (WA)
Termination of Pregnancy Act 2018 (Qld)
Termination of Pregnancy Act 2021 (SA)
Termination of Pregnancy Law Reform Act 2017 (No. 7 of 2017) (NT)
Termination of Pregnancy Law Reform Legislation Amendment Act 2021 (NT)
Therapeutic Goods Act 1989 (Cwlth)
Reproductive Health (Access to Terminations) Act 2013 (Tas)
R v Bayliss and Cullen (1986) 8 Qld Lawyer Reps 8.
R v Davidson [1969] VR 667, 672.
R v Wald (1972) 3 DCR (NSW) 25, 29.

Media

5AA
ABC News
ABC Radio
ABC RN
ABC Television
Adelaide Now
Al Jazeera
Australian Financial Review
BBC News
Brisbane Times
Buzzfeed News
Charity Times
CNBC
Crikey
Croakey Health Media
Courier Mail Weekend
Green Left
Junkee
National Indigenous Times
news.com

nine.com.au
NPR
SBS
Spectator Australia
Sunday Mail (QLD)
The Sydney Morning Herald
The Advertiser
The Age
The Australian
The Australian Magazine
The Border Mail
The Bulletin
The Canberra Times
The Examiner
The Guardian
The Mercury
The Saturday Paper
The Weekend Australian
WAtoday

Films and Television Programs

19 Weeks, theatre performance, written by Emily Steel, directed by Daisy Brown, 2017. https://www.19weeks.com.
19 Weeks, film, written and directed by Emily Steel, premiered 2023.
A Womb of Her Own: Four Women's Experiences of Abortion, VHS tape, directed by Catherine Gough-Brady, Fem TV and Red Emma Productions, Adelaide, 1994.
After Tiller, film documentary, directed by Martha Shane and Lana Wilson, 2013.
Christians Like Us, two-part television series, SBS television, 2019.
Inside the Clinic, episode 2 in Tough Jobs, directed by Maddie Parry, ABC television, 2015.
The Upside, television documentary, produced by Kim Akhurst, ABC television, 2020.

Websites

1800 My Options (Women's Health Victoria), https://www.1800myoptions.org.au
Australian Medical Association (AMA), https://www.ama.com.au
Blue Water Medical, https://www.bluewatermedical.com.au
Children By Choice, https://www.childrenbychoice.org.au
Clinic 66, https://www.clinic66.com.au
FPAA (Family Planning Alliance Australia), https://www.familyplanningallianceaustralia.org.au
Family Planning NSW, https://www.fpnsw.org.au
Family Planning Welfare Association NT (FPWANT), http://www.fpwnt.com.au/pages/Abortion.html
Gynaecare, https://gynaecare.com.au/
Gynaecology Centres Australia, https://gcaus.com.au
I Had One Too, https://ihadonetoo.com.au

Marie Stopes Australia, https://www.mariestopes.org.au

MSI Australia, https://www.mariestopes.org.au

MSI Reproductive Choices, https://www.msichoices.org

National Aboriginal Community Controlled Health Organisations, https://www.naccho.org.au

NSW Health, Pregnancy Options, https://www.health.nsw.gov.au/women/pregnancyoptions/Pages/default.aspx

Queensland Government: Termination of Pregnancy, https://www.qld.gov.au/health/children/pregnancy/termination-of-pregnancy

Royal Women's Hospital: Abortion And Contraception Education & Training, https://www.thewomens.org.au/health-professionals/clinical-education-training/abortion-and-contraception-education-training

Services Australia, https://www.servicesaustralia.gov.au/how-much-jobseeker-payment-you-can-get?context=51411

Sexual Health Quarters, https://shq.org.au

SHFPACT Unplanned Pregnancy Counselling Services, https://www.shfpact.org.au/unplanned-pregnancy-services

saaac, (South Australian Abortion Action Coalition), https://saabortionactioncoalition.com/about-us

SPHERE, NHMRC Centre of Research Excellence for Sexual and Reproductive Health for Women in Primary Care, https://www.spherecre.org/about

Support After Fetal Diagnosis of Abnormality (SAFDA), https://www.wch.sa.gov.au/patients-visitors/women/care-and-support/safda

The Tabbot Foundation, https://www.tabbot.com.au

Victorian Clinical Network For Abortion And Contraception Care, https://medicine.unimelb.edu.au/cersh/engage/clinical-network

Wellbeing SA, Pregnancy Outcome Statistics (SA Health) (for the reports of the South Australian Abortion Reporting Committee and Pregnancy Outcome in South Australia), https://www.wellbeingsa.sa.gov.au/evidence-data/pregnancy-outcome-statistics

Women's Health Tasmania, Pregnancy Choices Information, https://www.womenshealthtas.org.au/pregnancy-choices-information

Other Primary and Secondary Sources

56th Parliament Health, Communities, Disability Services and Domestic and Family Violence Prevention Committee, *Termination of Pregnancy Bill 2018, Report No. 11,* Queensland Parliament, Brisbane, 2018, https://documents.parliament.qld.gov.au/TableOffice/TabledPapers/2018/5618T1578.pdf.

Abortion Providers Federation of Australia, *Standards of Practice and Guidelines for Member Facilities,* Version 2.0, 2 July 1998.

Albury, Rebecca, *The Politics of Reproduction: Beyond the Slogans,* Allen & Unwin, St. Leonards, 1999.

——Too Many, Too Late and the Adoption Alternative: Shame and Recent Abortion Debates, paper presented at Public Policy Network Summer Conference, Adelaide, February 2007.

Allanson, Susie, *Murder on His Mind: The Untold Story of Australia's Abortion Clinic Murder,* Wilkinson Publishing, Melbourne, 2006.

——'Pregnancy/Abortion Counselling: False Providers, Mandatory Counselling, Ultrasound and "Cooling Off"', *Violence Against Women*, vol. 19, 2007, 5–9.

Allanson, Susie, with Lizzie O'Shea, *Empowering Women: From Murder and Misogyny to High Court Victory*, Wilkinson Publishing, Melbourne, 2021.

Anderson, Alison, 'The Abortion Struggle in Queensland', *Hecate*, vol. 6, no. 2, 1980, 7–13.

Anonymous, 'Just When You Thought It Was Safe … The Crisis in Public Abortion Services', *Health Issues*, vol. 18, March 1989, 27–31.

Arabena, Kerry, 'Preachers, Policies and Power: The Reproductive Health of Adolescent Aboriginal and Torres Strait Islander Peoples in Australia', *Health Promotion Journal of Australia*, vol. 17, no. 2, 2006, 85–90.

Atlay, Kemal, 'National "Cut-price" Postal Abortion Service to Close', *AusDoc*, 26 March 2019, https://www.ausdoc.com.au/news/national-cutprice-postal-abortion-service-close.

Australian Democrats, 'Democrats Move to Undo Harradine Block on RU-486', Press Release, 2 March 2001, https://parlinfo.aph.gov.au/parlInfo/download/media/pressrel/RSK36/upload_binary/rsk361.pdf;fileType=application%2Fpdf#search=%22media/pressrel/RSK36%22.

Australian Government Department of Health, *National Women's Health Strategy 2020–2030*, 2018, https://www.health.gov.au/sites/default/files/documents/2021/05/national-women-s-health-strategy-2020-2030.pdf.

Australian Lawyers for Human Rights, 'Human Rights Experts Warn against US-style Politicisation of Reproductive Rights in Australia', Media Release, 9 March 2023, https://alhr.org.au/children-born-alive-bill.

Australian Medical Association, 'Reproductive Health and Reproductive Technology Position Statement', *ama.com.au*, 1998, revised 2005, https://www.ama.com.au/sites/default/files/documents/Position_Satement_on_Reproductive_Health_And_Reproductive_Technology_1998_revised_2005.pdf.

Australian Medical Association (South Australia), 'AMA(SA) Submission to the South Australian Law Reform Institute (SALRI): Review of Abortion Law and Practice in South Australia', *AMA South Australia*, 2019, https://www.ama.com.au/sa/advocacy-policy/amasa-abortion-submission-recognises-diversity-of-members-views.

Australian Medical Association Tasmania, 'Submission to the Tasmanian Government on the Law Governing Termination of Pregnancy', *AMA Tasmania*, 5 April 2013, https://www.ama.com.au/tas/governing-termination-pregnancy-submission-tasmanian-government-april-2013.

Avant Media, 'Category of Cover Changed for GPs Involved in Medical Termination of Pregnancy', *Avant*, 1 December 2014, https://www.avant.org.au/news/20141201-category-of-cover-changed-for-gps/.

Axby, Helen, Abortion in the UK, paper presented at Abortion in Focus International Conference, November 1999.

Bacchi, Carol, and Susan Goodwin, *Poststructural Policy Analysis: A Guide to Practice*, Palgrave Macmillan, Basingstoke, 2016.

Bacon, Wendy, Pamela Curr, Carmen Lawrence, Julie Macken, and Claire O'Connor, *Protection Denied, Abuse Condoned: Women on Nauru at Risk*, Australian Women in Support of Women on Nauru, 2016, https://apo.org.au/sites/default/files/resource-files/2016/06/apo-nid64498.pdf.

Baird, Barbara, 'Abortion Politics During the Howard Years: Beyond Liberalisation', *Australian Historical Studies*, vol. 44, no. 2, 2013, 245–61.

——'The Futures of Abortion', in E McMahon and B Olubas (eds), *Women Making Time: Contemporary Feminist Critique and Cultural Analysis*, UWA Publishing, Perth, 2006, 116–51.

——*I Had One Too: An Oral History of Abortion in South Australia Before 1990*, Women's Studies Unit, Flinders University of South Australia, Bedford Park, 1990.

——'Maternity, Whiteness and National Identity: The Case of Abortion', *Australian Feminist Studies*, vol. 21, no. 50, 2006, 197–221.

——'Medical Abortion in Australia: A Short History', *Reproductive Health Matters*, vol. 23, no. 46, 2015, 169–76.

——'Tales Of Mobility: Women's Travel and Abortion Services in a Globalized Australia', in Christabelle Sethna and Gayle Davis (eds), *Abortion Across Borders: Transnational Travel and Access to Abortion Services*, Johns Hopkins University Press, Baltimore, 2019, 144–71.

——'Unforgetting: National Memory and Women's Personal Narratives about Abortion in Australian Public Spaces since 1970', *History Australia*, vol. 19, no. 2, 2022, 285–304.

Baird, Barbara, and Erica Millar, 'More Than Stigma: Interrogating Counter Narratives of Abortion', *Sexualities*, vol. 22, nos. 7–8, 2019, 1110–26.

Baker, Joanne, 'The Ideology of Choice: Overstating Progress and Hiding Injustice in the Lives of Young Women: Findings from a Study in North Queensland, Australia', *Women's Studies International Forum*, vol. 31, no. 1, 2008, 53–64.

Banwell, Stacy, 'Gender, North–South Relations: Reviewing the Global Gag Rule and the Defunding of UNFPA under President Trump', *Third World Quarterly*, vol. 41, no. 1, 2020, 1–19.

Barker, Lee, 'Establishing a Women's Controlled Abortion Clinic—The Tasmanian Experience', in *Abortion: Legal Right, Women's Right, Human Right: 1993 National Conference Papers*, Abortion Rights Network of Australia, South Brisbane, 1994, 41–45.

——'Who Wields the Scalpel? Limiting Access to Abortion Services in Tasmania', in R Moore (ed.), *Women and Surgery 1990 Conference Proceedings: Conference Papers, Workshop Reports and Program Details*, Healthsharing Women, Melbourne, 1991, 91.

Barnett, Belinda, The Perinatal Is Political: Community Advocacy for Implementation and Evaluation of the 2010–2016 Australian National Maternity Services Plan, paper presented at ACM 2019 National Conference, Canberra, 2019.

Bateson, Deborah J, Patricia A Lohr, Wendy V Norman, Caroline Moreau, Kristina Gemzell-Danielsson, Paul D Blumenthal, Lesley Hoggart, Hang-Wun Raymond Li, Abigail RA Aiken, and Kirsten I Black, 'The Impact of COVID-19 on Contraception and Abortion Care Policy and Practice: Experiences from Selected Countries', *BMJ Sexual & Reproductive Health*, vol. 46, no. 4, 2020, 241–3.

Baum, Fran, *The New Public Health*, 3rd edn, Oxford University Press, South Melbourne, 2008.

Beattie, Jennifer, "Gatekeepers" of Abortion in Australia: Abortion Law and the Protection of Doctors, PhD, Australian National University, 2018.

Behrendt, Larissa, Chris Cunneen, and Terri Libesman, *Indigenous Legal Relations in Australia*, Oxford University Press, South Melbourne, 2008.

Belton, Suzanne, Caroline de Costa, and Andrea Whittaker, 'Termination of Pregnancy: A Long Way to Go in the Northern Territory', *Medical Journal of Australia*, vol. 202, no. 3, 2015, 130–1.

Belton, Suzanne, and Karen Dempsey, Termination of Pregnancy: Trends, Women's Characteristics and Implications for Public Health Planning in the Northern Territory, unpublished paper, August 2016 (in possession of the author).

Belton, Suzanne, Georgia McQueen, and Edwina Ali, 'Impact of Legislative Change on Waiting Time for Women Accessing Surgical Abortion Services in a Rural Hospital in the Northern Territory', *Australian and New Zealand Journal of Obstetrics and Gynaecology*, vol. 60, no. 3, 2020, 459–64.

Belton, Suzanne, Ea Mulligan, Felicity Gerry, Paul Hyland, and Virginia Skinner, 'Mifepristone by Prescription: Not Quite a Reality in the Northern Territory of Australia', *Contraception*, vol. 94, no. 4, 2016, 378–9.

Berer, Marge, 'Medical Abortion: Issues of Choice and Acceptability', *Reproductive Health Matters*, vol. 13, no. 26, 2005, 25–34.

——'Provision of Abortion by Mid-level Providers: International Policy, Practice and Perspectives', *Bulletin of the World Health Organization*, vol. 87, no. 1, 2009, 58–63.

——'Reconceptualizing Safe Abortion and Abortion Services in the Age of Abortion Pills: A Discussion Paper', *Best Practice & Research Clinical Obstetrics & Gynaecology*, vol. 63, 2020, 45–55.

——'Telemedicine and Self-Managed Abortion: A Discussion Paper', *The Berer Blog*, 22 November 2020, https://bererblog.wordpress.com/2020/11/22/telemedicine-and-self-managed-abortion-a-discussion-paper.

Berer, Marge, and Lesley Hoggart, 'Medical Abortion Pills Have the Potential to Change Everything About Abortion', *Contraception*, vol. 97, no. 2, 2018, 79–81.

——'Progress Toward Decriminalization of Abortion and Universal Access to Safe Abortions: National Trends and Strategies', *Health and Human Rights*, vol. 21, no. 2, 2019, 79–83.

Berry, Wayne, Decriminalising Abortion in the ACT, address to public meeting presented by the Women's Studies Program, University of Tasmania, May 2003 (in possession of the author).

Berry, Yvette, and Rachel Stephen-Smith, 'Canberrans to Have Free Access to Safe Abortion Services', Joint Media Release, ACT Government, 4 August 2022, https://www.cmtedd.act.gov.au/open_government/inform/act_government_media_releases/rachel-stephen-smith-mla-media-releases/2022/canberrans-to-have-free-access-to-safe-abortion-services.

Black, Kirsten I, Heather Douglas, and Caroline de Costa, 'Women's Access to Abortion after 20 Weeks' Gestation for Fetal Chromosomal Abnormalities: Views and Experiences of Doctors in New South Wales and Queensland', *Australian and New Zealand Journal of Obstetrics and Gynaecology*, vol. 55, no. 2, 2015, 144–148.

Black, Kirsten, Jane Fisher, and Sonya Grover, 'Public Hospital Pregnancy Termination Services: Are We Meeting Demand?', *Australian and New Zealand*

Journal of Public Health, vol. 23, no. 5, 1999, 525–7.

Black, Kirsten I, and Helen Paterson, 'A Focus on Sexual and Reproductive Health Is Central to Achieving RANZCOG's Goal of Excellence in Women's Health Care', *Australian and New Zealand Journal of Obstetrics and Gynaecology*, vol. 59, no. 1, 2019, 18–20.

Brookes, Barbara, *Abortion in England 1900–1967*, Routledge, London, 1988.

Brown, Wendy, 'American Nightmare: Neoliberalism, Neoconservatism, and De-democratization', *Political Theory*, vol. 36, no. 6, 2006, 690–714.

Bryan, Amanda, 'Shy of Retiring', *The Medical Journal of Australia*, vol. 197, no. 9, 2012, https://www.mja.com.au/journal/2012/197/9/shy-retiring.

Buttfield, Barbara, and Katrina Allen, 'Can Education Influence the Shortage of Doctors Willing to Provide Abortion Services', in *Abortion—Politics, Access and Challenges: Conference Proceedings*, Abortion Providers Federation of Australasia Biennial Conference, Adelaide, 2001, 120–1.

Calkin, Sydney, 'One Year On, It's Clear That the New Irish Abortion Services Have Serious Limitations', *The Conversation*, 15 January 2020, https://theconversation.com/one-year-on-its-clear-that-the-new-irish-abortion-services-have-serious-limitations-129491.

——'Towards a Political Geography of Abortion', *Political Geography*, vol. 69, 2019, 22–29.

Calo, Brooke, 'The Violence of Misinformation: Compulsory Independent Counselling and the Current Abortion Debate', *Women Against Violence*, no. 19, 2006–07, 10–19.

Cameron, Sarah M, and Ian McAllister, *Trends in Australian Political Opinion: Results from the Australian Election Study, 1987–2013*, Australian National University, Canberra, 2008.

Cannold, Leslie, and Cait Calcutt, 'The Australian Pro-Choice Movement and the Struggle for Legal Clarity, Liberal Laws and Liberal Access: Two Case Studies', in B Klugman and D Budlender (eds), *Advocating for Abortion Access: Eleven Country Studies*, School of Public Health, Women's Health Project, University of Witwatersrand, Johannesburg, 2001, 46–57.

Carpenter, Morgan, Statement on Intersex and Abortion Law Reform, Intersex Human Rights Australia, 29 October 2019, https://ihra.org.au/35596/statement-intersex-abortion-law/.

Carson, Andrea, Martha Paynter, Wendy V Norman, Sarah Munro, Josette Roussel, Sheila Dunn, Denise Bryant-Lukosius, Stephanie Begun, and Ruth Martin-Misener, 'Optimizing the Nursing Role in Abortion Care: Considerations for Health Equity', *Canadian Journal of Nursing Leadership*, vol. 35, no. 1, 2022, 54–68.

Cations, Monica, Margie Ripper, and Judith Dwyer, 'Majority Support for Access to Abortion Care Including Later Abortion in South Australia', *Australian and New Zealand Journal of Public Health*, vol. 44, no. 5, 2020, 349–52.

Cavanagh, Greg, Coroner, Coroner's Court of Darwin, *Inquest into the Death of Jessica Jane ★★★★★★★*[2000] NTMC 37, Reference 9815022 101/98, 2 November 1999, https://justice.nt.gov.au/__data/assets/pdf_file/0017/206702/baby-j.pdf.

Cawley, A, 'Submission to the Inquiry into Therapeutic Goods Amendment (Repeal of Ministerial Responsibility for Approval of RU486), Bill 2005. No.

606', Broome Regional Aboriginal Medical Service, n.d.

Chambers, Dennis G, Ea C Mulligan, Anthony R Laver, Brownyn W Keller, Jane K Baird, and Wye Y Herbert, 'Comparison of Four Perioperative Misoprostol Regimens for Surgical Termination of First-Trimester Pregnancy', *International Journal of Gynecology & Obstetrics*, vol. 107, no. 3, 2009, 211–15.

Chambers, DG, RJ Willcourt, AR Laver, JK Baird, and WY Herbert, 'Comparison of Dilapan-s and Laminaria for Cervical Priming before Surgical Pregnancy Termination at 17–22 weeks' Gestation', *International Journal of Women's Health*, vol. 3, 2011, 347–52.

Chan, Annabelle et al., *Pregnancy Outcome in South Australia 1990*, Pregnancy Outcome Unit, Department of Human Services, Adelaide, 1991.

Chan, Annabelle, Joan Scott, Anh-Minh Nguyen, and Rosemary Keane, *Pregnancy Outcome in South Australia 2001*, Pregnancy Outcome Unit, Department of Human Services, Adelaide, 2002.

Cheng, Hon Chuen, Kirsten Black, Cindy Woods and Caroline de Costa, 'Views and Practices of Induced Abortion Among Australian Fellows and Trainees of The Royal Australian and New Zealand College of Obstetricians and Gynaecologists: A Second Study', *Australian and New Zealand Journal of Obstetrics and Gynaecology*, vol. 60, no. 2, 2020, 290–5.

Cheng, Hon Chuen, and Caroline de Costa, 'Abortion Education in Australian Medical Schools', *Australian and New Zealand Journal of Obstetrics and Gynaecology*, vol. 61, no. 5, 2021, 793–7.

Choudry, Aziz, and Dip Kapoor, 'Introduction', in A Choudry and D Kapoor (eds), *NGOization: Complicity, Contradictions and Prospects*, Zed Books, London, 2012, 1–23.

Clarke, Adele, and Theresa Montini, 'The Many Faces of RU486: Tales of Situated Knowledges and Technological Contestations', *Science, Technology, & Human Values*, vol. 18, no. 1, 1993, 42–78.

Clavant, Samantha, 'Women's Right to Choose—Political Barriers and Challenges', in *Abortion—Politics, Access and Challenges: Conference Proceedings*, Abortion Providers Federation of Australasia Biennial Conference, Adelaide, 2001, 94–103.

Collyer, Fran, Karen Willis, and Helen Keleher, 'The private health sector and private health insurance', in Eileen Willis, Louise Reynolds and Trudy Rudge (eds), *Understanding the Australian Health Care System*, 4th edn, Elsevier, Chatswood, 2020, 37–52

Commonwealth of Australia, *Inquiry into Therapeutic Goods Amendment (Repeal of Ministerial Responsibility for Approval of RU486) Bill 2005*, 8 February 2006, https://www.aph.gov.au/parliamentary_business/committees/senate/community_affairs/completed_inquiries/2004-07/ru486/report/index.

——*Item 16525 in Part 3 of Schedule 1 to the Health Insurance (General Medical Services Table) Regulations 2007*, November 2008, https://www.aph.gov.au/Parliamentary_Business/Committees/Senate/Finance_and_Public_Administration/Completed_inquiries/2008-10/health_insurance_regs/report/index.

Connors, Sarah, 'What do Consumers of Termination of Pregnancy Want?' in *Proceedings of APFA/RWH Conference: Sex, Lies and Dilemmas: Abortion into the Next Millennium*, Royal Women's Hospital, Carlton, 1997, 3–5.

Davenport, Cheryl, 'Achieving Abortion Law Reform in Western Australia', *Australian Feminist Studies*, vol. 13, no. 28, 1998, 299–304.

Davis, Jasmine Meredith, Casey Michelle Haining, and Louise Anne Keogh, 'A Narrative Literature Review of the Impact of Conscientious Objection by Health Professionals on Women's Access to Abortion Worldwide 2013–2021', *Global Public Health*, vol. 17, no. 9, 2021, 2190–205.

Dawson, Angela J, Rachel Nicolls, Deborah Bateson, Anna Doab, Jane Estoesta, Ann Brassil, and Elizabeth A Sullivan, 'Medical Termination of Pregnancy in General Practice in Australia: A Descriptive-Interpretive Qualitative Study', *Reproductive Health*, vol. 14, no. 1, 2017.

Deb, Seema, Asvini K Subasinghe, and Danielle Mazza, 'Providing Medical Abortion in General Practice: General Practitioner Insights and Tips for Future Providers', *Australian Journal of General Practice*, vol. 49, no. 6, 2020, 331–7.

de Costa, Caroline, 'Early Medical Abortion in Australia: More Common Than Statistics Suggest?', *Medical Journal of Australia*, vol. 185, no. 6, 2006, 341.

——'Medical Abortion for Australian Women: It's Time', *Medical Journal of Australia*, vol. 183, no. 7, 2005, 378–80.

——*Never, Ever, Again: Why Australian Abortion Law Needs Reform*, Boolarong Press, Moorooka, 2010.

——*RU-486: The Abortion Pill*, Boolarong Press, Moorooka, 2007.

——*The Women's Doc*, Allen & Unwin, Sydney, 2021.

de Costa, Caroline M, Kirsten I Black, and Darren B Russell, 'Medical Abortion: It Is Time to Lift Restrictions', *Medical Journal of Australia*, vol. 210, no. 6, 2019, E248–9.

de Costa, Caroline M, and Michael Carrette, 'Early Medical Abortion—Available and Safe', *Medical Journal of Australia*, vol. 197, no. 5, 2012, 257–8.

de Costa, Caroline, and Heather Douglas, 'Abortion Law in Australia: It's Time for National Consistency and Decriminalisation', *Medical Journal of Australia*, vol. 203, no. 9, 2015, 349–50.

de Costa, Caroline M, Darren B Russell, and Michael Carrette, 'Views and Practices of Induced Abortion among Australian Fellows and Specialist Trainees of the Royal Australian and New Zealand College of Obstetricians and Gynaecologists', *Medical Journal of Australia*, vol. 193, no. 1, 2010, 13–16.

de Costa, Caroline, Darren B Russell, Naomi R de Costa, Michael Carrette, and Heather M McNamee, 'Early Medical Abortion in Cairns, Queensland: July 2006–April 2007', *Medical Journal of Australia*, vol. 187, no. 3, 2007, 171–3.

de Crespigny, Lachlan, 'Australian Abortion Laws: Do They Pose a "Health Hazard"?' *O&G Magazine*, vol. 7, no 1, 2005, 52–4.

de Crespigny, Lachlan, F Chervenak, P A Coquel, Y Ville, and L McCullough, 'Practicing Prenatal Diagnosis Within the Law', *Ultrasound in Obstetrics and Gynecology: The Official Journal of the International Society of Ultrasound in Obstetrics and Gynecology*, vol. 24, no. 5, 2004, 489–94.

de Crespigny, Lachlan J, and Julian Savulescu, 'Abortion: Time To Clarify Australia's Confusing Laws', *Medical Journal of Australia*, vol. 181, no. 4, 2004, 201–3.

de Crespigny, Lachlan J, Dominic J Wilkinson, Thomas Douglas, Mark Textor, and Julian Savulescu, 'Australian Attitudes to Early and Late Abortion', *Medical Journal of Australia*, vol. 193, no. 1, 2010, 9–12.

Dean, Rebecca, and Susie Allanson, 'Abortion in Australia: Access Versus Protest', *Journal of Law and Medicine*, vol. 11, no. 4, 2004, 510–15.

de Moel-Mandel, Caroline, Melissa Graham, and Ann Taket, 'Expert Consensus on a Nurse-Led Model of Medication Abortion Provision in Regional and Rural Victoria, Australia: A Delphi Study', *Contraception*, vol. 100, no. 5, 2019, 380–5.

de Moel-Mandel, Caroline, and Julia M Shelley, 'The Legal and Non-Legal Barriers to Abortion Access in Australia: A Review of the Evidence', *The European Journal of Contraception & Reproductive Health Care*, vol. 22, no. 2, 2017, 114–22.

Department of Community Services and Health, *National Women's Health Policy: Advancing Women's Health in Australia*, Australian Government Publishing Service, Canberra, 1989.

Department of Health, Government of Western Australia, *Abortion Legislation: Proposal for Reform in Western Australia*, Discussion Paper, November 2022, https://consultation.health.wa.gov.au/pahd-ocho-alr/abortion-laws/user_uploads/abortion-legisation----proposal-for-reform-in-western-australia---november-2022-1.pdf.

Department of Health, Victoria State Government, *Victorian Women's Sexual and Reproductive Health Plan 2022–30*, Victorian Government 2022, Melbourne, https://www.health.vic.gov.au/publications/victorian-womens-sexual-and-reproductive-health-plan-2022-30.

Department of Health and Human Services, Victoria State Government, *Women's Sexual And Reproductive Health: Key Priorities 2017–2020*, State of Victoria, Melbourne, 2017, https://content.health.vic.gov.au/sites/default/files/migrated/files/collections/policies-and-guidelines/w/womens-sexual-health-priorities-20172020-pdf.

Dickinson, Jan E, 'Late Pregnancy Termination Within a Legislated Medical Environment', *Australian and New Zealand Journal of Obstetrics and Gynaecology*, vol. 44, no. 4, 2004, 337–41.

Dodd, Jodie, Lauri O'Brien, and Judy Coffey, 'Misoprostol for Second and Third Trimester Termination of Pregnancy: A Review of Practice at the Women's and Children's Hospital, Adelaide, Australia', *Australian and New Zealand Journal of Obstetrics and Gynaecology*, vol. 45, no. 1, 2005, 25–9.

Doherty, P, The GP Connection: Improving Medical Abortion Access, paper presented at Public Health Association Australia 2nd National Sexual & Reproductive Health Conference, Melbourne, 2014.

Doran, Frances, and Julie Hornibrook, 'Rural New South Wales Women's Access to Abortion Services: Highlights From an Exploratory Qualitative Study', *Australian Journal of Rural Health*, vol. 22, no. 3, 2014, 121–6.

Douglas, Heather, Kirsten Black, and Caroline de Costa, 'Manufacturing Mental Illness (and Lawful Abortion): Doctors' Attitudes to Abortion Law and Practice in New South Wales and Queensland', *Journal of Law and Medicine*, vol. 20, no. 3, 2013, 560–76.

Down Syndrome Australia, 'Submission to Disability Royal Commission Health Issues Paper', *Down Syndrome Australia*, 2020, https://www.downsyndrome.org.au/wp-content/uploads/2020/05/Submission_RoyalCommission_Health_PDF.pdf.

Downing, Sandra G, Colette Cashman, and Darren B Russell, 'Ten Years On: A Review of Medical Terminations of Pregnancy Performed in a Sexual Health Clinic', *Sexual Health*, vol. 14, no. 3, 2017, 208–12.

Duffy, Deirdre Niamh, Claire Pierson, Caroline Myerscough, Diane Urquhart, and Lindsey Earner-Byrne, 'Abortion, Emotions, and Health Provision: Explaining Health Care Professionals' Willingness to Provide Abortion Care Using Affect Theory', *Women's Studies International Forum*, vol. 71, 2018, 12–18.

Dwyer, Judith M, 'Australian Health System Restructuring—What Problem is Being Solved?', *Australia and New Zealand Health Policy*, vol. 1, no. 1, 2004, 6.

Dwyer, Judith, Mark Rankin, Margie Ripper, and Monica Cations, 'Is There Still a Need for Abortion-Specific Laws? The Capacity of the Health Framework to Regulate Abortion Care', *Alternative Law Journal*, vol. 46, no. 2, 2021, 141–8.

Eddington, John, 'Conquering the Last Frontier: Development of an Abortion Service in Regional Australia', in Key Centre for Women's Health in Society, The University of Melbourne, Royal Women's Hospital, Family Planning Victoria, and Women's Health Victoria, *Abortion in Victoria. Where Are We? Where Do We Want to Go?* 30 November 2007, The University of Melbourne, 31–6.

Edwards, Sandy, Sue McKinnon, Jane Tassie, and Vicki Toovey, 'Women's Health Centres – Survival and Future in a New Political Era', in J Davis, S Andrews, DH Broom, G Gray and M Renwick (eds) *Changing Society for Women's Health: Proceedings of the Third National Women's Health Conference, 17–19 November 1995*, Australian Women's Health Network and Women's Electoral Lobby, 1996, 42–46.

Eisenstein, Hester, *Inside Agitators: Australian Femocrats and the State*, Allen & Unwin, St Leonards, 1996.

Elliott, Eliza (Lander and Rogers), 'General Practitioner Reprimanded For Unprofessional Conduct In Late Stage Pregnancy Termination', *Lexology*, 15 November 2017, https://www.lexology.com/library/detail. aspx?g=61710bf9-824e-4d37-b8ae-fee22392e61c.

Ellwood, David, 'Late Terminations of Pregnancy—An Obstetrician's Perspective', *Australian Health Review*, vol. 29, no. 2, 2005, 139–42.

El-Murr, Alissar, 'Representing the Problem of Abortion: Language and the Policy Making Process in the Abortion Law Reform Project in Victoria, 2008', *Australian Feminist Law Journal*, vol. 33, no. 1, 2010, 121–40.

Endler, M, A Lavelanet, A Cleeve, B Ganatra, R Gomperts, and K Gemzell–Danielsson, 'Telemedicine for Medical Abortion: A Systematic Review', *BJOG: An International Journal of Obstetrics & Gynaecology*, vol. 126, no. 9, 2019, 1094–102.

Erdman, Joanna, 'Put Abortion Pills into Peoples' Hands', *Policy Options*, 11 May 2022, https://policyoptions.irpp.org/magazines/may-2022/abortion-pills-canada/.

——'Theorizing Time in Abortion Law and Human Rights', *Health & Human Rights Journal*, vol. 19, no. 1, 2017, 29–40.

Erdman, Joanna N, Kinga Jelinska, and Susan Yanow, 'Understandings of Self-Managed Abortion as Health Inequity, Harm Reduction and Social Change', *Reproductive Health Matters*, vol. 26, no. 54, 2018, 13–19.

Erny-Albrecht, Katrina, and Petra Bywood, 'Corporatisation of General Practice—Impact and Implications', *PHCRIS Policy Issue Review*, Primary Health Care Research & Information Service, Adelaide, 2016.

Estimates and Financial Operations Committee, *Question on Notice Supplementary Information (Questions 16 and 17 from Hon N Goiran)*, 24 June 2015, https://www.parliament.wa.gov.au/parliament/commit.nsf/($lookupRelatedDocsByID)/A6E3FC2BC81B2D8948257E680018A60D/$file/ef.ehw16.150619.qpa.001.kh.pdf.

Evatt, Elizabeth, Felix Arnott, and Anne Deveson, *Royal Commission on Human Relationships, Final Report, Volume 3*, Australian Government Publishing Service, Canberra, 1977.

Family Planning NSW, Women's Health NSW and Chair of Sexual and Reproductive Health Special Interest Group of RANZCOG, *Framework for Abortion Access in NSW*, October 2020, https://www.fpnsw.org.au/sites/default/files/assets/Report_Abortion-Access-in-NSW_202010.pdf.

Faruqi, Mehreen, 'End12—A Campaign To Decriminalise Abortion In New South Wales', http://www5.austlii.edu.au/au/journals/UNSWLawSocCConsc/2017/7.pdf.

Finch, Lynette, *The Classing Gaze: Sexuality, Class and Surveillance*, Allen & Unwin, St. Leonards, 1993.

Finch, Lyn, and Jon Stratton, 'The Australian Working Class and the Practice of Abortion 1880–1939', *Journal of Australian Studies*, vol. 12, no. 23, 1988, 45–64.

Flowers, Prudence, *Late Termination of Pregnancy: An Internationally Comparative Study of Public Health Policy, the Law, and the Experiences of Providers*, Report for the Catherine Helen Spence Scholarship 2018, November 2020, https://www.sa.gov.au/__data/assets/pdf_file/0004/713290/Late-Termination-of-Pregnancy-CHS-Report.pdf.

Franzway, Suzanne, Dianne Court, and RW Connell, *Staking a Claim: Feminism, Bureaucracy and the State*, Allen & Unwin, Sydney, 1989.

Fraser, Nancy, 'Feminism, Capitalism and the Cunning of History', *New Left Review*, vol. 56, March/April 2009, 97–117.

Funston, Leticia, and Sigrid Herring, 'When Will the Stolen Generations End?: A Qualitative Critical Exploration of Contemporary "Child Protection" Practices in Aboriginal and Torres Strait Islander Communities', *Sexual Abuse in Australia and New Zealand*, vol. 7, no. 1, 2016, 51–8.

Galrao, M, M Hutchinson, and A Joyce, *Induced Abortions in Western Australia 2016–2018: Sixth Report of the Western Australian Abortion Notification System*, Department of Health, Western Australia, 2019.

Gay, Rennie, 'Mid-Trimester Abortion in South Australia', *Women and Surgery 1990 Conference Proceedings: Conference Papers, Workshop Reports and Program Details*, Healthsharing Women, Melbourne, 1991, 100–01.

Gerber, Paul, 'Late-term Abortion: What Can Be Learned from Royal Women's Hospital v Medical Practitioners Board of Victoria?', *Medical Journal of Australia*, vol. 186, no. 7, 2007, 359–62.

Gill, Andrew W, Peter Saul, John McPhee, and Ian Kerridge, 'Acute Clinical Ethics Consultation: The Practicalities', *Medical Journal of Australia*, vol. 181, no. 4, 2004, 204–6.

Gill, Rosalind, and Christina Scharff, *New Femininities: Postfeminism, Neoliberalism and Subjectivity*, Palgrave Macmillan, Basingstoke, 2010.

Gleeson, Kate, 'The Limits of "Choice": Abortion and Entrepreneurialism', in Meredith Nash (ed.), *Reframing Reproduction: Conceiving Gendered Experiences*,

Palgrave, New York, 2014, 69–83.

——'The Other Abortion Myth—The Failure of the Common Law', *Journal of Bioethical Inquiry*, vol. 6, no. 1, 2009, 69–81.

Goldstone, Philip, Jill Michelson, and Eve Williamson, 'Early Medical Abortion Using Low-dose Mifepristone Followed by Buccal Misoprostol: A Large Australian Observational Study', *Medical Journal of Australia*, vol. 197, no. 5, 2012, 282–86.

——'Effectiveness of Early Medical Abortion Using Low-Dose Mifepristone and Buccal Misoprostol in Women with No Defined Intrauterine Gestational Sac', *Contraception*, vol. 87, no. 6, 2013, 855–58.

Goldstone, Philip, Clara Walker, and Katherine Hawtin, 'Efficacy and Safety of Mifepristone–Buccal Misoprostol for Early Medical Abortion in an Australian Clinical Setting', *Australian and New Zealand Journal of Obstetrics and Gynaecology*, vol. 57, no. 3, 2017, 366–71.

Goodwin, Susan, and Kate Huppatz, *The Good Mother: Contemporary Motherhoods in Australia*, Sydney University Press, Sydney, 2010.

Graham, Melissa, Hayley McKenzie, Greer Lamaro, and Ruth Klein, 'Women's Reproductive Choices in Australia: Mapping Federal and State/Territory Policy Instruments Governing Choice', *Gender Issues*, vol. 33, no. 4, 2016, 335–49.

Gray Jamieson, Gwendolyn, *Reaching for Health: The Australian Women's Health Movement and Public Policy*, ANU Press, Canberra, 2012.

Graycar, Reg, and Jenny Morgan, 'Law Reform: What's In It For Women', *Windsor Yearbook of Access to Justice*, vol. 23, 2005, 419.

——'Unnatural Rejection of Womanhood and Motherhood: Pregnancy, Damages and the Law—A Note on CES v Superclinics (Aust) Pty Ltd', *Sydney Law Review*, vol. 18, no. 3, 1996, 323.

Grayston, Stephanie, 'Changing Attitudes and Services: Abortion in Western Australia, 1970–1990', in P Hetherington and PC Maddern (eds), *Sexuality and Gender in History: Selected Essays,* Centre for Western Australian History, Perth, 1993, 242–54.

Greble, Ruth, 'Western Australian Report', in *Abortion: Legal Right, Women's Right, Human Right: 1993 National Conference Papers,* Abortion Rights Network of Australia, South Brisbane, 1994, 41–2.

Grundmann, David, Abortion and the Law: Twenty Five Years. A Personal Perspective, paper presented at the Australian Institute of Criminology, Law, Medicine and Criminal Justice Conference, Surfers Paradise, 1993, 1–5 (in possession of the author).

Grzeskowiak, Luke E, Helen Calabretto, Natalie Amos, Danielle Mazza, and Jenni Ilomaki, 'Changes in Use of Hormonal Long-acting Reversible Contraceptive Methods in Australia Between 2006 and 2018: A Population-based Study', *Australian and New Zealand Journal of Obstetrics and Gynaecology*, 61, no. 1, 2021, 128–134.

Haggis, Jane, and Susanne Schech, 'Meaning Well and Global Good Manners: Reflections on White Western Feminist Cross-cultural Praxis', *Australian Feminist Studies*, vol. 15, no. 33, 2000, 387–99.

Hayes, Trish, 'Reproductive Coercion and the Australian State: A New Chapter', *Australian Community Psychologist*, vol. 28, no. 1, 2016, 90–100.

Hayes, Trish, Chanel Keane, and Suzanne Hurley, 'Counselling "Late Women":

The Experience of Women Seeking Abortion in the Eighteen to Twenty-Four-Week Gestational Period: Critical Reflections From Three Abortion Counsellors', *Women's Studies International Forum*, vol. 78, 2020, 102307.

Healy, David, and Amanda J Evans, 'Mifepristone and Emergency Contraception: Unavailability of Mifepristone Represents a Neglect of Australian Women's Health', *Medical Journal of Australia*, vol. 161, 1994, 403–4.

Healy, David L, and Hamish M Fraser, 'The Antiprogesterones Are Coming: Menses Induction, Abortion, and Labour?', *British Medical Journal*, vol. 290, no. 6468, 1985, 580–1.

Hemmings, L 'Medical Abortion in Tasmania: Nursing Implications', in *Abortion—Politics, Access, and Challenges: Conference Proceedings*, Abortion Providers Federation of Australia Biennial Conference, Adelaide, 2001, 123.

Henckels, Caroline, Ronli Sifris, and Tania Penovic, 'High Court Delivers Landmark Ruling Validating Abortion Clinic "Safe Access Zones"', *The Conversation*, 12 April 2019, https://theconversation.com/high-court-delivers-landmark-ruling-validating-abortion-clinic-safe-access-zones-115062.

Hulme-Chambers, Alana, Meredith Temple-Smith, Ange Davidson, Lauren Coelli, Catherine Orr, and Jane E Tomnay, 'Australian Women's Experiences of a Rural Medical Termination of Pregnancy Service: A Qualitative Study', *Sexual & Reproductive Healthcare*, vol. 15, 2018, 23–7.

Human Rights Law Centre, 'NSW Decriminalisation Campaign Launches', 2 May 2019, https://www.hrlc.org.au/news/2019/5/2/nsw-abortion-decriminalisation-campaign-launches.

——'NSW Votes Down Bill to Modernise Abortion Law', 11 May 2017, https://www.hrlc.org.au/news/2017/5/11/nsw-votes-down-bill-to-modernise-abortion-law.

Hutchinson, M, and T Ballestas, *Induced Abortions in Western Australia 2013–2015: Fifth Report of the Western Australian Abortion Notification System*, Department of Health, Western Australia, 2018.

Hyland, Paul, Elizabeth G Raymond, and Erica Chong, 'A Direct-to-Patient Telemedicine Abortion Service in Australia: Retrospective Analysis of the First 18 Months', *Australian and New Zealand Journal of Obstetrics and Gynaecology*, vol. 58, no. 3, 2018, 335–40.

INCITE! Women of Color Against Violence (eds), *The Revolution Will Not Be Funded: Beyond the Non-Profit Industrial Complex*, Duke University Press, Durham, 2007.

Ireland, Sarah, Suzanne Belton, and Frances Doran, '"I Didn't Feel Judged": Exploring Women's Access to Telemedicine Abortion in Rural Australia', *Journal of Primary Health Care*, vol. 12, no. 1, 2020, 49–56.

Jamieson, Audrey, Coroner, Coroner's Court of Melbourne, 'Finding into Death with Inquest Court. Inquest into the Death of Delta Diawo Poke', Reference COR 2011 4738, 26 May 2016, https://www.coronerscourt.vic.gov.au/sites/default/files/2018-12/deltadiawopoke_473811.pdf.

Joffe, Carole E, *Doctors of Conscience: The Struggle to Provide Abortion Before and After Roe v. Wade*, Beacon Press, Boston, 1996.

Johnson, Carol, *Governing Change: Keating to Howard*, University of Queensland Press, St. Lucia, 2000.

Jones, Mark, 'Clinical Issues in Mid Trimester Abortion', in *Proceedings of APFA/*

RWH Conference: Sex, Lies and Dilemmas: Abortion into the Next Millennium, Royal Women's Hospital, Melbourne, 1997, n.p.

Jones, Rachel, Ushma D Upadhyay, and Tracy Weitz, 'At What Cost?: Payment for Abortion Care by US Women', *Women's Health Issues*, vol. 23, no. 3, 2013, e173–8.

Jones, Rachel K, Elizabeth Witwer, and Jenna Jerman, *Abortion Incidence and Service Availability in the United States, 2017*, Guttmacher Institute, New York, 2019.

Kelly, Janet, and Yoni Luxford, 'Yaitya Tirka Madlanna Warratinna: Exploring What Sexual Health Nurses Need to Know and Do in Order to Meet the Sexual Health Needs of Young Aboriginal Women in Adelaide', *Collegian*, vol. 14, no. 3, 2007, 15–20.

Kelly, Susan, 'Mid Trimester Counselling', in *Proceedings of APFA/RWH Conference: Sex, Lies and Dilemmas: Abortion into the Next Millennium*, Royal Women's Hospital, Melbourne, 1997, n.p.

Keogh, Louise Anne, Lynn Gillam, Marie Bismark, Kathleen McNamee, Amy Webster, Christine Bayly, and Danielle Newton, 'Conscientious Objection to Abortion, the Law and its Implementation in Victoria, Australia: Perspectives of Abortion Service Providers', *BMC Medical Ethics*, vol. 20, no. 1, 2019.

Keogh, Louise A, Lyle C Gurrin, and Patricia Moore, 'Estimating the Abortion Rate in Australia from National Hospital Morbidity and Pharmaceutical Benefits Scheme Data', *The Medical Journal of Australia,* vol. 215, no. 8, 2021, 375–6.

Keogh, Louise A, Danielle Newton, Christine Bayly, Kelly McNamee, Anne Hardiman, Angela C Webster, and Marie M Bismark, 'Intended and Unintended Consequences of Abortion Law Reform: Perspectives of Abortion Experts in Victoria, Australia,' *Journal of Family Planning and Reproductive Health Care*, vol. 43, no. 1, 2017, 18–24.

Kevin, Catherine, and Karen Agutter, 'Failing "Abyan", "Golestan" and "the Estonian Mother": Refugee Women, Reproductive Coercion and the Australian State', *Immigrants & Minorities*, vol. 36, no. 2, 2018, 87–104.

Key Centre for Women's Health in Society, The University of Melbourne, Royal Women's Hospital, Family Planning Victoria, and Women's Health Victoria, *Abortion in Victoria. Where Are We? Where Do We Want to Go?*, The University of Melbourne, 30 November 2007.

Keys, Zoe, Media Discourses of Abortion Law Reform, unpublished PhD thesis, Flinders University, 2023.

Kirkby, Margaret, Discussion Paper Regarding the Bessie Smyth Foundation, unpublished paper, March 2010 (in possession of the author).

Klein, Renate, Janice G Raymond, and Lynette J Dumble, *RU 486: Misconceptions, Myths and Morals*, new edn, Spinifex, North Melbourne, 2013.

Krassnitzer, Lindsay, 'The Public Health Sector and Medicare', in Eileen Willis, Louise Reynolds and Trudy Rudge (eds), *Understanding the Australian Health Care System*, 4th edn, Elsevier, Chatswood, 2020, 18–36.

Lancaster, Paul, Jishan Huang, and Elvis Pedisich, *Australia's Mothers and Babies 1991*, AIHW National Perinatal Statistics Unit, Sydney, 1994.

LaRoche, Kathryn J, LL Wynn, and Angel Foster, '"We Have to Make Sure You Meet Certain Criteria": Exploring Patient Experiences of the Criminalisation of Abortion in Australia', *Public Health Research and Practice*, vol. 31, no. 3, 2021, e0342011.

——"'We've Got Rights and Yet We Don't Have Access'": Exploring Patient Experiences Accessing Medication Abortion in Australia', *Contraception*, vol. 101, no. 4, 2020, 256–60.

Larkins, Sarah L, R Priscilla Page, Kathryn S Panaretto, Melvina Mitchell, Valerie Alberts, Suzanne McGinty, and P Craig Veitch, 'The Transformative Potential of Young Motherhood for Disadvantaged Aboriginal and Torres Strait Islander Women in Townsville, Australia', *Medical Journal of Australia*, vol. 194, no. 10, 2011, 551–5.

Lee, Ellie, Sally Sheldon, and Jan Macvarish, 'The 1967 Abortion Act Fifty Years On: Abortion, Medical Authority and the Law Revisited', *Social Science & Medicine*, vol. 212, 2018, 26–32.

Lee, Rebekah Yeaun, Rebekah Moles, and Betty Chaar, 'Mifepristone (RU486) in Australian Pharmacies: The Ethical and Practical Challenges', *Contraception*, vol. 91, no. 1, 2015, 25–30.

Legislative Council Standing Committee on Social Issues, *Reproductive Health Care Reform Bill 2019 [Provisions] Report 55*, August 2019, https://www.parliament. nsw.gov.au/lcdocs/inquiries/2547/Final%20report%20-%20Reproductive%20 Health%20Care%20Reform%20Bill%202019.pdf.

Lie-Spahn, Cecelia Brun, The Pharmocratics of Misoprostol: Race, Drugs, and Reproductive Neoliberalism, PhD, University of California, Santa Cruz, 2019.

Lohr, Patricia A, Jonathon Lord and Sam Rowlands, 'How Would Decriminalisation Affect Women's Health?', in S Sheldon and K Wellings (eds), *Decriminalising Abortion in the UK: What Would it Mean?*, Policy Press, Bristol, 2020, 37–56.

Maddison, Sarah, and Richard Denniss, 'Democratic Constraint and Embrace: Implications for Progressive Non-government Advocacy Organisations in Australia', *Australian Journal of Political Science*, vol. 40, no. 3, 2005, 373–89.

Maddox, Marion, *God Under Howard: The Rise of the Religious Right in Australian Politics*, Allen & Unwin, Crows Nest, 2005.

Mainey, Lydia, 'Empower Nurses to Improve Abortion Care', *The Hive*, 2 December 2019, https://www.acn.edu.au/the-hive-2019/empower-nurses-improve-abortion-care.

Mainey, Lydia, Catherine O'Mullan, and Kerry Reid-Searl, 'Unfit for Purpose: A Situational Analysis of Abortion Care and Gender-based Violence', *Collegian*, vol. 29, no. 5, 2022, 557–565.

——'Working With or Against the System: Nurses' and Midwives' Process of Providing Abortion Care in the Context of Gender-based Violence in Australia', *Journal of Advanced Nursing*, 2022.

Mamers, Pam M, Amanda J Evans, David L Healy, Anna L Lavelle, Sandra M Bell, and Jen R Rusden, 'Women's Satisfaction with Medical Abortion with RU486', *Medical Journal of Australia*, vol. 167, no. 6, 1997, 316–17.

Marcotte, Jessica, 'The Agnotology of Abortion: A History of Ignorance about Women's Knowledge of Fertility Control', *Outskirts: Feminisms Along the Edge*, vol. 34, 2016, 1–20.

Marie Stopes Australia, 'Big Changes in a New Strategy Coming—The New Team to See It Through', Media Statement, 12 November 2020, https://www. mariestopes.org.au/your-choices/new-strategy-coming-new-team.

Marie Stopes Australia, *Hidden Forces: A White Paper on Reproductive Coercion in*

Contexts of Family and Domestic Violence, 2nd edn, 2020, https://www.
mariestopes.org.au/wp-content/uploads/Hidden-Forces-Second-Edition-.pdf.

——*Impact Report 2018*, 2019, https://www.mariestopes.org.au/wp-content/
uploads/0596-MSA-Impact-Report-Web-200108.pdf.

——*Impact Report 2019*, 2020, https://www.mariestopes.org.au/wp-content/
uploads/MSA-Impact-Report-2019.pdf.

——*Impact Report 2020*, 2021, https://www.mariestopes.org.au/wp-content/
uploads/MSA-Impact-Report-2020.pdf.

——*Pre-Budget Submission 2021–2022: A Call to Increase Access to Sexual and
Reproductive Health in Australia*, 29 January 2021, https://treasury.gov.au/sites/
default/files/2021-05/171663_marie_stopes_australia.pdf.

——*Situational Report: Sexual and Reproductive Health Rights in Australia*, October
2020, https://resources.mariestopes.org.au/SRHRinAustralia.pdf.

Marie Stopes Australia, University of Queensland's Pro Bono Centre and
Australian Women Against Violence Alliance, *Safe Access Zones in Australia:
Legislative Considerations*, 2020, https://awava.org.au/wp-content/uploads/
2020/10/Safe-Access-Zones-in-Australia.pdf.

Marie Stopes Australia, University of Queensland's Pro Bono Centre, SPHERE
and ASHM, *Nurse-Led Termination of Pregnancy in Australia: Legislative Scan*, 2nd
edn, 2022, https://www.mariestopes.org.au/wp-content/uploads/Nurse-led-
MToP-in-Australia-legislative-scan.pdf.

Maury, Susan, 'Poverty in Australia in 2020: What Does a Gendered Analysis
Reveal?', *The Power to Persuade*, 21 February 2020, http://www.
powertopersuade.org.au/blog/poverty-in-australia-2020-what-does-a-
gendered-analysis-reveal/19/2/2020.

Mazza, Danielle, Cathy J Watson, Angela Taft, Jayne Lucke, Kevin McGeechan,
Marion Haas, Kathleen McNamee, M Epi, Jeffrey F Peipert, and Kirsten I
Black, 'Increasing Long-Acting Reversible Contraceptives: The Australian
Contraceptive ChOice pRoject (ACCORd) Cluster Randomized Trial',
American Journal of Obstetrics and Gynecology, vol. 222, no. 4, 2020, S921.e1–e13.

McCalman, Janet, *Sex and Suffering: Women's Health and a Women's Hospital*,
Melbourne University Press, Carlton, 1999.

McCulloch, Alison, *Fighting to Choose: The Abortion Rights Struggle in New Zealand*,
Victoria University Press, Wellington, 2013.

McDonald, Catherine, and Charlesworth, Sara, 'Outsourcing and the Australian
Nonprofit Sector', in Ian Cunningham and Philip James (eds), *Voluntary
Organizations and Public Service Delivery*, Routledge, New York, 2011, 197–213.

McGuinness, Sheelagh, and Michael Thomson, 'Medicine and Abortion Law:
Complicating the Reforming Profession', *Medical Law Review*, vol. 23, no. 2,
2015, 177–99.

McKinney, Claire, 'A Good Abortion is a Tragic Abortion: Fit Motherhood and
Disability Stigma', *Hypatia*, vol. 34, no. 2, 2019, 266–85.

McLaren, Kirsty, 'The Emotional Imperative of the Visual: Images of the Fetus in
Contemporary Australian Pro-life Politics', in Nicole Doerr, Alice Mattoni and
Simon Teune (eds), *Advances in the Visual Analysis of Social Movements*, Emerald
Group Publishing Limited, Bingley, 2013, 81–104.

McQuillan, Julia, Arthur L Griel, and Karina M Shreffler, 'Pregnancy Intentions
Among Women Who Do Not Try: Focusing on Women Who Are Okay Either

Way', *Maternal and Child Health Journal*, vol. 15, no. 2, 2011, 178–87.

Mengesha, Zelalem B, Janette Perz, Tinashe Dune, and Jane Ussher, 'Refugee and Migrant Women's Engagement with Sexual and Reproductive Health Care in Australia: A Socio-Ecological Analysis of Health Care Professional Perspectives', *PLoS One*, vol. 12, no. 7, 2017, 1–22.

Miani, Céline, 'Medical Abortion Ratios and Gender Equality in Europe: An Ecological Correlation Study', *Sexual and Reproductive Health Matters*, vol. 29, no. 1, 2021, 214–31.

Mikhailovich, Katja, and Kerry Arabena, 'Evaluating an Indigenous Sexual Health Peer Education Project', *Health Promotion Journal of Australia*, vol. 16, no. 3, 2005, 189–93.

Miles, Steven, 'Abortion Legal in Queensland', Media Statement, 3 December 2018, http://statements.qld.gov.au/statement/2018/12/3/Abortion-Legal-In-Queensland.

Millar, Erica, *Happy Abortions: Our Bodies in the Era of Choice*, Zed Books, London, 2017.

——'Maintaining Exceptionality: Interrogating Gestational Limits for Abortion', *Social & Legal Studies*, vol. 31, no. 3, 2022, 439–58.

——'Mourned Choices and Grievable Lives: The Anti-Abortion Movement's Influence in Defining the Abortion Experience in Australia Since the 1960s', *Gender & History*, vol. 28, no. 2, 2016, 501–19.

Miller, Chris, and Lionel Orchard, *Australian Public Policy: Progressive Ideas in the Neoliberal Ascendancy*, Policy Press, Bristol, 2016.

Miller, Peter, and Nikolas Rose, *Governing the Present: Administering Economic, Social and Personal Life*, Wiley, Oxford, 2013.

Mitchell, Dundi, Maria Nugent, and Veronica Arbon, '"Shame and Blame": How Sexuality and Confidentiality Feature in Urban Australian Aboriginal Women's Discourses About Experiences of Health Institutions', in Mary Spongberg, Jan Larbalestier and Margaret Winn (eds), *Women Sexuality Culture: Cross Cultural Perspectives on Sexuality*, Women's Studies Centre, Sydney, 1996, 64–78.

Moore, Paddy, and Aimee Kent, Equality of Access to Late Gestation Abortion in Victoria: The RWH Experience, paper presented at Children By Choice Conference, Brisbane, August 2022.

Moore, P, and K Stephens, Can We Decentralise Abortion Services in Victoria? A Case Study Of Collaboration in Northeast Victoria, paper presented at Public Health Association Australia 2nd National Sexual & Reproductive Health Conference, November 2014.

Moreton-Robinson, Aileen, 'The Possessive Logic of Patriarchal White Sovereignty: The High Court and the Yorta Yorta Decision', *Borderlands E-Journal*, vol. 3, no. 2, 2004, 1–9.

Morgan, Jenny, 'Abortion Law Reform: The Importance of Democratic Change', *UNSW Law Journal*, 35, 2012, 142–74.

MS Health, Medical Abortion Provider and Dispenser Update December 2022, https://www.mshealth.com.au/publications/.

MSI Australia, 'Apology for Forced Medical Procedures Linked to Colonisation and Racism in Australia', 3 August 2022, https://www.mariestopes.org.au/your-choices/apology-for-forced-medical-procedures-linked-to-colonisation-and-racism-in-australia/.

MSI Reproductive Choices, *Australian Strategic Plan 2021–2023*, 2021, https://
www.mariestopes.org.au/wp-content/uploads/MSI-Australia-Strategic-
Plan-2021-2023.pdf.

——*MSI 2030: Your Body, Your Choice, Your Future*, November 2020, https://www.
msichoices.org/media/3919/msi-2030-external-strategy-11112020.pdf.

Multicultural Centre for Women's Health, *Data Report: Sexual and Reproductive
Health* , MCWH, 2021, https://www.mcwh.com.au/wp-content/uploads/
SRH-Report-2021-for-web-accessible.pdf.

Mulligan, Ea C, 'Striving for Excellence in Abortion Services', *Australian Health
Review*, vol. 30, no. 4, 2006, 468–73.

Mulligan, Ea, and Hayley Messenger, 'Mifepristone in South Australia: The First
1343 Tablets', *Australian Family Physician*, vol. 40, no. 5, 2011, 342–5.

Munroe, Erik, Brandan Hayes, and Julia Taft, 'Private-sector Social Franchising to
Accelerate Family Planning Access, Choice, And Quality: Results from Marie
Stopes International', *Global Health: Science and Practice*, vol. 3, no. 2, 195–208.

Murdoch, Jacqueline, Kirsten Thompson, and Suzanne Belton, 'Rapid Uptake of
Early Medical Abortions in the Northern Territory: A Family Planning-Based
Model', *Australian and New Zealand Journal of Obstetrics and Gynaecology*, vol. 60,
no. 6, 2020, 970–5.

Mutua, Michael, 'Kenya's Marie Stopes Ban May Drive More Women to Unsafe
Abortions', *The Conversation*, 2 December 2018, https://theconversation.com/
kenyas-marie-stopes-ban-may-drive-more-women-to-unsafe-abortions-107911.

Nash, Judith, 'GP Bias Clouds Termination Advice', *Medical Forum*, vol. 5, 2011, 3.

Newton, Danielle, Chris Bayly, Kathleen McNamee, Annarella Hardiman, Marie
Bismark, Amy Webster, and Louise Keogh, 'How Do Women Seeking Abortion
Choose Between Surgical and Medical Abortion? Perspectives from Abortion
Service Providers,' *Australian and New Zealand Journal of Obstetrics and
Gynaecology*, vol. 56, no. 5, 2016, 523–529.

NHMRC (National Health & Medical Research Council), *An Information Paper
on Termination of Pregnancy in Australia*, NHMRC, Canberra, 1996.

Nickson, Carolyn, Julia Shelley, and Anthony Smith, 'Use of Interstate Services for
the Termination of Pregnancy in Australia', *Australian and New Zealand Journal of
Public Health*, vol. 26, no. 5, 2002, 421–5.

Nieman, Lynette K, Teresa M Choate, George P Chrousos, David L Healy, Martin
Morin, David Renquist, George R Merriam, Irving M Spitz, C Wayne Bardin,
Étienne-Émile Baulieu, and D Lynne Loriaux, 'The Progesterone Antagonist
RU 486', *New England Journal of Medicine*, vol. 316, no. 4, 1987, 187–91.

NSW Government, *Policy Directive: Framework for Termination of Pregnancy in New
South Wales*, PD2021_018, June 2021, https://www1.health.nsw.gov.au/pds/
ActivePDSDocuments/PD2021_018.pdf.

*NT Termination of Pregnancy Law Reform, 12 Month Interpretive Report, 1 July
2017–30 June 2018*, Department of Health, Darwin, 2020.

Oberman, Michelle, *Her Body, Our Laws: On the Front Lines of the Abortion War,
from El Salvador to Oklahoma*, Beacon Press, Boston, 2018.

Ogden, Kathryn, Emily Ingram, Joanna Levis, Georgia Roberts, and Iain
Robertson, 'Termination of Pregnancy in Tasmania: Access and Service
Provision from the Perspective of GPs', *Australian Journal of Primary Health*,
vol. 27, no. 4, 2021, 297–303.

Oppegaard, Kevin Sunde, Margaret Sparrow, Paul Hyland, Francisca García, Cristina Villarreal, Aníbal Faúndes, Laura Miranda, and Marge Berer, 'What If Medical Abortion Becomes the Main or Only Method of First-trimester Abortion? A Roundtable of Views', *Contraception*, vol. 97, no. 2, 2018, 82–5.

O'Rourke, Anne, 'A Legal and Political Assessment of Challenges to Abortion Laws by Anti-choice Activists in Australia and the Progression of Abortion Law in Australia and the United States', *The American Journal of Comparative Law*, 2022, 162–204.

——'The Discourse of Abortion Law Debate in Australia: Caring Mother or Mother of Convenience', *Women's Studies International Forum*, vol. 56, 2016, 37–44.

O'Rourke, Anne, Suzanne Belton, and Ea Mulligan, 'Medical Abortion in Australia: What Are the Clinical and Legal Risks? Is Medical Abortion Over-Regulated?', *Journal of Law and Medicine*, vol. 24, no. 1, 2016, 221–38.

Palmer, Charis, 'Tasmania to Amend Law to Decriminalise Abortion', *The Conversation*, 8 March 2013, https://theconversation.com/tasmania-to-amend-law-to-decriminalise-abortion-12721.

Parliament of Australia, *Research Brief: How Many Abortions are There in Australia? A Discussion of Abortion Statistics, Their Limitations, and Options for Improved Statistical Collection*, Parliament of Australia, Parliamentary Library, no. 9, 2005.

Peat, Brian, 'Intra-operative Ultra-sound for Improved Safety in Training in Termination of Pregnancy', in *Abortion—Politics, Access and Challenges: Conference Proceedings*, Abortion Providers Federation of Australasia Biennial Conference, Adelaide, 2001, 119.

Penovic, Tania, 'The Fall of Roe v Wade: The US Anti-Abortion Movement and Its Influence in Australia', *Alternative Law Journal*, vol. 47, no. 4, 2022, 253–60.

Perks, Robert, and Alistair Thomson (eds), *The Oral History Reader*, Routledge, London, 1997.

Petersen, Kerry, *Abortion Regimes*, Dartmouth, Aldershot, 1993.

Petroechevsky, Judy, 'The Story of Children by Choice', in W Weeks (ed.), *Women Working Together: Lessons from Feminist Services,* Longman Cheshire, Melbourne, 1994, 195–207.

Piepmeier, Alison, 'The Inadequacy of "Choice": Disability, and What's Wrong with Feminist Framing of Reproduction', *Feminist Studies*, vol. 39, no. 1, 2013, 159–86.

Pitts, Marian K, Murray Couch, Hunter Mulcare, Samantha Croy, and Anne Mitchell, 'Transgender People in Australia and New Zealand: Health, Well-being, and Access to Services', *Feminism & Psychology*, vol. 19, no. 4, 2009, 475–95.

Price, Elizabeth, Leah S Sharman, Heather A Douglas, Nicola Sheeran, and Genevieve A Dingle, 'Experiences of Reproductive Coercion in Queensland Women', *Journal of Interpersonal Violence,* vol. 37, no. 5–6, 2022, NP2823-43.

Pridmore, BR, and DG Chambers, 'Uterine Perforation During Surgical Abortion: A Review of Diagnosis, Management and Prevention', *Australian and New Zealand Journal of Obstetrics and Gynaecology*, vol. 39, no. 3, 1999, 349–53.

Pringle, Rosemary, *Sex and Medicine: Gender, Power and Authority in the Medical Profession*, Cambridge University Press, Cambridge, 1998.

Pusey, Michael, *Economic Rationalism in Canberra: A Nation-Building State Changes Its Mind*, Cambridge University Press, Cambridge, 1991.

Queensland Government, 'Maternity and Neonatal Clinical Guideline Supplement: Therapeutic Termination of Pregnancy', Queensland Health, 2022, https://www.health.qld.gov.au/__data/assets/pdf_file/0032/735296/s-top.pdf.

Queensland Government, 'Palaszczuk Government Delivers Historic Abortion Laws', Media Statement, 17 October 2018, https://statements.qld.gov.au/statements/85768.

Queensland Health, *Queensland Clinical Guidelines: Termination of Pregnancy*, Guideline No. MN19.21-V7-R24, 2020, http://www.health.qld.gov.au/qcg.

QLRC (Queensland Law Reform Commission), *Review of Termination of Pregnancy Laws*, Report No. 76, June 2018.

RANZCOG (Royal Australian and New Zealand College of Obstetricians and Gynaecologists), 'Abortion', March 2019, https://ranzcog.edu.au/wp-content/uploads/2022/05/Abortion.pdf.

——'RANZCOG Advanced Training Module: Sexuality and Reproductive Health: Contraception and Abortion', *ranzcog.edu.au*, 2021, https://ranzcog.edu.au/wp-content/uploads/2022/06/Fellowship-of-RANZCOG-FRANZCOG-Sexual-and-Reproductive-Health_Contraception-and-Abortion-ATM-Guide.pdf.

——'Late Abortion', *ranzcog.edu.au*, 2016, https://ranzcog.edu.au/wp-content/uploads/2022/05/Late-Abortion.pdf.

——Mifepristone (RU486), Statement C-Gyn 14, First Endorsed by Council 2001, November 2005.

—— 'Pathways to FRANZCOG', https://ranzcog.edu.au/og-magazine/franzcog-advanced-training-modules/.

——'Senate Inquiry into Abortion Access', News, 29 September 2022, https://ranzcog.edu.au/news/senate-inquiry-into-abortion-access/.

——Termination of Pregnancy Statement C-Gyn 17, March 2005, updated March 2019, 3, 4.

——'The Use of Misoprostol in Obstetrics and Gynaecology', Best Practice Statement, November 2021, https://ranzcog.edu.au/wp-content/uploads/2022/05/The-use-of-misoprostol-in-obstetrics-and-gynaecology.pdf.

Raymond, Elizabeth G, Caitlin Shannon, Mark A Weaver, and Beverly Winikoff, 'First-trimester Medical Abortion with Mifepristone 200 mg and Misoprostol: A Systematic Review', *Contraception*, vol. 87, no. 1, 2013, 26–37.

Rebouché, Rachel, 'A Functionalist Approach to Comparative Abortion Law', in Rebecca J Cook, Joanna N Erdman and Bernard M Dickens (eds), *Abortion Law in Transnational Perspective*, University of Pennsylvania Press, Philadelphia, 2014, 98–117.

——'The Public Health Turn in Reproductive Rights', *Washington and Lee Law Review*, vol. 78, no. 4, 2021, 1355–432.

Report To the Minister For Health on the Review of Provisions of The Health Act 1911 *and* The Criminal Code *Relating to Abortion As Introduced by the* Acts Amendment (Abortion) Act 1998, Government of Western Australia, Department of Health, 17 June 2002, https://ww2.health.wa.gov.au/~/media/Files/Corporate/general-documents/Data-collection/PDF/Report_Abortion_Legislation_Review_WA_2002.pdf.

Ripper, Margie, 'Abortion: The Shift in Stigmatisation from Those Seeking Abortion to Those Providing It', *Health Sociology Review*, vol. 10, no. 2, 2001, 65–77.

Ripper, Margie, and Lyndall Ryan, 'The Role of the "Withdrawal Method" in the Control of Abortion', *Australian Feminist Studies*. vol. 13, no. 28, 1998, 313-21.

Robertson, S, L Edney, M Wheeler, T Hunter, and D Bateson, Access to Medical Abortion: Experiences of Women Calling FPNSW Talkline, paper presented at Public Health Association Australia 2nd National Sexual & Reproductive Health Conference, November 2014.

Romans-Clarkson, Sarah E, 'Psychological Sequelae of Induced Abortion', *Australian and New Zealand Journal of Psychiatry*, vol. 23, no. 4, 1989, 555–65.

Rose, Nikolas, *Powers of Freedom: Reframing Political Thought*, Cambridge University Press, Cambridge, 1999.

Rosenthal, Doreen, Heather J Rowe, Shelley Mallett, Annarella Hardiman, and Maggie Kirkman, *Understanding Women's Experiences of Unplanned Pregnancy and Abortion, Final Report*, Key Centre for Women's Health in Society, Melbourne School of Population Health, The University of Melbourne, Melbourne, 2009.

Ross, Loretta J, 'Reproductive Justice as Intersectional Feminist Activism', *Souls*, vol. 19, no. 3, 2017, 286–314.

Rushton, Gina, *The Most Important Job in the World*, Pan Macmillan Australia, Sydney, 2022.

Ryan, Lyndall, Margie Ripper, and Barbara Buttfield, *We Women Decide: Women's Experience of Seeking Abortion in Queensland, South Australia and Tasmania 1985–1992*, Flinders University, Women's Studies Unit, 1994.

Saad-Filno, Alfredo, and Deborah Johnston, *Neoliberalism: A Critical Reader*, Pluto Press, London, 2004.

Samandari, Ghazaleh, Nathalie Kapp, Christopher Hamon, and Alison Campbell, 'Challenges in the Abortion Supply Chain: A Call to Action for Evaluation Research', *Reproductive Health*, vol. 18, no. 1, 2021.

Sampson, Louise, 'Australian Capital Territory Report', in *Abortion: Legal Right, Women's Right, Human Right: 1993 National Conference Papers*, Abortion Rights Network of Australia, South Brisbane, 1994, 33–34.

Sawer, Marian, *The Ethical State? Social Liberalism in Australia*, Melbourne University Press, Carlton, 2003.

Schiebinger, Londa, 'West Indian Abortifacients and the Making of Ignorance', in Robert N Proctor and Londa Schiebinger (eds), *Agnotology: The Making and Unmaking of Ignorance*, Stanford University Press, Stanford, 2008, 149–62.

Schoen, Johanna, *Abortion After Roe: Abortion After Legalization*, University of North Carolina Press, Chapel Hill, 2015.

Shand, Carol, and Margaret Sparrow, The Value and Future of Abortion Provider Organisations, paper presented at Unplanned Pregnancy and Abortion Conference, Brisbane, 2019.

Shankar, Mridula, Kirsten I Black, Philip Goldstone, Safeera Hussainy, Danielle Mazza, Kerry Petersen, Jayne Lucke, and Angela Taft, 'Access, Equity and Costs of Induced Abortion Services in Australia: A Cross-Sectional Study', *Australian and New Zealand Journal of Public Health*, vol. 41, no. 3, 2017, 309–14.

Sheldon, Sally, *Beyond Control: Medical Power and Abortion Law*, Pluto Press, London, 1997.

——'The Decriminalisation of Abortion: An Argument for Modernisation', *Oxford Journal of Legal Studies*, vol. 36, no. 2, 2015, 334–65.

——'How Can a State Control Swallowing? The Home Use of Abortion Pills in

Ireland', *Reproductive Health Matters*, vol. 24, no. 48, 2016, 90–101.

Sheldon, Sally, Gayle Davis, Jane O'Neill, and Clare Parker, *The Abortion Act (1967): A Biography of a UK Law*, Cambridge University Press, Cambridge, 2021.

Sheldon, Sally, Jane O'Neill, Clare Parker, and Gayle Davis, '"Too Much, Too Indigestible, Too Fast"? The Decades of Struggle for Abortion Law Reform in Northern Ireland', *The Modern Law Review*, vol. 83, no. 4, 2020, 761–96.

Siedlecky, Stefania, and Diana Wyndham, *Populate and Perish: Australian Women's Fight for Birth Control*, Allen and Unwin, Sydney, 1990.

Sifris, Ronli, 'State by State, "Safe Access Zones" Around Clinics Are Shielding Women From Abortion Protesters', *The Conversation*, 30 November 2015, https://theconversation.com/state-by-state-safe-access-zones-around-clinics-are-shielding-women-from-abortion-protesters-51407.

——'Tasmania's Reproductive Health (Access to Terminations) Act 2013: An Analysis of Conscientious Objection to Abortion and the "Obligation to Refer"', *Journal of Law and Medicine*, vol. 22, 2015, 900–14.

Sifris, Ronli, Tania Penovic, and Caroline Henckels, 'Advancing Reproductive Rights Through Legal Reform: The Example of Abortion Clinic Safe Access Zones', *University of New South Wales Law Journal*, vol. 43, no. 3, 2020, 1078–97.

Simons, Margaret, 'Duty of Care', *The Monthly*, 5 August 2010, 42–6.

Singh, Susheela, Lisa Remez, Gilda Sedgh, Lorraine Kwok, and Tsuyoshi Onda, *Abortion Worldwide 2017: Uneven Progress and Unequal Access*, Guttmacher Institute, New York, NY, 2018.

SPHERE, NHMRC Centre of Research Excellence in Sexual and Reproductive Health for Women in Primary Care, *2019–2021 Achievement Report*, https://3fe3eaf7-296b-470f-809a-f8eebaec315a.filesusr.com/ugd/410f2f_3a33f53e60444d74b5fadf21a57c49b4.pdf?index=true.

Straton, J, K Godman, V Gee, and Q Hu, *Induced Abortion in Western Australia 1999-2005, Report of the WA Abortion Notification System*, Department of Health, Perth, 2006.

Stringer, Rebecca, *Knowing Victims: Feminism, Agency and Victim Politics in Neoliberal Times*, Routledge, London, 2013.

Subasinghe, Asvini K, Seema Deb, and Danielle Mazza, 'Primary Care Providers' Knowledge, Attitudes and Practices of Medical Abortion: A Systematic Review', *BMJ Sexual & Reproductive Health*, vol. 47, no. 1, 2021, 9–16.

Suha, Mariyam, Linda Murray, Deborah Warr, Jasmin Chen, Karen Block, Adele Murdolo, Regina Quiazon, Erin Davis, and Cathy Vaughan, 'Reproductive Coercion as a Form of Family Violence Against Immigrant and Refugee Women in Australia', *PLoS One*, vol. 17, no. 11, 2022, e0275809.

Supreme Court of Queensland, *Medical Board of Queensland v Freeman* [2010] QCA 93, https://archive.sclqld.org.au/qjudgment/2010/QCA10-093.pdf.

Swannell, Cate, 'Medical Abortion Access Extended', *InSight*, 27 January 2015, https://insightplus.mja.com.au/2015/2/medical-abortion-access-extended/.

Swerissen, Hal, Stephen Duckett, and Greg Moran, *Mapping Primary Care in Australia*, Grattan Institute, Carlton, 2018, https://grattan.edu.au/wp-content/uploads/2018/07/906-Mapping-primary-care.pdf.

Swinn, Louise, *Choice Words: A Collection Of Writing About Abortion*, Allen & Unwin, Sydney, 2019.

Szporluk, Michael, 'A Framework for Understanding Accountability of International NGOs and Global Good Governance', *Indiana Journal of Global Legal Studies*, vol. 16, no. 1, 2009, 339–61.

Taft, Angela J, Mridula Shankar, Kirsten I Black, Danielle Mazza, Safeera Hussainy, and Jayne C Lucke, 'Unintended and Unwanted Pregnancy in Australia: a Cross-sectional, National Random Telephone Survey of Prevalence and Outcomes', *Medical Journal of Australia,* vol. 209, no. 9, 2018, 407–8.

Tankard Reist, Melinda, *Giving Sorrow Words: Women's Stories of Grief after Abortion,* Duffy & Snellgrove, Potts Point, 2000.

Therapeutic Goods Administration, *Australian Public Assessment Report for mifepristone/misoprostol,* Australian Government, Department of Health and Aged Care, October 2014, https://www.tga.gov.au/sites/default/files/auspar-mifepristone-misoprostol-141013.pdf.

——*Registration of Medicines for the Medical Termination of Early Pregnancy,* Australian Government, Department of Health and Aged Care, 30 August 2012, https://www.tga.gov.au/registration-medicines-medical-termination-early-pregnancy.

Thompson, Terri-Ann, Jane W Seymour, Catriona Melville, Zara Khan, Danielle Mazza, and Daniel Grossman, 'An Observational Study of Patient Experiences with a Direct-To-Patient Telehealth Abortion Model in Australia', *BMJ Sexual & Reproductive Health*, vol. 48, no. 2, 2022, 103–9.

Tilley, Elizabeth, Jan Walmsley, Sarah Earle, and Dorothy Atkinson, '"The Silence is Roaring": Sterilization, Reproductive Rights and Women With Intellectual Disabilities', *Disability & Society*, vol. 27, no. 3, 2012, 413–26.

Tomnay, Jane E, Lauren Coelli, Ange Davidson, Alana Hulme-Chambers, Catherine Orr, and Jane S Hocking, 'Providing Accessible Medical Abortion Services in a Victorian Rural Community: A Description and Audit of Service Delivery and Contraception Follow Up', *Sexual and Reproductive Healthcare*, vol. 16, 2018, 175–80.

Travers, Bonnie, 'Choice/No Choice? The Courage and Selflessness of the Second Trimester Woman: Counselling Women for Second Trimester Abortion', in *Abortion—Politics, Access and Challenges: Conference Proceedings,* Abortion Providers Federation of Australasia Biennial Conference, Adelaide, 2001, 125–8.

Treloar, Susan, Emmi Snyder, and Charles Kerr, 'Effect of a New Service on Women's Abortion Experience', *Journal of Biosocial Science*, vol. 9, no. 4, 1977, 417–27.

Ulmann, André, 'The Development of Mifepristone: A Pharmaceutical Drama in Three Acts', *Journal of the American Medical Women's Association (1972)*, vol. 55, no. 3 Suppl., 2000, 117–20.

Utting, Selena, Susan Stark, and Nicola Sheeran, 'Hidden Women: The Impact of Poverty on Abortion Access', Powerpoint presentation at Unplanned Pregnancy and Abortion in Australia conference, Children by Choice, Brisbane, August 2017, n.p.

VLRC (Victorian Law Reform Commission), *Law Of Abortion. Final Report,* 2008, https://www.lawreform.vic.gov.au/wp-content/uploads/2021/07/VLRC_Abortion_Report-1.pdf.

Wainer, Jo, 'Abortion as an Indicator of the Value of Women: Women and Surgery Conference' in R Moore (ed.), *Women and Surgery 1990 Conference Proceedings:*

Conference Papers, Workshop Reports and Program Details, Healthsharing Women, Melbourne, 1991, 108–10.

——'The Social Impact of RU 486', *New Doctor*, Spring 1991, 9–11.

Watego, Chelsea, Alissa Macoun, David Singh, and Elizabeth Strakosch, 'Carceral Feminism and Coercive Control: When Indigenous Women Aren't Seen as Ideal Victims, Witnesses or Women', *The Conversation*, 25 May 2021, https://theconversation.com/carceral-feminism-and-coercive-control-when-indigenous-women-arent-seen-as-ideal-victims-witnesses-or-women-161091.

Williams, John, David Plater, Anita Brunacci, Sarah Kapadia, and Melissa Oxlad, *Abortion: A Review of South Australian Law and Practice*, South Australian Law Reform Institute, Adelaide, 2019.

Williamson, Angela, 'The Apple Isle', in L Swann (ed.), *Choice Words*, Allen & Unwin, Sydney, 2019, 31–41.

Willis, Eileen, Louise Reynolds, and Trudy Rudge, 'Understanding the Australian Health Care System' in Willis, Reynolds and Rudge (eds), *Understanding the Australian Health Care System*, 4th edn, Elsevier Chatswood, 2020, 1–16.

Withers, Rachel, 'Culture Cowards', *The Monthly*, 22 July 2022, https://www.themonthly.com.au/the-politics/rachel-withers/2022/07/22/culture-cowards.

Women's Electoral Lobby (WEL), Report to the Chairperson, Committee on the Elimination of Discrimination against Women (CEDAW), *Continuing Threats of Curtailment of Family Planning Services and Abortion in Particular, in Australia in 1989*, Women's Electoral Lobby, Perth, 1990.

Women's Health Matters, *Women's Health Matters! Recommendations Paper: Publicly Funded Abortion for the ACT*, Women's Health Matters, Canberra, 9 March 2023.

Women With Disabilities Australia (WWDA), *WWDA Submission on Sexual and Reproductive Rights of Women and Girls With Disability to the Royal Commission into Violence, Abuse, Neglect and Exploitation of People With Disability*, Women With Disabilities, Hobart, December 2022.

Woodrow, Nicole L, 'Termination Review Committees: Are They Necessary?', *Medical Journal of Australia*, vol. 179, no. 2, 2003, 92–94.

Working Party to Examine the Adequacy of Existing Services for Termination of Pregnancy and South Australian Health Commission, *Report of the Working Party to Examine the Adequacy of Existing Services for Termination of Pregnancy in South Australia*, South Australian Health Commission, Adelaide, 1986.

World Health Organization (WHO), *Abortion Care Guideline*, World Health Organization, Geneva, 2022, https://apps.who.int/iris/handle/10665/349316.

Wright, Alyson, Karl Briscoe and Ray Lovett, 'A National Profile of Aboriginal and Torres Strait Islander Health Workers', *Australian and New Zealand Journal of Public Health*, vol. 43, no. 1, 2019, 24–6.

Wyatt, Donna, and Katie Hughes, 'When Discourse Defies Belief: Anti-Abortionists in Contemporary Australia', *Journal of Sociology*, vol. 45, no. 3, 2009, 235–53.

Ziegler, Mary, *After Roe: The Lost History of the Abortion Debate*, Harvard University Press, Cambridge, 2015.

Index